C. Ellis (Charles Ellis) Stevens

Sources of the Constitution of the United States

Considered in Relation to colonial and english History

C. Ellis (Charles Ellis) Stevens

Sources of the Constitution of the United States
Considered in Relation to colonial and english History

ISBN/EAN: 9783337153557

Printed in Europe, USA, Canada, Australia, Japan

Cover: Foto ©ninafisch / pixelio.de

More available books at **www.hansebooks.com**

SOURCES

OF THE

CONSTITUTION OF THE UNITED STATES

CONSIDERED IN RELATION TO COLONIAL
AND ENGLISH HISTORY

BY

C. ELLIS STEVENS, LL.D., D.C.L.

F.S.A. (EDINBURGH)

New York

MACMILLAN AND CO.

AND LONDON

1894

In Tribute

TO THE

NATIONS WHICH IN VARYING WAYS BORE

RELATION TO

The Founding of America

SPAIN, ITALY, FRANCE, THE NETHERLANDS

SWEDEN, GERMANY, AND

GREAT BRITAIN

THIS WORK IS INSCRIBED

.

PREFACE.

AMERICA is sometimes said to be a nation without a past. The remark may mean much or little, according to its application. It is made most frequently in referring to civil institutions. In particular, there has been a tendency to regard the Constitution of the United States as without sources or antecedents, — a new invention in political science.

Mr. Gladstone has observed, that "as the British Constitution is the most subtle organism which has proceeded from progressive history, so the American Constitution is the most wonderful work ever struck off at a given time by the brain and purpose of man." His words, though not necessarily carrying such meaning, have been often quoted as expressive of this old-time idea, that the American Constitution is wholly new, — that it is, in fact, an original creation of the convention which met in Philadelphia in 1787.[1] What Dr.

[1] Professor Morey well expresses this idea: "The organic law under which he [the American] lives is set forth in a written document. It was put into form at a given time and place. It was fashioned in the heat of discussion by a chosen body of men, whose

Von Holst aptly calls the "worship of the Constitution"[1] has largely stimulated the idea. The philosophy of modern democracy — which, under the influence of the theories of Rousseau, long ignored historical facts — has steadily cultivated it. And there is in it some truth ; for not only was this constitution established as a written document by the convention, and in circumstances quite unique, but it has elements — many of them very important — which *are* altogether peculiar and characteristic. Hardly strange is it, that such traits of singularity should attract, as points of differentiation usually do, a somewhat disproportionate attention.

But it is beginning to be realized that the Constitution of the United States, though possessing elements of novelty, is not, after all, the new creation that this idea would imply. It is not, properly speaking, the original composition of one body of men, nor the outcome of one definite epoch, — it is more and better than that. It does not stand in historical isolation, free of antecedents. It rests upon very old principles, — principles laboriously worked out by long ages of constitutional struggle. It looks back to the annals of

work in its outlines and its details, he is accustomed to think, was *solely the product of their creative wisdom.* This idea was formerly so prevalent, that the apotheosis of the fathers occupies a large place in American political literature; and this view is not confined to native writers." — *Annals of the American Academy of Political and Social Science,* April, 1891, p. 530.

[1] Von Holst, *Constitutional and Political History of the United States,* I. 65.

the colonies and of the mother-land for its sources and its explanation. And it was rendered possible, and made what it is, by the political development of many generations of men.

When the preparation of the present work was undertaken, some years ago, there existed no popular recognition of these facts. The tendency was still to regard this constitution as solely the creation of the Philadelphia Convention; and the scant allusions to constitutional genesis, scattered in American literature, had seemingly left no impression on the general mind. While, however, the work has been in progress, American universities have gradually taken up the study of constitutional sources, occasional articles touching phases of the subject have been published in periodicals, and explicit references to it have found their way into current books, so that public opinion has been ripening.[1] The path now seems opened for a comprehensive investigation. Yet, down to the present, no volume devoted to the theme has appeared.

The American Constitution is, strictly speaking, the *document* which goes by that name. The present work treats of the document, and of the sources of its contents, — avoiding all side issues. Whatever influence

[1] Bryce, *American Commonwealth*, has some references. Hannis Taylor, *Origin and Growth of the English Constitution*, gives in the Introduction a brief but lucid outline. Douglas Campbell, *Puritan in Holland, England, and America*, treats of American institutions in general, but says little of the Constitution itself, and that little is practically limited to the question of Dutch antecedents.

various European races may have exerted upon American institutions in general, as existing to-day,[1] the antecedents of this great national document are traceable so directly and so almost exclusively through colonial and English channels, that no apology is necessary for taking such channels as the true line of investigation. The aim has been to place in the hands of scholars and the general public, a clear and concise survey of the salient features of such constitutional evolution.

There may still be persons in America who are unprepared to regard with favour such a study, and who look unwillingly to England or other countries for the origin of institutions they have long been accustomed to consider characteristically modern and American. But surely Americanism can never be more truly American, than when it welcomes, not merely such isolated fragments of fact as differentiate the United States from other nationalities, but every fact, whatever it be, that has to do with the nation; and among these, a most important fact is that of progression from the Anglo-Teutonic past. In reality, the light that comes from historical comparison will be found to give new and heightened colour to the national institutions, and to bring out more clearly than anything else could do, their true meaning and value.

Englishmen and dwellers on the Continent, who often appear to believe that the example of America leads toward a limitless democratic advance, may find in the

---

[1] Recent claims have been made for Dutch, Scotch-Irish, etc.

American Constitution, if they will, a balancing element of conservatism that should not be lost to sight. The American loves liberty, but liberty regulated by precedent and law. In an age when democratic and socialistic theories are threatening the foundations of the political and social fabric of the civilized world, it can scarcely be unprofitable for earnest thinkers to pause and consider, that the great republic possesses in its method of government the result, not merely of a philosophy, but of an historical upgrowth.

And it is proper to observe, that there are Americans who regard with dismay the tendency of those in England who seem in haste to modify or destroy old English institutions, appearing to believe that America sets the example of such destructiveness, and that such a road is the way of progress. England would do well to realize that the American institutions which have proved the most successful have been, very often at least, the working out of ancient English principles of free government. If the case of America is to count for anything, it may count, certainly in some respects, on the side of a careful handling of those old principles. There is many a true-hearted and loyal American who would deplore the spectacle of Englishmen breaking with their own great past.

The author would be justly deemed ungrateful, if he failed to express sincere appreciation of the important aid given him by distinguished legal and historical scholars in Europe and America. Special mention should be made of the earnest help and interest accorded by the late Sir Henry Maine. Thanks are also due to many kind friends, — among them the Rev. Henry B. Ensworth, who has supplied a number of valuable works; and a lady who has aided materially in the task of final revision for the press. Despite carefulness, the author is fully conscious that he has not improbably fallen into mistakes, — for all which he begs a generous indulgence. He has tried to see the facts clearly, fairly, fearlessly, — and to let the facts tell their tale.

JANUARY 1, 1894.

CONTENTS.

―――∘◦∘―――

CHAPTER I.

IT has been a prevalent error in political writings to overestimate intelligence, and underestimate the power of what, for want of a better term, may be called instinct. This error appears notably in the writings of Grotius, Hobbes, Spinoza, Puffendorf, Locke, Rousseau, — in fact, in all writings where the origin of government is explained by the hypothesis, now exploded, of an original social contract, based upon the element of intelligent selection. A safer course is adopted by some recent writers, who may be said to incline to the view believed to have been first advanced by Aristotle, which regards government as a result of natural social growth.[1]

---

[1] Aristotle says: "It is evident that a state is one of the works of nature, and that man is naturally a political animal, and that whosoever is naturally and not accidentally unfit for society must be either inferior or superior to man." — Welford's translation of Aristotle's *Politics and Economics*, 6. Mr. Hannis Taylor gives modern expression to this old thought: "The cityless man (ἄπολις) — the natural man of Hobbes and Rousseau — must be more or less than man, — either superhuman or a monster." — *Origin and Growth of the English Constitution*, 5. "He is the unit," Pollock remarks.

The later theory has been aptly stated thus : "The long continuance of a people under any given political order engenders a habit and action, which ripens into a political instinct and becomes powerful in determining the form of institutions and the direction of political progress.[1]   In the early stages of political life, changes

"out of whom, if there be only enough of them, theorists of the Social Contract school undertake to build up the state. This is an enterprise at which Aristotle would have stared and gasped." — *History of the Science of Politics*, 9. "The influence of this contract theory on political thought lingers even to this day, though in a constantly diminishing degree. At present it may be considered as having generally given place to the view first advanced by Aristotle." — Crane and Moses, *Politics*, 68.

[1] "Intelligence," substantially says Professor Joseph Le Conte, "works by experience, and is wholly dependent on individual experience for the wisdom of its actions; while instinct, on the other hand, is wholly independent of individual experience. If we regard instinct in the light of intelligence, then it is not individual intelligence, but cosmic intelligence, or the laws of nature working through inherited brain structure to produce wise results. Intelligence belongs to the individual, and is therefore variable, that is, different in different individuals, and also improvable in the life of the individual by experience. Instinct belongs to the species, and is therefore the same in all individuals, and unimprovable with age and experience. . . . In a word, intelligent conduct is self-determined and becomes wise by individual experience. Instinctive conduct is predetermined in wisdom by brain structure. The former is free; the latter is, to a large extent, automatic." — *Popular Science Monthly*, October, 1875. "As to the origin of instinct, it can hardly be said that any theory has as yet gained universal assent, but no hypothesis appears more worthy of acceptance than that which regards it as habit grown to be hereditary. An act frequently performed in the consciousness of a specific purpose may continue to be performed, through the determinative force of struc-

are less frequent than in the later stages, and opportunity is thereby offered for the ideas of social organization peculiar to primitive times to impress themselves upon the mind, and in the course of centuries of political monotony to ripen into a firmly fixed instinct. Thus the political instincts of a race have their origin in a prehistoric age, in an age when generation after generation passes away, leaving no record of change in social forms, or of the acquisition of new ideas. And it is this political instinct that must be taken account of, if we would fully understand political progress ; it is in its force and persistence that we discern the main cause of that tendency displayed in kindred nations to preserve in their governments the essential features of the primitive political institutions of the race to which they belong." [1]

Whether such philosophy be sound or not, attention is being increasingly drawn at the present day to the ascertained fact of racial influence on political development, — the essential and continuous potency of racial institutions in the life of nations. Historical writers have directed observation to the actual rise of modern governmental systems from ancient originals, and scientific writers have applied the theory of heredity to

ture, after the consciousness of the purpose of the act has been lost. When this peculiarity of structure or the mental bias caused by the frequent and continued exercise of the mind in a given direction has become hereditary, the habit has grown into an instinct." — Crane and Moses, *Politics*, 69.

[1] Ibid. 70.

politics, and have asserted the well-nigh automatic play of hereditary traits upon national career and destiny. Quite aside from possible extremes of speculation, few persons will nowadays question the reality of this racial force.

In examining into the sources of the Constitution of the United States, it will be found necessary to bear in mind from the outset that the nation was founded by men, the great majority of whom were of the English branch of the Teutonic race.[1]   The colonists were, for

[1] Mr. Douglas Campbell (*Puritan in Holland, England, and America*), in his effort to make out a Dutch origin for American institutions, has fallen into the mistake of underestimating English influence.   One of his main contentions is that the American people are not of English race; and he bases this assumption upon the fact that there were resident along with the English in the colonies Welshmen, Scotchmen, Irishmen, Scotch-Irishmen, Dutch, Germans, Frenchmen and Swedes.   But, for the purposes of the present inquiry, it is sufficient to remember: —

1. The above statement is strictly accurate: "The great majority" of the settlers were of "the English branch of the Teutonic race."   Mr. Campbell admits that the English majority was overwhelming.

2. The Scotch, Welsh, Irish, and Scotch-Irish had lived under British institutions before journeying to America.   They had passed through an English constitutional experience as really as had their English fellow-countrymen.

3. Those of other races resident in the colonies had personal contact for several generations with English government in its imperial and colonial forms.

4. All colonists alike were British subjects; and English administration dominated all, as completely as did the English language.

5. The Constitution of the United States as a legal document is traceable not to race influences in any vague sense, but to race

the most part, of one blood. Their language and social
usages were those of Great Britain. They took with
them to America not merely memories of political institutions, but, to a considerable extent, the English law
itself. And they continued for a century or more,
despite changing conditions, in political union with
England as members of one empire.[1]

influences as worked out in the form of laws. And those laws were
English.

In simple truth, the presence in America, during colonial days,
of the representatives of other races than the English has left
scarcely a trace in the national Constitution. This is so, notwithstanding the fact that these races have contributed in several ways
to the formation of the national spirit of the Americans. Thus an
acknowledgment is due to the Dutch — themselves Teutonic — who
did much to promote the love of freedom. And Mr. Campbell, in
his second volume, shows that the influence of the Scotch-Irish was
in the same direction. The free school, the use of a written ballot,
certain features of the land laws and of the township system, which
Mr. Campbell mentions, are doubtless traceable, in part at least, to
Dutch sources; and though *not included in the Constitution*, have
exercised an influence in moulding the American nation. It would
be easy to exaggerate this influence, especially if English government in America, which forms the great fact of early American history, should be left out of the account. In opening for investigation a most interesting question — the question of Dutch influences
— Mr. Campbell has seemingly erred on this side. His very able
treatment of his theme renders this bias the more regrettable.

[1] "The people were proud to call themselves 'Englishmen away
from home,' and they were prompt to claim all the rights and liberties of English subjects." — Landon, *Constitutional History and Government of the United States*, 20. Referring to the persistence of the
English traits in the race, even among Americans of our own day,
Professor Hosmer says: " Can it be said that the stock is still funda-

That they possessed a common nationality in, and
were thus subject to England is in itself an important
fact ; for a strong nation never fails to make an impress
upon the minds of its citizens or subjects, and it edu-

mentally English, however large may have been the inpouring into
its veins of foreign blood?   When among our kin beyond sea it
was urged, not long since, that in the people of England the Anglo-
Saxon had been superseded; that Celt, Frank, Scandinavian, Hol-
lander, and Huguenot — the multitude of invaders and immigrants
through a thousand years — had reduced the primitive element to
insignificance, it was well replied by Mr. Freeman: 'In a nation
there commonly is a certain element which is more than an element, something which is its real kernel, its real essence; something which attracts and absorbs all other elements, so that other
elements are not co-ordinate elements, but mere infusions into
a whole which is already in being. . . .   If, after adopting so
many . . . we remain Englishmen, none the less surely a new witness is brought to the strength of the English life within us, — a
life which can thus do the work of the alchemist, and change every
foreign element into its own English being.' [*Four Oxford Lectures,* 1887, p. 80.]   A similar statement might be made as regards
America. . . .   The stranger, indeed, has been with us from the
beginning: Frenchman and Spaniard preceded us; Celt, Swede,
Dutchman, and German came with us in the earliest ships.   The
overflow of Europe . . . has poured in upon us in an inundation;
yet the English stock remains, — the element which is more than
an element, the real kernel, the real essence; something that attracts
and absorbs all other elements, so that other elements are not
co-ordinate, but mere infusions into a whole which is already in
being." — Hosmer, *Anglo-Saxon Freedom,* 312, 313.   He gives
evidence of this, and quotes the testimony of the late Professor
Richard A. Proctor: " I have had better opportunities than most
men of comparing the two nations; and I profess I find the difference between them even less than I should have expected from the
difference in the conditions under which the two nations have sub-

cates and powerfully moulds their political opinions.
Nationality creates characteristic traits of thought and
tendency. And, possibly for this reason, the political
development of colonies has been usually, in all the

sisted during the last few generations." Sir Edwin Arnold, commenting upon the same fact, says of America: " I have found myself
everywhere in a transatlantic England. I do not say that in any
foolish idea that to be 'quite English' is a point of perfection. . . .
Half an American as I am, by marriage and by sympathies, I must
confess that it has been wholly delightful to observe this unmistaka-
ble and minute identification of the races." Mr. Bryce points out
the process of foreign absorption, by which, though immigrants
usually retain their foreign traits in the first generation, the rising
generation rapidly loses its old nationality. "The younger sort,"
he says truthfully, "when they have learned English; when, working
among Americans, they have imbibed the sentiments and assimilated
the ideas of the country, are henceforth scarcely to be distinguished
from the native population. They are more American than the
Americans in their desire to put on the character of their new
country." — *American Commonwealth*, II. 328. Professor Hosmer
comments: "The Anglo-Saxon stock has been made rich and
strong by a score of crossings with the most vigorous and intellectual of modern races; but it remains, nevertheless, Anglo-Saxon.
In 1886, at the great Colonial Exhibition in London, what especially
struck the American visitor was the identity with his own civilization of the civilization represented in the products set forth; and
the similarity to himself of the English-speaking men who had
gathered there, though they came from the farthest corners of the
world. Such clothing we wear . . . with such appliances we, too,
mine, work the soil, sail the sea, . . . and teach the young idea how
to shoot; in the paintings of towns at the antipodes, which sometimes were hung on the walls, the streets looked like those of any
American town; the frontiersman's hut in the remote clearing, as
the model showed it, was a reproduction of the log cabin of Dakota
or Kansas. If the American fell into talk with a group pausing in

history of the world, through forms similar to those which dominate the parent people.

When in the early part of the seventeenth century English colonization of America began, England had

an aisle before some attractive object, though one might be from New Zealand, another from the Faulkland Islands, a third from Natal, and a fourth from Athabasca, a close spiritual and intellectual relationship was at once developed. All had read, to a large extent, the same books, been trained in the same religious faith, disciplined and made strongly virile by that priceless polity, so free and yet so carefully ordered, which had been inherited from Anglo-Saxon ancestors, or thoroughly assimilated through contact with Englishmen. 'Should you know,' said the American, 'that my home is in the valley of the Mississippi?' 'By no means,' was the reply; 'you seem to me like my neighbours in Aukland.' And yet it was two hundred and fifty years since the ancestor of the American had left his home in Kent to go to the New World, and the New Zealander had never left his island until he took ship a month before for London. 'You seem like my neighbours,' also could say the man from Cape Town, from Fort Garry, from Puget Sound, from the gold fields of Ballarat. 'You might all come from this or that English county,' said a Londoner, who had joined the group; 'you are no more diverse from one another, or from us, than the man of Yorkshire from the man of Dorset; the Cumberland shepherd from the Leicestershire farmer. . . . Substantially, they were identical with one another — identical too with the American — all with blood enriched by infusion, . . . but not changed in frame or speech or soul from the champions who, under Alfred, or Earl Simon, or Cromwell, or Washington, or Lincoln, fought to sustain Anglo-Saxon freedom." — *Anglo-Saxon Freedom*, 318–320. So speaks a writer of our time, of the race as it is to-day in America, notwithstanding the changes of two centuries, and those other changes wrought by modern immigration. The race during the American colonial period —which is the sole point that the present volume has to consider — was thoroughly and intensely English.

long been a fully developed, homogeneous nation. The
Englishmen of the reigns of Elizabeth and James I.
possessed a certain stock of political ideas in common.
There was agreement in the conception of certain elements of government; and the principal of these elements were : (1) a single executive ; (2) a legislative
body consisting of two houses, the upper conservative,
and the lower representative of the people at large ; (3)
a distinctive judiciary. There was also agreement in (4)
a number of general principles — such as trial by jury,
the essential relation of representation to taxation, and
the like — derived from the old struggle of the nation
for its freedom. It was natural that colonies, set off
from the home land as these were, should manifest a
tendency to develop such governmental institutions.
And this was the actual course of their development.
The American colonies were settled mainly by Englishmen, and were subject to Great Britain. And their
institutions were mainly of an English nature, except as
modified by the provisions of the royal charters under
which their governments were organized, and by the
circumstances that attended transplanting to a new soil.[1]

[1] Professor William C. Morey (*Annals of American Academy of
Political and Social Science*, April, 1891) lays emphasis upon the
fact that the charters granted by the sovereigns for the colonies
were really charters of commercial corporations. The further fact
that the governmental provisions of these charters closely resem-
bled the outlines of the English government, greatly aided the
colonists in establishing English institutions. The colonists, however, did not confine themselves to charter provisions. What

This essential political fact is made forcibly clear by any examination of colonial origin and progress. Such examination, at least in brief, is called for, as introducing the present theme. In entering upon it, we will first consider the government of each colony separately, and then the relation of the colonies collectively to the home administration.

The earliest permanent English settlement, within the present territory of the United States, was in Virginia, under a charter granted by James I. in 1606.[1] This charter, which was followed by others in 1609 and 1612, provided for a company having a council resident in England with power to govern under regulations and instructions from the king. As the colonists began to increase, a demand was set up for a voice in the making of the laws. "They grew restless and impatient," Judge Story expresses it, "for the privileges enjoyed under the

these lacked they supplemented by a direct copying from British originals, until there resulted, by action of the people themselves, a close assimilation of each colonial government to the model of the government of the mother-land. "The constitutional development of the American colonies began very early. The colonial system hampered them but slightly, and that chiefly in regard to trade. Assemblies were not instituted, but grew up of themselves, because it was of the nature of Englishmen to assemble."—Seeley, *Expansion of England*, 67. As Hutchinson expresses it, "This year (1619) a House of Burgesses *broke out* in Virginia." See Robinson, *Publications of the American Academy of Political and Social Science*, No. 9, p. 207.

[1] This charter is given in Poore's *Charters and Constitutions*, Part II., p. 1888. Also it may be found in Stith, and in Hazard's *Historical Collections*.

government of their native country."[1] And to meet
this uneasiness, Governor Yeardly called together representatives in a general assembly at Jamestown in 1619,
and allowed them legislative powers.[2] Story adds:
"Thus was formed and established the first representative legislature that ever sat in America. And this
example of a domestic parliament to regulate all the
internal concerns of the country was never lost sight of,
but was ever afterwards cherished throughout America as
the dearest birthright of freemen."[3] So acceptable was
it to the people, and so essential to the real prosperity of
the colony, that the council in England issued an ordinance in 1621, which gave it a complete and permanent
sanction.[4] In imitation of the constitution of the British

---

[1] *Commentaries on the Constitution of the United States,* I. 21,
§ 46.

[2] Robertson's *America,* B. 9. "The first representative legislative assembly ever held in America was convened in the chancel of
the [Episcopal] church at James City or Jamestown, and was composed of twenty-two burgesses from the eleven several towns, plantations, and hundreds styled Burroughs." — *Narrative and Critical
History,* III. 143. In 1874 the manuscript account of the transactions of this assembly, from the State Paper Office, London, was
published as a State Senate Document; *Colonial Records of Virginia.* In 1857 it was published in the *Collections of the New York
Historical Society.*

[3] *Commentaries on the Constitution of the United States,* 1. 21,
§ 46.

[4] Referring to the Jamestown assembly of 1619, Professor Thorp
remarks: "Two years later, on the 24th of July, the council of the
company in England approved the course of the assembly by passing an ordinance establishing a written constitution for Virginia.

Parliament, the legislative power was lodged partly in the governor, who held the place of the sovereign ; partly in a council of state named by the company, and partly in an assembly composed of representatives chosen by the people. Each branch of the legislature might decide by a majority of votes, and a negative was reserved for the governor. But no law was to be in force, though approved by all three parts of the legislature, until it had been ratified by a general court of the company, and returned to the colony under seal of the court. The ordinance further required the general assembly and the council of state "to initiate and follow the policy of the forms of the laws, customs, and manner of trial, and the administration of justice used in the realm of England, as near as may be."

Thus the government of Virginia, even at that early date, included a personal executive in the governor, representing the sovereign ; two houses of legislature, the lower one elected by the people ; and a system of justice.

By the annulling of the charter and the dissolution of the company in 1624, the colony came under the rule of the king, exercised through a governor and twelve councillors of his own appointment ; and it remained a royal province down to the American Revolution. For

This earliest written constitution for an American commonwealth was modelled after the unwritten constitution of England, and it is the historical foundation of all later constitutions of government in this country." — *Story of the Constitution*, 26. See Henning, *Stat.*, 111; Stith's *Virginia*, App. No. 4, 321. The boasted Connecticut constitution was of later date.

many years following this change, there was no second
house of legislature ; and during the greater part of the
reign of Charles I., the sovereign who sought to govern
without a Parliament at home, succeeded in governing
by his own will in the colony.   But after complaints, and
some open resistance, Charles sent over Sir William
Berkeley, with instructions to summon elected representatives, who should form, with the governor and council, an assembly clothed with full legislative powers.   He
also set up courts of justice.   And thus for the second
time by popular demand, Virginia obtained a government embracing the essential points of that of the
mother land.   English common law underlay the colonial jurisprudence.   Trial by jury, taxation by the representatives of the people in assembly, and other characteristic English principles, were incorporated into custom
and regulation.   Such was Virginia before she became a
State of the American union, and her State constitution
was essentially an outgrowth of this colonial adaptation
of English usage.

To the "Governor and Company of Massachusetts Bay
in New England" Charles I. granted a charter in 1628,[1]
intending that the corporation should administer its affairs
from England.   Provision was made for a governor,
deputy governor, and eighteen assistants, to serve as a
council, with permission to freemen of the company to
attend and take part in certain general meetings annually.
Laws for the benefit of the distant colony were allowed

[1] Poore's *Charters*, I. 932; *Massachusetts Records*, I. 3.

to be made, "so as such laws and ordinances be not contrary or repugnant to the laws and statutes of this our
realm of England." But in the year following the grant
of the charter, by a bold stroke on the part of the company the document was transferred to Massachusetts ; and
it became thenceforth, until its abrogation under James
II., the basis of government by the colonists within the
colony itself.[1] For a few succeeding years, the administration was conducted by a General Court composed of
the governor and assistants, with the assembling of such
freemen as were capable of attending in person. But in
1634 the towns sent elected delegates to represent them,
though no provision for such a course was to be found in
the charter ; and ten years later, the governor and assistants on one hand, and the representatives on the other,
definitely separated into two houses of legislature. Thus
in Massachusetts, as in Virginia, the outlines of English
government were worked out in local usage by movement of the colonists themselves.

[1] " What was originally organized as an English trading company
thus became an American colony, with its constitution and government unchanged. The charter of 1628 remained the colonial constitution of Massachusetts until 1691, when it was superseded by a
new royal charter, which, however, confirmed the previous frame of
government in its essential points, save that the governor was now
appointed by the crown. It should be noticed that by this charter
of 1691 the colony of pilgrims at Plymouth, Massachusetts, who
had developed an independent government of their own, without
any royal sanction, was united to Massachusetts Bay, and became incorporated into the same political organization." — *Annals of American Academy of Political and Social Science*, April, 1891, p. 550.

In 1646 the General Court of Massachusetts sent an address to the Long Parliament, declaring: "For our government itself, it is framed according to our charter, and the fundamental and common laws of England, and conceived according to the same — taking the words of eternal truth and righteousness along with them as that rule by which all kingdoms and jurisdictions must render account of every act and administration in the last day — with as bare allowance of the disproportion between such an ancient populous, wealthy kingdom, and so poor an infant, thin colony as common reason can afford." They then endeavoured to demonstrate the accuracy of their statement by setting forth in parallel columns the fundamental laws of England from Magna Charta, and their own laws.[1]

For New Hampshire, the king issued a commission in 1679, erecting a government with the executive power vested in a president. The president was appointed by the sovereign, and was aided by a council, also of royal appointment, which, together with popularly elected representatives or burgesses, composed the legislature. The council also possessed judicial powers; and it was required in the charter that "the form of proceedings in such cases, and the judgment thereon to be given, be as consonant and agreeable to the laws and statutes of this our realm of England, as the present state and condition of our subjects inhabiting within the limits

[1] Palfrey, *History of New England*, II. 174; Hutchinson, *History*, I. 145, 146.

aforesaid, and the circumstances of the place will admit."[1]

The colonies of Connecticut[2] and New Haven, without awaiting a charter, established governments of their

[1] *New Hampshire Provincial Laws*, ed. 1771, pp. 1, 3.

[2] "In 1639 a written instrument was signed by which the three towns of Windsor, Wethersfield, and Hartford became associated as one body politic. Citizens of Connecticut, with very just pride point to this instrument as the first American written constitution, for the compact on the Mayflower was merely an agreement to found a government, leaving its character to be determined in the future. But in view of the fact, that the Netherland republic had for about half a century been living under the 'Union of Utrecht,' which was a written constitution pure and simple, writers are hardly warranted in calling this the first instrument of the kind known to history." — Campbell, *Puritan in Holland, England, and America*, II. 417. "This enactment of the Connecticut colonists has been extolled as 'the first example in history of a written constitution, — an organic law constituting a government and defining its powers.'" — Bacon, *Constitutional History of Connecticut*, 5, 6. Mr. Bryce calls it the oldest truly political constitution in America. — *American Commonwealth*, I. 414, note. "It was, no doubt, the first written constitution which was enacted by the independent act of the people. The form of government, however, which it constituted was simply a reproduction of that of the Massachusetts Bay Company, sanctioned by the charter of 1628. Whether the independent authority exercised by the Connecticut colonists was alone sufficient to constitute a legal government was, to them at least, a matter of question. Aware of the doubtful nature of their title to exercise sovereignty, the colonists appealed to the king, and in 1662 received a royal charter, which erected the colony into a corporate company, with powers and privileges similar to those already given to the Massachusetts Bay Company. The phraseology of this charter throughout is almost precisely the same as that employed in the Massachusetts charter of 1628." — Morey, *Annals*

own, consisting of governor, assistants, and deputies com-
posing a general court. The two colonies were merged
by the charter granted to Connecticut at the restoration
of Charles II., 1662 ; which document — escaping seizure
at the hands of Sir Edmund Andros in the reign of the
last Stuart king, by being secreted in an oak — remained
in force until so late as 1818, when the State constitution
succeeded to it and was modelled upon it. A bill of
rights similar to that of Massachusetts was early passed
by the colony, and trial by jury was, with other English
customs, established in common practice.

Rhode Island, also a union of two previously existing
colonies, received from Charles II., in 1663, after a succession of political vicissitudes, a charter constituting the
usual elements of government. And the colony itself set
forth the customary bill of rights. For about thirty years
afterwards, the general assembly met as a single chamber ; but from 1696, the governor and assistants acted
as an upper house, and the deputies as a lower house.[1]
The original charter remained until 1842 the fundamental law of the State, and was not until then superseded by a State constitution.

Maryland was granted by a patent of Charles I., in
1632, to Cecilius Calvert, Lord Baltimore, and his heirs,
in full and absolute property, saving only the rights of

---

of *American Academy of Political and Social Science*, April, 1891,
p. 551. As a matter of fact, the royal charters were the first
American written constitutions.

[1] *Rhode Island Colony Laws* (1744), 24.

the crown.[1] The patent vested in the proprietor full executive power, and the privilege of making laws, with the co-operation of the colonists. All freemen were permitted to take part in legislation; and the first gatherings for the purpose were held in 1634 and 1635. But in 1639, in consequence of the increase of population, deputies were elected to represent the freemen. Eventually, as in other colonies, the assembly was divided into two houses.[2] And among the earliest laws adopted was one declaring "that the inhabitants shall have all their rights and liberties according to the great charter of England."[3]

Originally colonized by the Dutch, New York and New Jersey did not pass into English hands until 1664. Singularly, however, the Dutch occupation left very

---

[1] " The Province was made a county palatine, and the Proprietary was invested with all the royal rights, privileges, and prerogatives which had ever been enjoyed by any Bishop of Durham within his county palatine." — *Narrative and Critical History*, III. 520.

[2] "The details of political organization were in a great measure confided to the discretion of the proprietor, whose original conception of a constitution consisted of a governor, council, and primary assembly — a veritable old English gemote — in which every freeman had the right to represent himself and to vote. Gradually, as the primary plan grew inconvenient, it was supplanted by a representative system, and in 1647 the governing body was divided into two chambers: the lower consisting of an elective house of burgesses; the upper, of the councillors and of those specially summoned by the proprietor." — Taylor, *Origin and Growth of the English Constitution*, 24.

[3] Bacon, *Laws of Maryland*, c. 2, 1638; c. 1, 1650. *Assembly Proceedings of Maryland*, 1637 to 1658, p. 129.

little permanent result of a constitutional character.[1]
The territory was granted to the Duke of York by two
charters of Charles II., one given before and the other
after the final acknowledgment of the conquest on the
part of the government of the Netherlands.[2]

[1] "The Dutch did not trouble themselves much about forms of
government." — Landon, *Constitutional History of the United States*,
23.

[2] In consequence of this a large proportion of the Dutch inhabitants left the colony and returned to Europe.

Since Mr. Douglas Campbell made his assertion of Dutch as
against English influence upon the institutions of the United States,
it has become customary in New York and some other localities
to repeat and amplify his allegations. When this is done by
Americans of Dutch ancestry, no one need wonder; but when the
utterances proceed from other sources, and are marked by a rhe-
torical rather than historical tone, they are to be regarded differently. The lines of argument used by such writers commonly
repeat themselves. (1) It is claimed that America was influenced
by Holland, because Holland exerted an influence over England.
But it is evident that this particular line of influence, whatever
it may have been, reached America through England. Little is
said by these one-sided writers of any influence exerted by England
over Holland. (2) It is claimed that because the Pilgrims and
some of the early Puritans passed through Holland on their way to
America, they were controllingly influenced by the Dutch. But
there is practically an ignoring of the fact that these men had spent
the greater part of their lives in England, and were by birth and
blood Englishmen. (3) It is claimed that by means of commercial
transactions, Holland and New Amsterdam influenced the social
life of the colonists. But the long and bitter hostility of the colonists toward the Dutch is unmentioned. And the fact is left out
of sight, that the main contact and commerce of the colonies down
to the very last, was with England. It is not worth while to follow
these writers further in such irresponsible toying with sober history.

Under the second charter, the Duke ruled New York until his own accession to the crown as James II. No general assembly was summoned for eight years, but popular clamour became so great, that in 1682 the governor was authorized to establish one, with the right of making laws subject to approval by the proprietor.[1] Six years later the colony declared for William and Mary; and thereafter, although without charter, it was governed as a royal province by crown-appointed governors, and with regular sessions of the legislature. The laws indicate closer adherence to the policy of England than do those of any other colony, and the British common law was the basis of jurisprudence.[2]

Undoubtedly nations do affect one another through example, institutions, literature, and commerce. England and Holland have thus exerted an influence upon each other. So also have England and France. So have America and European peoples other than the Dutch. Dutch influence upon the United States has doubtless been real in several ways. But nothing can be gained by the effort of enthusiasts to exaggerate that influence, or to assert for it a place comparable with the influence of England.

[1] This assembly "was formally called by the governor, as the duke's representative, in answer to a popular petition for a government *like that of the New England colonies.* These enactments, under the name of a ' charter of liberty,' vested the government in the hands of a governor, council, and representative assembly, with powers similar to those possessed by the corresponding branches *in New England;* and these enactments were approved, not only by the governor and the duke, but also by the king." — *Annals of American Academy of Political and Social Science*, April, 1891, p. 553.

[2] As New York was originally settled by the Dutch, the complete supremacy of English constitutional law and usage is the more remarkable. Some Dutch usages linger (see Campbell, *Puritan in*

New Jersey was granted by the Duke of York, in 1664, to Lord Berkeley and Sir George Carteret, on the same terms as he himself held New York; and these proprietors in 1664-65 made to the people a concession

Holland, England, and America); but their number seems to be relatively small, — so small that Dutch influence was until recently almost forgotten. When the first charter was granted to the Duke of York, "no laws contrary to those of England were allowed." — Story, *Commentaries on the Constitution*, I. 75, § 112. The supremacy of the Englishmen, with their characteristic claims of liberty, is evidenced by the exclamation of the governor to the legislature in 1697: "There are none of you but what are big with the privileges of Englishmen and Magna Charta." — Landon, *Constitutional History of the United States*, 24. Among the earliest acts was one declaring the right to enjoy the liberties and privileges of Englishmen by Magna Charta. — Smith, *New York*, 127, 75, 76; *Acts* of 1691. Story remarks: "In examining the subsequent legislation of the province, there do not appear to be any very striking deviations from the laws of England; and the common law, beyond all question, was the basis of its jurisprudence. . . . Perhaps New York was more close in adoption of the policy and legislation of the parent country before the Revolution, than any other colony." — *Commentaries on the Constitution*, I. 77, 78, § 114. The facts are well summarized by Crane and Moses: "New York we find owed its first settlement, like many other colonies, to a speculative corporation. The Dutch West India Company, under its charter from the government of the Netherlands, undertook to colonize the new territory in the neighbourhood of the Hudson River. It is not necessary to our purpose to examine very closely the history of this commercial venture, because the Dutch *régime* made little or no impression politically, however great its impression socially, upon the future State. . . . The elements of local self-government then existing in Holland were not transplanted. It is from the capture by the English, in 1664, that the political life of New York dates." — *Politics*, 117.

of the customary forms of government. After political vicissitudes, the proprietary control terminated in the reign of Queen Anne. But though the colony had no charter, and was ruled under royal commissions, the local model of government remained practically unchanged.[1]

The settlement of Pennsylvania and Delaware by the Dutch and Swedes was, as in the case of the original settlement of New York, without much political result. William Penn obtained a patent as proprietor in 1631, and purchased in the following year the rights of the Duke of York over the Three Lower Counties of Delaware. The patent empowered Penn and his successors to make laws and raise taxes, with the consent of the freemen of the country, the king reserving right of veto. The proprietor was permitted to appoint judicial and other officials, to grant pardons and reprieves, to erect courts, to establish corporations, manors, and ports, and to execute locally other functions of the crown.[2]

---

[1] "In all these changes of authority, the form of government established . . . retained the general form which already prevailed in New England, which type was more consciously followed than that of the south, although there was no essential difference between the political forms of the two sections." — *Annals of American Academy*, April, 1891, p. 554.

[2] It has been remarked, as a strange omission in this charter, that no provision exists to the effect that the inhabitants and their children shall be deemed British subjects, and entitled to all the liberties and immunities thereof, such a clause being found in every other charter. Chalmers has observed that the clause was unnecessary, as allegiance to the crown was reserved; and the common law thence

After some variation in the system of government, a final charter was established in 1701, providing for a governor, council of state, and assembly of deputies.[1] Delaware sent representatives until accorded a legislature of her own in 1703.

Carolina was granted to Lord Clarendon and others by Charles II. The earliest government was set aside in 1669 by a plan originating in the brain of the philosopher Locke, which contemplated an elaborate system of offices of state, an hereditary nobility, and similar features, impossible of realization in an infant settlement of scattered planters.[2] But in 1691 this system was

inferred that all the inhabitants were subjects, and of course were entitled to all the privileges of Englishmen. See *Annals*, 639, 658.

[1] See Campbell, *Puritan in Holland, England, and America.* He claims that a few Dutch elements crept into the institutions of Pennsylvania, and partly accounts for their existence by pointing out that the mother of William Penn was Dutch. However this may be, Penn's father and family were English, and he always accounted himself an Englishman. That, with local modifications, the institutions of Pennsylvania were essentially English, cannot be historically questioned; and the presence of an occasional feature of possibly Dutch origin only serves to accentuate the predominance of the English features that make up the whole body of the laws.

[2] "The proprietors attempted to create a political fabric through the aid of Locke — a philosopher of the Social Contract school — whose Fundamental Constitutions quickly illustrated how vain it was to attempt to govern Englishmen by a paper constitution whose complicated and artificial details offended the national instinct by departing from the primitive tradition."—Taylor, *Origin and Growth of the English Constitution*, 24. These constitutions may be seen in their first state in Carroll, II. 361; and the modifications are given under the years of issue in the *Shaftesbury Papers*. See,

abrogated by popular demand. Carolina became a royal province in 1729, with the usual form of colonial government. The governor convened, prorogued, and dissolved the legislature, and had the right of veto on its enactments. He appointed civil and military officers, and, as has been tersely said, was "invested, as far as compatible, with the executive and judicial powers of the English monarch."[1] North and South Carolina, long practically divided for reasons of convenience, were eventually separated, each having a government of its own.

Georgia was founded in 1732 with a charter from George II. Its earliest administration, by a company resident in England, was so unsuccessful that this charter was soon surrendered, and the colony became a royal province with government of the customary form.[2]

The necessary repetition in these details of the political systems of the colonies is not without value, as evidence of the unanimity with which the colonies followed a common model. Where, at first, in charter or usage, some features of this model were lacking, popular de-

also, *Carolina Charters*, London, 33, etc. A recent biographer of Locke (II. R. Bourne) notes that the plan was initiated by Shaftesbury, and modified by other proprietors; and although Locke had a large share in the work, not all the features were such as he himself approved.

[1] Crane and Moses, *Politics*, 123.

[2] "In respect to its ante-revolutionary jurisprudence, a few remarks may suffice. The British common and statute law lay at the foundation. The same general system prevailed as in the Carolinas, from whence it sprung." — Story, *Commentaries on the Constitution of the United States*, I. 99, § 145.

mand invariably was made by the colonists themselves, for the supply of the lack, until the full outline of English governmental institutions was completed, as far as was applicable to colonial conditions.[1]

Referring to this subject, and to the persistence of the old tendency even in later and more modern States of the American Union, Mr. Bryce observes: "The similarity of the frame of government in the thirty-two republics which make up the United States — a similarity which appears the more remarkable when we remember that each of the republics is independent and self-determined as respects its frame of government — is due to the common source whence the governments flow.   They

[1] The scope of the present volume does not admit of a discussion of the interesting questions associated with the history of American townships and local government. It is just possible those questions have been pressed too far. But the student of ancient institutions must recognize their great importance. Nor can he fail to appreciate the force with which evidence drawn from such sources confirms the truth of the development of American governments from the historic past. See Scott, *Development of Constitutional Liberty*, 174; Fiske, *American Political Ideas*, 17–56; Fiske, "Town Meeting," *Harper's Magazine*, January, 1885; Professor Adams, "Germanic Origin of New England Towns," in *Johns Hopkins University Studies*, 1st Series, II.; E. Channing, "Town and County Government," *Ibid.*, 2d Series, X.; Doyle, *English Colonies in America, Puritan*, etc., II. 7–26; Professor Andrews, "Origin of Conn. Towns," *Annals of American Academy*, Vol. I.; Hildreth, *History*, I. chap. vii.; De Tocqueville, *Bowen's Translation, Democracy in America*, I. chap. v.; Parker, *Origin, Organization and Influence of Towns of New England;* Massachusetts Historical Society, 1866–67, etc. See also Statutes of New England States, Law Reports, etc.

are all copies, some immediate, some mediate, of ancient English institutions; viz. chartered self-governing corporations, which under the influence of English habits and with the precedent of the English parliamentary system before their eyes, developed into governments resembling that of England in the eighteenth century. Each of the thirteen colonies had, up to 1776, been regulated by a charter from the British crown, which, according to the best and oldest of all English traditions, allowed it the practical management of its own affairs. The charter contained a sort of skeleton constitution which usage had clothed with nerves, muscles, and sinews, till it became a complete and symmetrical working system of free government." [1]

"The English Constitution was generally the type of these colonial governments," remarks Sir Erskine May. "The governor was the viceroy of the crown; the legislative council, or upper chamber, appointed by the governor, assumed the place of the House of Lords, and the representative assembly, chosen by the people, was the express image of the House of Commons." [2] In the words of the author of the *History of the English People,* "The colonists proudly looked on the constitutions of their various States as copies of that of the mother-country. England had given them her law, her language, her religion, and her blood." [3]

[1] Bryce, *American Commonwealth*, I. 458.
[2] *Constitutional History of England*, II. 511.
[3] Green, *History*, V. 217, § 1440.

But the American colonies not only copied English institutions; they long remained politically united to Great Britain, and her government long continued to be their own supreme or imperial government. Though every colony was independent of every other colony, and possessed much freedom of local administration, yet allegiance to the mother-country and to the throne bound all together, and prepared the way for the subsequent federal system of the United States. There was, in fact, even then, a beginning of the federal system, and London was the colonial capital, as Washington of to-day is the federal capital.[1] The colonists were British subjects. The king was "supreme and sovereign lord" of all alike. — the central executive. Parliament, with whatever limitations in practice, was the central legislature, and the Privy Council exercised the jurisdiction of supreme judicial tribunal.

The authority of the king was employed with a varying degree of directness in different colonies. His prerogatives were, for the most part, put in operation by the local governors. In crown colonies, where the royal contact was closest, civil government largely depended upon special instructions and commissions issued from time to time directly from the throne. Colonial legislation was subject to the sovereign's approval or veto. All charters were granted by him, and his powers were exercised on occasion in other acts affecting the fundamental status of colonial administration.[2]

[1] The analogy is not close, but it is real as far as it goes.

[2] "The fact that the soil upon which the English colonies in

Parliament made laws for the supreme government of the colonies. While some confusion of ideas existed as to the proper exercise of this power, the power was always claimed unlimitedly by Parliament itself, and its operation was willingly conceded by the colonists in cases affecting foreign, commercial, and Indian affairs, and what might be called imperial as distinct from internal interests. The legislation of the colonial assemblies was, indeed, occasionally annulled by a board or council in England, as well as by Parliament. And denial of all parliamentary authority, though made in some of the colonies after the passage of the Stamp

America were planted, came to them through royal grants, the fact that every form of political organization established thereon rested upon royal charters, were the foundation stones upon which the colonists gradually built up, in the light of their actual experience, their theory of the political relations which bound them to the mother-country. Their rights as Englishmen endowed with ' all liberties, franchises, and immunities of free denizens and natural subjects' flowed from their charters, which, as between themselves and the crown, were irrevocable though not non-forfeitable contracts. The earliest form of direct legislative control to which any of the colonies were subjected in the form of ordinances or instructions for their government emanated, not from the law-making power of the king in Parliament, but from the ordaining power of the king in council. And at a later day, when the colonial assemblies began the work of legislation on their own account, the validity of their enactments depended, not upon the approval of the English Parliament, but upon that of the royal governor, who stood as the ever-present representative of his royal master. With the founding of the colonies, and with the organization of their political systems, the crown had everything to do." — Taylor, *Origin and Growth of the English Constitution*, 25, 26.

Act of 1765, was not general until the verge of actual separation from the mother-country.

The jurisdiction of the Privy Council as a supreme court for colonial affairs, in appeals from decisions of the colonial judiciary, and in other matters, was constantly exercised. And it was fully recognized by all the colonies at the period of the American Revolution, and regarded as a benefit and protection.

Yet notwithstanding mutual ties of blood and institutions, it is easy to perceive, looking back from our own time, that there existed fair opportunity for friction, and even for eventual separation in the somewhat complex and vaguely defined relations, and in the gradually diverging interests of Great Britain and her distant children. Among causes of uneasiness is often mentioned the development of a democratic tendency among the colonists, manifesting itself in varied forms, but chiefly in contests between the legislatures and the royal governors. This tendency, which eventually became characteristic, is, perhaps, not to be wondered at, if it be remembered that the colonists were commoners, without the restraining presence of a resident nobility, and that the colonial period was a period which witnessed the overthrow of Charles I. by his House of Commons, the rise of the English Commonwealth, and the Revolution of 1688, as contemporaneous movements in the mother-country, ending in the modern control of the crown by the popular branch of Parliament. But the truth is, that as the colonists grew in numbers and material wealth, and began to realize their own power, interference across seas came to be less and less easy to maintain on one side, or to endure on the other. And with the fall of Canada and the consequent overthrow of a threatening French power in the north and west, America ceased to feel the need of dependence upon the empire.

Yet although a sense of the inevitable approach of American independence came to find expression even among keen foreign observers on the continent of Europe,[1] the colonists themselves, up to the very eve of war, were averse to the thought of actual separation. The records of the time are filled with evidences of the powerful hold which the mother-country had upon their hearts. They loved Great Britain as their old home.[2] "They regarded," remarks Froth-

---

[1] "Turgot and Choiseul had very early recognized that the separation of the colonies from the mother-country was only a question of time." — Von Holst, *Constitutional History of the United States*, I. 1. See also Bancroft, *History of the United States*, IV. 399. Durand wrote in August, 1766, "They are too rich to remain in obedience." See also, Frothingham, *Rise of the Republic of the United States.*

[2] "This feeling was not an easy one to eradicate, for it was based in blood, training, and sympathies of every nature. It would not have been easy to distinguish the American from the Englishman; it would, indeed, have been less easy than now, when the full effects of a great stream of immigration have begun to appear. American portraits of the time show typical English faces. Whenever life was relieved of the privations involved in colonial struggle, the person at once reverted to the type which was then the result of corresponding conditions in England. The traditions of American

ingham, "their connection with the mother-country to
be a fountain of gcod. They looked upon the English
Constitution as their own."[1]   Even in the midst of the
final contest, so great a leader as the elder Adams could
write : "Would to God, all, even our enemies, knew
the warm attachment we have for Great Britain."[2]   And
John Adams,[3] referring to "the habitual affection for
England," during colonial times, was able to declare
truthfully that "no affection could be more sincere."[4]

officers were English; their methods were English; even the attitude which they took towards the private soldiers of their armies
was that which was characteristic of the English officer of the time.
In the south, the men who led and formed public opinion had
almost all been trained in England, and were ingrained with English
sympathies and even prejudices. In the north, the acute general
intellect had long ago settled upon the 'common rights of Englishmen' as the bulwark behind which they could best resist any
attempt on their liberties. The pride of the colonists in their position as Englishmen found a medium of expression in enthusiasm
for 'the young king'; and it would be hard to imagine a more loyal
appendage of the crown than its English colonies in North America in 1760."— Professor Johnson, of Princeton, in *Encyclopædia
Britannica*, 9th ed., XXIII. 736.

[1] Frothingham, *Rise of the Republic of the United States*, 123.
The following extract from the American press of the time fairly
expresses the popular feeling : "Our constitution is English, which
is another name for free and happy, and is without doubt the per-
fectest model of civil government that has ever been in the world."
— *Independent Advertiser*, May 29, 1749.

[2] Letter to Charles Thompson, 1774, *Life of Warren*, 232.

[3] *Works*, X. 282.

[4] Referring to the period preceding the Revolution, Frothingham says : "A town under the lead of zealous Whigs voted that the
union between the colonies and Great Britain was not worth a rush;

When the contest came, it came as a struggle over ancient English constitutional principles. The drift had long been toward an opening of the whole question of mutual civil relations, when George III. forced the question to an issue by attempted taxation through act of Parliament. England was proud of America as her

occasionally a writer urged in an essay in the newspapers that the only way to place American liberty on a firm foundation was to form an independent nation ; but these were the views of extremists, and were generally disavowed. The great body of the Whigs united with the Tories in prizing this union as of incalculable value. They regarded themselves as fellow-subjects with Britons. They looked on the people of both countries as being one in the essential elements of nationality, political ideas, language, and the Christian religion; and one in the love of a noble literature and precious historic memories. They kindled at the sight of the old flag and at thoughts of the mother-land —

> " 'A land of just and old renown,
>   Where freedom broadens slowly down
>   From precedent to precedent; '

and it was the prevailing sentiment that a recognition of coequal rights would enable the people of both countries to live long under the same flag. The popular leaders averred that they did not deny the sovereignty, but opposed the administration. They did not ascribe the obnoxious measures to the king whom they revered, or to the constitution which they venerated, or to the nation which they loved, but to despotic ministers and corrupt majorities." — *Rise of the Republic of the United States*, 294, 295. In another place he well remarks: "I cannot but think that much error has crept into American history by not keeping in view the difference between opposition to the measures of an administration and resistance to the supreme power of the empire, or to the sovereignty." And looking back over the period of colonial history, adds, "The immigrants . . . bore toward [England] a noble affection." — *Ibid.* 67.

chief imperial possession; but she had not yet learned
the secret of imperial administration, and her old customs and legal theories, lingering from days when she
had been but an island kingdom, were inapplicable to
the new conditions. By those theories, the colonists,
being British subjects, were as completely subordinated
to Parliament as were all other British subjects. True,
they had long been permitted to regulate their internal
affairs, and above all, to vote their own taxes; but Parliament had on sundry occasions asserted its right of taxation, and held such right to be a necessary part of its
own position as supreme legislature. As the legal theory
of Parliament had grown up under purely national conditions, this parliamentary claim was theoretically correct. But it did not accord with the new imperial facts.
On the other hand, the colonists held that the imperial
facts ought to be conceded. Though British subjects,
they were separated by wide seas from the older land,
and were unable to take active part in its political life.
A fundamental principle of the liberties of Englishmen
associated, as the colonists understood it, the right of
representation with the right of taxation. The principle
had been enunciated in their colonial legislation almost
from the beginning of colonial settlement, and had been
steadily acted upon by them. They were without representatives in Parliament, and therefore Parliament could
not, in their view, rightfully tax them. They were un-
willing to pay the parliamentary tax, though, through
their own representatives in the colonial legislatures,

they were ready to vote more liberal supplies than those proposed by Parliament. Their plea was conservative, for it desired that the then existing state of affairs should be continued. The war that ensued was fought on the part of the colonists in defence of what they thus held to be their rights as men of the English blood ; and American independence resulted from this constitutional struggle.

CHAPTER II.

MAKING OF THE AMERICAN CONSTITUTION.

THE political steps that led to American independence were taken gradually. At the beginning
of the war, an intercolonial or "continental" Congress
assembled. Gatherings, similar in principle, had been
held on other occasions in colonial experience without
involving a denial either of the civil rights of individual
colonies or of the authority of the mother-country.
Indeed, the colonists, though in no gentle mood, contemplated at first not political separation, but only
defence against what they claimed to be an unconstitutional attack upon their liberties as English subjects ; and
Englishmen had many a time in the history of the
mother-land itself taken up arms for the preservation of
liberties.[1] But the logic of events on American soil

[1] " A separation from Great Britain was viewed with alarm and
trepidation, and was not only opposed by the Tory party as a
whole, but also by many Whigs, who feared it might lead to
anarchy and its attendant evils." — Straus, *Origin of Republican
Form of Government in the United States*, 5. " It was long before
the ill will, which the systematic disregard by Parliament of the
rights of the colonists had excited, triumphed over this feeling.
Even in August and September, 1775 — that is, half a year after the

slowly shaped the issue, and the Congress was forced
more and more into acts involving the assumption of
sovereign power, and plainly inconsistent with loyalty to

battle of Lexington — so strong was the Anglo-Saxon spirit of conservatism and loyalty among the colonists, that the few extremists
who dared to speak of a violent disruption of all bonds, entailed
chastisement upon themselves and were universally censured." —
Von Holst, *Constitutional History of the United States*, I. 2. See also
Works of John Adams, II. 423, and *American Archives*, III. 21,
196, 644, etc. "In May, 1775, Washington said: 'If you ever
hear of me joining in any such measure [as separation from Great
Britain], you have my leave to set me down for everything wicked.'
He had also said: 'It is not the wish or interest of the government [meaning Massachusetts], or of any other upon this continent,
separately or collectively, to set up for independence.' And in the
same year, Benjamin Franklin assured Chatham, that no one in
America was in favour of separation. As a matter of fact, the people of the colonies wanted a redress of their grievances — they
were not dreaming of separation, of independence. . . . We
must also remember that the Revolution was begun and carried on
by a noble minority — that the majority were really in favour of
Great Britain." — Ingersoll, *North American Review*, CLV. No. 2,
August, 1892, p. 183. It is proper in this connection to add,
that in the opening period of the war, the feeling in England in
favour of American brethren " was intense. Officers resigned their
commissions rather than serve in America; the great cities took
open ground in favour of the colonies; and some of the English
middle classes were mourning the dead at Lexington. As the war
increased in its intensity, this sentiment necessarily decreased; but
even while Parliament was supporting the war by votes of more than
two to one, the ministry was constantly hampered by the notorious
consciousness that the real heart of England was not in it. Even
when 25,000 men were voted at the king's wish, provision had to
be made to obtain them from Germany." — Johnson, *Encyclopædia
Britannica*, 9th ed., XXIII. 742.

the crown. For awhile even these were excused, on the plea of temporary emergency. Repeatedly, and even to the last, did the colonies address petitions to the king, regretting the necessity to which they were driven, and urging, in the old words of English usage, "redress of grievances" for the restoration of peace and unity. Yet, step by step, as by a resistless destiny, were they swept on toward the complete severance of the old relations. Opinion changed with the progress of the conflict, and a popular demand for independence arose and grew into a controlling motive. The Declaration of 1776 thus resulted, and the war finally developed into a struggle for national existence.

But it is important to bear in mind, that the Revolution disarranged but slightly the fabric of government in the individual colonies. "It did not," Webster has affirmed, "subvert the local laws and local legislation." It "did not," Chancellor Kent has said, "involve in it any abolition of the common law."[1] When independence came, and the old colonies were turned into new States, no real political break occurred ; but constitutions embracing the essential principles of the colonial system were adopted in all the States save two : in Delaware, Maryland, New Jersey, Pennsylvania, North Carolina, and Virginia in 1776 ; in New York and Georgia in 1777 ; in South Carolina and Massachusetts in 1778 ; and

---

[1] "British and colonial statutes made prior to the Revolution continued also in force, unless expressly repealed." — *The Critical Period*, etc., 69.

in New Hampshire in 1784.[1] Connecticut and Rhode Island were the exceptions, and, as already seen, the former continued under its royal charter until 1818, and the latter until so late as 1842, *i.e.* until within living memory.[2] As Professor Johnson has said, these " new constitutions were the natural outgrowths of the colonial system, established by charters, or by commissions to royal or proprietary governors ; and the provisions of the constitutions were only attempts to adopt such features as had grown up under the colonial systems, or to cut out such features as colonial or State experience had satisfied the people were dangerous."[3] And as the political usage of the colonies had come originally from Great Britain, and had been adapted and modified in

[1] " On the 10th of May, 1776, the Continental Congress recommended to the several conventions and assemblies of the colonies the establishment of independent governments ' for maintenance of internal peace, and the defence of their lives, liberties, and properties.' Before the end of the year in which this recommendation was made, by far the greater part of the colonies had adopted written constitutions, in which were restated in a dogmatic form all of the seminal principles of the English constitutional system. Thus ended that marvellous process of growth, through which the English colonies in America were rapidly developed into a group of independent commonwealths, in which each individual member was, in its organic structure, a substantial reproduction of the English kingdom." — *Origin and Growth of English Constitution,* 45.

[2] " It was not possible that the term American should suddenly supplant that of Englishman; but the successive steps by which the change was accomplished are easily perceptible." — Johnson, *Encyclopædia Britannica,* 9th ed., XXIII. 739.

[3] *New Princeton Review,* September, 1887.

colonial practice, so now that political usage passed on
to the constitutions of the new States, to be again
adapted and modified by varying wants as such might
arise, but with essential characteristics still maintained
and steadily transmitted.

From the nature of the case, there could be no settled
central government for the newly forming nationality
in the early stages of the contest, and before independence had been formally proclaimed.   In assuming
governmental functions, the Continental Congress became essentially a revolutionary body.   Its existence was
simply the result of an emergency created by the need
of united opposition to the home authorities.   Its powers
rested upon the acquiescence of the several colonies
and were temporary and transitional.   And it was regarded, while it lasted, as an advisory assembly rather
than a government.

But when the centre of colonial unity in the crown
was lost by the Declaration of Independence of 1776,
a permanent union on American soil became a political
necessity.   And on the very day that saw the Declaration
put forth, steps were taken which led to the adoption,
in the following year, of "Articles of Confederation
and Perpetual Union," binding all the States in a "firm
league of friendship with each other."   This earliest
attempt at the construction of a national government
established what, as the sequel proved, was neither
national nor a government.   In reality it was a mere
league of States, allied for common aims, but with each

State reserving to itself almost all elements of power, and conceding to the common administration little else than responsibilities without the means of meeting them. Its main feature was a congress of one house, without an executive, and without any proper judiciary. It was, perhaps, the nearest approach to central authority then attainable ; but, modelled upon the previous Revolutionary government, and perhaps, in part upon Dutch ideas borrowed from the Netherlands, it was a radical departure from long-established usage of the English race.[1] Not to trace its disastrous history in detail, enough to say, that its incompetency for all the purposes for which it was established, brought about, after ten years of failure, its utter breakdown, and led to the calling, by general demand, of the Constitutional Con-

[1] It is to be doubted whether there was in the Articles of Confederation any *intended* following of Dutch institutions, though as a matter of fact, several close analogies may be drawn. But Campbell is entitled to speak on the subject. He says: "When the rebellious American colonies framed a government for themselves during the Revolutionary War, they adopted articles of confederation in which this feature of the Netherland republic was incorporated in all its fulness. Under these articles, a congress was established in which each State, whatever the number of its representatives, from two to seven, had but a single vote. This Congress also, like the States General of the Netherlands in the early days, exercised all executive powers. Neither republic had a president or other executive officer, as did their separate states. In each the legislative body made war and peace, appointed all officers, civil and military, and exercised all the functions of government except those purely judicial." — *Puritan in Holland, England, and America*, II. 422.

vention which met in Philadelphia in 1787, and framed the present Constitution of the United States.[1]

The moment for final constitutional action was well chosen. A healthy change from the spirit of reaction against all authority — a spirit which manifested itself at the close of the war — had gradually come over the young nation. Modern democracy, bred of the French Revolution, was not yet the dangerous force it was so soon to be in America and Europe.[2] The leaders of opinion and action had learned wisdom by their unsuccessful experiment with constitutional novelties under the Confederation, and were inclined to distrust political theory, as distinct from sound and practical political experience. "The spirit of 1787 was an English spirit, and therefore a conservative, tinged, no doubt, by the hatred of tyranny developed in the Revolutionary struggle, tinged also by the nascent dislike of inequality, but in the

---

[1] "The government under the Articles of Confederation had proved so weak that by 1787 the American people were left as 'thirteen distinct communities under no effective superintending control.' [Randolph's letter, Elliot, I. 484.] The condition of the country was one in which no indication of 'national disorder, poverty, or insignificance' was wanting. [Hamilton, *Federalist*, No. 15.] To substitute for the decayed fabric of the Confederation a central power sufficient to cope with the existing evils was thus the task of the convention." — *Publications of American Academy of Political and Social Science*, No. 9, p. 204. See also Curtis, *History of Constitution*, etc.

[2] "Many of the fifty delegates shared Hamilton's contempt for a democracy." — Landon, *Constitutional History of the United States*, 64.

main an English spirit, which desired to walk in the old paths of precedent." [1]

No attempt was made by the Philadelphia Convention to reconstruct or even to amend the Confederation. Both it, and the peculiarities it stood for, were abandoned as by common consent. The constitution adopted was something very different. It was a return to the older forms, and a recognition of the abiding facts of English constitutional usage in America. It provided for a personal executive, a legislature of two branches, a judiciary, and — in completed stage — a bill of rights based upon the historic liberties. The Convention practically took the model of colonial government as it had long and familiarly existed, and as adapted in the State governments then freshly set up, and applied it to the nation ; introducing certain features made necessary by the new civil conditions in America, and others drawn directly from the Constitution and contemporaneous laws and customs of Great Britain.

"No one familiar with the common law of England," remarks Mr. Justice Miller, "can read the Constitution of the United States without observing the great desire of the Convention which framed that instrument to make it conform as far as possible with that law. . . . To look at the general outlines organizing the new government into its various branches, there is but little departure from that of the English government. The President, the Senate, and the House of Representatives

[1] Bryce, *American Commonwealth*, I. 300.

correspond in essential features with the King, Lords, and Commons of Great Britain. And although there was a necessity arising from the bringing together of thirteen different States into one general government, with a recognition of many of the most important powers of government left in the States themselves, to vary in some respects the powers which were confided to the President, the Senate, and the House of Representatives from those which had by immemorial usage come to be the powers of the King, the House of Lords, and the House of Commons of Great Britain, yet the analogy is very close." [1]

Accustomed as we are to the progress of free institutions in civilized lands during the present century, it is difficult to realize that in 1787, at the time this Convention met, the only nations that actually possessed such liberties were England and little Switzerland.[2] Had the

---

[1] Miller, *Lectures on the Constitution of the United States*, 486, 487. As the words of a recent justice of the Supreme Court of the United States, these words are exceedingly significant. The decisions of the Supreme Court have recognized the principle of historic continuity between English and American law.

[2] No one claims that the Constitution of the United States is indebted to Switzerland for its characteristics. In the debates of the Philadelphia Convention, Swiss institutions were mentioned only to be criticised. — See Elliot's *Debates*, V. 201, 208, 236. Nor is the republic of Venice worth mentioning in this connection, for it was in a state of dissolution when the Philadelphia Convention met, and it went to pieces in 1798, having in no way influenced American affairs. Douglas Campbell makes a claim, however, for the Netherlands. He says: "To the fathers of the American republic, who carried through the war of the Revolution, and after-

citizens of the new commonwealth possessed no kinship
with England, and no inheritance from her political
system, they would still have been affected and swayed,

wards formed the American Constitution, it was a living reality, as
much so as the monarchy of England." — *Puritan in Holland, England, and America*, II. 420. But we may search in vain to find
conscious copying from contemporaneous Dutch institutions in the
American Constitution. At that time, as Straus remarks, "The republic of Holland was in a very precarious state, so much so, that
Mr. Adams says of it, in his 'Defence of the Constitutions of Government,' 'Considering the critical situation of it, prudence dictates
to pass it over!'" — *Works of John Adams*, IV. 356, quoted in
Straus, *Origin of Republican Form of Government in the United
States*, 83. The fact is, that notwithstanding the spirit of freedom
which illumines the history of Holland, republican principles, as
Americans understand them, are not to be looked for in that quarter. Charles Francis Adams, in a note to the quoted passage from
the works of John Adams, remarks: "The government of Holland
grew out of the immediate necessities of the heroic struggle with the
power of Spain. It never could be presented as a model for imitation by any people; it was a singular combination of corporation
and aristocratical influence with a federal principle. The author
had good reason for avoiding, at the moment of publication, any
analysis of a system which was then crumbling, and which has since
been swept completely away." — p. 357. For these reasons, reference to Venice and Holland have been omitted above. It is the
simple truth, that at the time of the meeting of the Constitutional
Convention, the only two nations actually possessing liberties were
England and Switzerland. With Venice and Holland, liberties were
then little more than a memory, and neither nation was a fit model
for free government. ?

Mr. Campbell claims that Dutch usages have crept into the Constitution by having been first incorporated into State usage, though
the cases he specifies are few and doubtful. One such case, for
instance, is that of the process of voting in the national Senate by
States. But when this was proposed in the Philadelphia Convention,

almost of necessity, by the force of her experience and her example.

A source of literary influence in favour of English

in committee of the whole, it was introduced by Roger Sherman of Connecticut, with a reference to England, not to the Netherlands.

The real attitude of the Philadelphia Convention can be gathered from a study of the debates of the members while the Constitution was being put together. So far as Dutch institutions are concerned, no one can read those debates without being forced to the conviction that Mr. Campbell has been misled, and that touching the Constitution, his book is misleading. There is no trace in the debates of any tendency on the part of the members to copy or even to admire Dutch institutions. And the few references to Holland that are to be found are usually in the form of disapproval and warning. Thus we hear Butler, when arguing in favour of a single executive, refer to "distracted Holland" as a warning of what to avoid. — Elliot's *Debates*, V. 149. We hear Wilson say: "Switzerland and Holland are supported in their confederation, not by its intrinsic merit, but by the incumbent pressure of surrounding bodies." — *Ibid.* 1. 430. We hear Madison say: "The Dutch are in a most wretched situation, — weak in all its parts, and only supported by surrounding contending powers." — *Ibid.* 424. And we listen to the warning of Gouverneur Morris: "The United Netherlands are at this time torn in factions. With these examples before our eyes, shall we form establishments which must necessarily produce the same effects?" — *Ibid.* V. 287; see, also, *Ibid.* 154, 219, 342. *The Federalist*, addressing the people in favour of the new Constitution, contrasts it with the constitution of the Netherlands. The writer of No. XX. (Madison), after summarizing the Dutch system, adds: "What are the characters which practice has stamped upon it? Imbecility in the government; discord among the provinces; foreign influence and indignities; a precarious existence in peace; and peculiar calamities from war. It was long ago remarked by Grotius, that nothing but the hatred of his countrymen to the house of Austria kept them from being ruined

models existed in the chief political writing of the time, Montesquieu's *Esprit des Lois.* Though of recent date,

by the vices of their constitution." He refers to that constitution as a "melancholy and monitory lesson of history."

In contrast with all this is the frank avowal of Hamilton in the Convention: "I believe the British government forms the best model the world ever produced." — Elliot's *Debates,* I. 421. And again, Pinckney's declaration: "Much has been said [in the Convention] of the Constitution of Great Britain. I am free to confess that I believe it to be the best constitution in existence." — *Ibid.* V. 234. Both of these men would have liked to see the British Constitution copied more nearly than the differing conditions of America permitted. References to English usages and precedents are scattered thickly through the debates, as also to the State usages which had grown up under English influence and example. Butler breaks out in complaint of this: "We are always following the British Constitution, when the reason for it does not apply." — *Ibid.* V. 163. Mason also complains: "We all feel too strongly the remains of ancient prejudices and view things too much through a British medium." — *Ibid.* V. 387. Some in the Convention *opposed* following English usages, — but only to find themselves in minority. Citations from the debates showing English influence could easily be multiplied. See *Ibid.* I. 394, 399, 409, 415, 422; V. 141, 150, 151, 152, 163, 165, 171, 178, 180, 202, 203, 231, 321, 346, 347, 370, 418, etc. Wilson refers to Anglo-colonial usage in connection with the proposal to initiate money bills in the House of Representatives: "He had observed that this discrimination had been transcribed from the British into several American constitutions."— *Ibid.* V. 282. And Randolph argued for the same proposal: "It would make the plan [of the Constitution] more acceptable to the people, because they will consider the Senate as the more aristocratic body, and will expect that the usual guards will be provided according to the example of Great Britain." — *Ibid.* V. 410. Gouverneur Morris, objecting to the extent to which the arguments from English usage were carried, exclaimed: "We should either take the British Constitution altogether, or make one for ourselves." — *Ibid.* V. 284.

this work had reached the position of a recognized authority on both sides of the Atlantic ; and it was accepted by the leaders of the Convention as in many ways a guide for their deliberations. This political writer, impressed by the despotisms of continental Europe, had taken England as an ideal, in his philosophical disquisition on free institutions. And as Madison expresses it in the *Federalist,* " The British Constitution was to Montesquieu what Homer has been to the didactic writers of epic poetry. As the latter have considered the works of the immortal bard the perfect model from which the principles and rules of the epic art were to be drawn, and by which all similar works were to be judged, so the great political critic appears to have viewed the Constitution of England as the standard, or, to use his own expression, as the mirror of political liberty ; and to have delivered in the form of elementary truths, the several characteristic principles of that system."[1] Notably Montesquieu's analysis of government in the threefold division of executive, legislative, and judicial, which gained world-wide acceptance as a political doctrine, was based upon the fact of the nearly complete separation of these functions in the British system. And he drew from it the special maxim : "There is no liberty if the judicial power be not separated from the legislative and the executive,"[2]—a maxim that has powerfully affected the course of American politics, though abandoned by a later political philosophy.

[1] *Federalist,* No. 47.   [2] *L'Esprit des Lois,* C. VI., LIV., XI.

The law commentaries of Sir William Blackstone also influenced the Convention in the same direction. "Whenever the power of making and that of enforcing the laws are united together, there can be no public liberty," is a statement in which Blackstone evidently echoes Montesquieu.[1] And his own analysis of the English Constitution accentuates the principle of an approximately threefold division. As being the highest authority on the laws of England, his book was apparently followed by the makers of the Constitution in all branches of their work, and with a fidelity which has even called forth criticism from modern English writers.

But American political experience was, after all, the principal factor on which the Philadelphia Convention relied in its constructive task. The idea of a sharply defined threefold division of government fell in with this experience; for in all the colonies such a division had long existed, the separation of functions being more evident and extending further than in the mother-country. The colonial governor, though associated with the legislature, was independent of its control, and derived his powers from the central executive, the crown; which, also, as a matter of course, was beyond the reach of the local legislature. This latter body was never a supreme authority such as the Parliament in England, but always a separate branch of government under definite limitations. And the judiciary had its essentially distinct field of operations. Such threefold division was

---

[1] Blackstone, Book I., Chap. III.

continued in the governments of the newly formed States. And the influence of this colonial and State usage upon the delegates was direct and powerful by reason of their lifelong contact with these governments, and also and notably because of the active part most of them had recently taken in the process of State constitution-making, — a task well fitting them for a national labour on similar lines.[1]

[1] Speaking of the division of government, Madison has said: "On the slightest view of the British Constitution we must perceive that the legislative, executive, and judiciary departments are by no means totally separate and distinct from each other." — *Federalist,* No. 46. Referring to the constitutions of the States he adds: "If we look into the constitutions of the several States, we find that, notwithstanding the emphatical and, in some instances, the unqualified terms in which the axiom has been laid down, there is not a single instance in which the several departments of power have been kept absolutely separate and distinct." — *Ibid.* Taylor accurately states the case: "The English maxim as to the division of powers was followed in the structure of the State constitutions only in the limited and qualified sense in which it was understood in England. . . . The 'literary theory' of the English Constitution misled neither Madison nor Hamilton." — *Origin and Growth of the English Constitution,* 46, n. 1. "The maxim as to the division of powers was accepted in the qualified sense in which it was understood by Montesquieu, who accepted it in the form in which it existed in the English system." — *Ibid.* 68, n. 3. Referring to this maxim of Montesquieu, Madison remarks: "He did not mean that these departments ought to have no partial agency in or no control over the acts of each other." — *Federalist,* No. 46. See also Paul Janet's *Histoire de la Science Politique.* In the Constitutional Convention at Philadelphia, "after the federal head had been split into the three departments, legislative, executive, and judicial, in the qualified sense in which such division was understood in the State constitutions, each department was organized in accordance with English ideas, in so far as could be applied to a 'composite state'

But American experience, let it be remembered, was not limited to the colonies and States. There had been contact all along with the English Constitution itself as the supreme constitution of the united British empire. And the Englishmen of the colonies had sympathized with and been profoundly affected by its vicissitudes. The fall of Charles I., the accession of Cromwell, the restoration of Charles II., the arbitrary reign of James II., the Revolution of 1688, and the coming in of the House of Hanover, were constitutional events, felt by them quite as really as, if less directly than, by their brethren at home, — events which left permanent results upon even their local institutions. The Constitution of the mother-land had been more than an ideal model; it had been a vital factor in the life of the American people. And there was a controlling force in the fact that until 1776 they had thus continued in unbroken touch with the ancient political fabric, in addition to having lived under an adaptation of it in their several provinces. The delegates at the Philadelphia Convention, in taking the State constitutions as a model for the new Constitution of the United States, took also the English Constitution itself, considered not merely as a theory or an ideal, but as a contemporaneous fact, and as an essential element in American political experience.

Yet the elements of the English Constitution which were thus adopted into the Constitution of the United

at once federal and republican." — Taylor, *Origin and Growth of the English Constitution*, 68.

States differ in many respects from those existing in
the England of to-day. "The comparison is the more
difficult," lucidly remarks an American law professor, "because the English Constitution is not a constant quantity.
Like the glacier, which, though seeming fixed and rigid,
is yet plastic and suffers a continual change, it has
varied in each century, and sometimes in each successive generation."[1] And Sir Henry Maine touches the
same point : "The Constitution of the United States is
coloured throughout by political ideas of British origin,
and it is in reality a version of the British Constitution
as it must have presented itself to an observer in the
second half of the last century."[2] And again : "The
Constitution of the United States is a modified version
of the British Constitution, but the British Constitution
which served as its original was that which was in existence between 1760 and 1787. The modifications
introduced were those, and those only, which were
suggested by the new circumstances of the American
colonies, now become independent."[3]

It is certainly strange that, until very recently, no
general realization of this historical truth of the
derivation of the American Constitution from English
originals has appeared to exist either in the mother
or the daughter land. Facts bearing on the subject

---

[1] J. I. Clark Hare, *Notes of a Course of Lectures on American
Constitutional Law*, Philadelphia, 1885, p. 86.

[2] *Popular Government,* 249, 253.

[3] *Ibid.* 253.

have been familiar to most English-speaking persons.
But from the first a singular silence has prevailed on
the whole question of sources, — a silence which is so
noteworthy for the period of the adoption and ratification of the new Constitution by the States, as to seem
to require explanation. Whatever may be said of later
times, how was it possible that so little was spoken or
published regarding English sources at the eventful
epoch when the question of the new central government profoundly agitated the people? How can the
comparative ignoring of the matter by all parties during the very season when turbulent debate was conducted upon the merits and demerits of the freshly
constructed document, be accounted for?

Sir Henry Maine refers to this remarkable silence,
especially as affecting the pages of the *Federalist*, and
ventures an explanation. "There is one fountain of
political experience upon which the *Federalist* seldom
draws, and that is the political experience of Great
Britain. The scantiness of these references is at first
sight inexplicable. The writers must have understood
Great Britain better than any other country except
their own. They had been British subjects during most
of their lives. They had scarcely yet ceased to breathe
the atmosphere of the British Parliament, and to draw
strength from its characteristic disturbances. . . . On
the whole it cannot but be suspected that the fewness
of the appeals to British historical examples had its
cause in their unpopularity. The object of Madison,

Hamilton, and Jay was to persuade their countrymen ; and the appeal to British experience would only have provoked prejudice and repulsion."[1]

The reaction of popular sentiment, which turned the old love of England into a new feeling of hostility, certainly goes far to account for this contemporaneous silence.   It is true that the Americans had but recently emerged from British rule, but that rule had been put aside in consequence of a hard-fought war, and the passions of war were still too fresh to permit the use of arguments based upon British experience in favour of any document commended for adoption by the people.

Yet the noted author just quoted but partly indicates the reason for the phenomenon in question.   He appears to be thinking of the public utterances of the leaders, and to have in mind only the English Constitution of that period.   And a distinction is important to remember, — that the American Constitution, though reflecting a contemporaneous stage, was not a mere imitation of the Constitution of the mother-land, but an historical development from it.   Its similarity to its prototype resulted not from any copying process first undertaken in the Convention at Philadelphia.   Rather was it a reaffirmation of principles already American by hereditary usage or long-established custom.   The earliest attempt at a national constitution, that of the Confederation, had been a failure precisely as to the points in which it departed from these principles ; and the present Constitution was

[1] *Popular Government,* 206, 207.

a return to a system from which the colonies themselves had never departed.[1] Hamilton, Madison, Jay, and others had no need to argue for the adoption of English constitutional usage as such, to a people who were already accustomed to it as their own. Little was said, for little needed to be said. The people thought and acted from long-acquired habit. Even the members of the Convention, though consciously taking much from the old system, were doubtless incompletely aware of the extent to which they themselves were influenced by their training under such institutions.[2] The establishment of a

[1] "No unbiassed student of political history is disposed to ignore the great merits which are attributed to the English Constitution, due to the fact that it is the result of growth and not of manufacture. The history of fiat-constitutions . . . illustrates the pitiful failures of organic law made to order; and the unhappy experiences of the many South American republics whose constitutions have been patterned after that of the United States, show that a successful form of government cannot be introduced into a country by mere importation, especially if it find no support in the political habits and character of the people." — *Annals of the American Academy of Political and Social Science*, April, 1891, p. 529.

[2] "An assembly could hardly have been convened in the United Kingdom more English as to race and political training than that made up of the fifty-three delegates who composed the Federal Convention. The Virginia delegation was simply a brilliant group of English country gentlemen who had been reared on the right side of the Atlantic. Alexander Hamilton and Robert Morris were born English subjects; the father of Franklin was an English emigrant from Northamptonshire; Charles Cotesworth Pinckney had been educated at Oxford and the Middle Temple; Rutledge had studied law at the Temple; and James Wilson, the most far-sighted man perhaps in the whole Convention, was born near St. Andrew's,

permanent constitution of any other than an English character would probably have been an impossibility. This is quite sufficient to account for the silence as to sources at the time and ever since. Americans then regarded and still regard their constitutional principles as essentially their own, — English constitutional principles having become American constitutional principles.[1]

By a process of adoption and adaptation, rather than of new creation, the Convention at Philadelphia gave the highest evidence of its sagacity. "The American Constitution," says Mr. Bryce, "is no exception to the rule that everything which has power to win the obedience and respect of men must have its roots deep in the past, and that the more slowly every institution has grown, so much the more enduring is it likely to prove. There is little in that Constitution that is ab-

Scotland. As to political training, they had all been reared under the English system of local self-government which had grown up alongside of the English customary law in the several States which they represented. Those States they had helped to transform from English provinces into independent commonwealths, whose constitutions were substantial reproductions of that of the English kingdom." — Taylor, *Origin and Growth of the English Constitution*, 62.

[1] "Although the framers of our Constitution were without any grasp of the modern conception of the historical continuity of the race, they revered the ancient constitutional traditions of England. And thus it came to pass that Magna Charta, the Acts of the Long Parliament, the Declaration of Independence, and the Constitution of 1787 constitute the record of an evolution." — W. T. Brantly's essay, "Formation of the Federal Constitution," *Southern Law Review*, August, 1880, VI. 352.

solutely new. There is much that is as old as Magna
Charta." [1]   The delegates of the Convention " had neither the rashness nor the capacity for constructing a
constitution *a priori.*   There is wonderfully little genuine inventiveness in the world, and perhaps least of
all has been shown in the sphere of political institutions.
These men, practical politicians, who knew how infinitely
difficult a business government is, desired no bold ex-
periments.   They preferred, so far as circumstances
permitted, to walk in the old paths, to follow methods
which experience had tested." [2]   Professor Johnson
speaks in the same strain : " If the brilliant success of
the American Constitution proves anything, it does not
prove that a viable constitution can ever be struck
off at a given time by the brain and purpose of man.
Man may be a political animal, but in no such sense
as this. . . .   To accuse the members of having deliber-
ately hazarded the destinies of their country upon the
outcome of an entirely new and untried instrument of
government, would be an injustice against which they would
have been the first to protest ; and yet the intensity of

---

[1] *American Commonwealth*, I. 26.

[2] *Ibid.* I. 31.   "The American Constitution of 1787 was a faithful copy, so far as it was possible to make one out of the materials
at hand, of the contemporary Constitution of England. . . .   Allow-
ing for the more democratic character of the constituencies, the
organization of the supreme power in the United States is nearer
the English type of the last century — is less modern, in fact — than
is the English Constitution of the present day." — *Encyclopædia
Britannica*, 9th ed., VI. 310, "Constitution."

posterity's admiration for their success is continually
tempting new writers into what is in reality just such
an accusation."[1] And Mr. James Russell Lowell has
observed, with his usual grace : " They had a profound
disbelief in theory, and knew better than to commit
the folly of breaking with the past. They were not
seduced by the French fallacy, that a new system of
government could be ordered like a new suit of clothes.
They would as soon have thought of ordering a suit
of flesh and skin. It is only on the roaring loom of
time that the stuff is woven for such a vesture of thought
and expression as they were meditating."[2]

[1] *New Princeton Review*, September, 1887.

[2] *Address on Democracy*, October 6, 1884. " What gives colour to
the notion, that the American constitutions, both State and Federal,
are the voluntary creation of man, is the fact that they are written
(so-called), and that these writings have been formulated, enacted,
and promulgated by representative conventions. This opinion has
been so prevalent that the national habit is to look upon the members of the Convention of 1787 as demi-gods, giant heroes, far
surpassing the foremost men of to-day, while the Constitution itself
has been placed upon a pedestal and worshipped as a popular
idol. . . . But by making a popular idol of it we are apt to lose
the very benefits which its excellencies insure. It is the complete
harmony of its principles with the political evolution of the nation
which justly challenges our admiration, and not the political acu-
men of the convention which promulgated it. Instead, therefore,
of being the voluntary creation of the American people in the
eighteenth century, the Federal and State constitutions of the
United States are but natural and sequential developments of
the British Constitution, modified as to detail and as to a few fundamental principles by the new environment. This claim is easily
substantiated by the most superficial comparison of the British and

American constitutions. . . . And a closer study of the two systems reveals the fact that every principle brought into play by the American constitutions, that has endured and proved effectual in the attainment of the ends aimed at, was either of English origin or was the direct product of the social forces that were at play in American life." — C. D. Tiedman, *Unwritten Constitution of the United States*, 20, 25.

CHAPTER III.

THE *Germania* of Tacitus describes the ancient Teutonic assembly as twofold in operation, with a conservative element in the conference of chiefs and a popular element in the gathering of the armed host of freemen. "About minor matters," he tells us, "the chiefs deliberate ; about the more important, the whole tribe. Yet even when the formal decision rests with the people, the affair is always thoroughly discussed by the chiefs. They assemble, except in the case of sudden emergency, on certain fixed days, either at new or at full moon, for this they consider the most auspicious season for the transaction of business. . . . Their freedom has this disadvantage, that they do not meet simultaneously, or as they are bidden, but two or three days are wasted in the delays of assembling. When the multitude think proper, they sit down armed. Silence is proclaimed by the priests, who have on these occasions the right of keeping order. Then the king or the chief, according to age, birth, distinction in war, or eloquence, is heard, more because he has influence to persuade, than because he has power to command. If

59

his sentiments displease them, they reject them with murmurs; if they are satisfied, they brandish their spears. The most complimentary form of assent is to express approbation with their weapons."[1]

Such was the earliest form of our racial legislature of which there is record. And in it were the germs of all that came after it. The essential features of Saxon markmoot, shiremoot, folkmoot and Witenagemot, of Norman Great Council, of Parliament, of colonial and State legislature, and of the American Congress, were historically derived from this ancient and original Teutonic source.[2]

[1] *Agricola and Germania of Tacitus*, translated by A. J. Church and William J. Brodribb, 95, 96.

[2] The purest Teutonic institutions are to be looked for in England, rather than on the continent of Europe. " While the Germans of Gaul, Italy, and Spain became Romans, the Saxons retained their language, their genius, and manners, and created in Britain a Germany outside of Germany." — Taine, *History of English Literature*, I. 50. Commenting upon this, Hannis Taylor remarks: " By this statement the difference between Teutonic conquest and settlement in Britain, and Teutonic conquest and settlement upon the Continent is clearly defined. In the one case the invaders were absorbed in the mass of the conquered; Teutonic life simply became an element in the older Roman society. In the other, the invaders absolutely annihilated, within the limits which they made their own while they were still heathens, every vestige of the existing civilization, and established in its stead their whole scheme of barbaric life. The Teutonic polity thus established in Britain in its purity has been able to survive and to preserve not only its identity, but its primitive instinct, in all the vicissitudes of change and of growth through which it has passed. The invaders who thus established a new nationality in Britain were of the purest Teutonic

"This immortal constitution," observes Mr. Freeman, in commenting upon the passage, " was the constitution of our forefathers in their old land of northern Germany, before they made their way to the isle of Britain. And that constitution, in all the essential points, they brought with them into their new homes ; and there transplanted to a new soil, it grew and flourished, and brought forth fruit rich and more lasting than it brought forth in the land of its earlier birth. On the Teutonic mainland the old Teutonic freedom, with its free assemblies, national and local, gradually died out before the en-croachments of a brood of petty princes. In the Teutonic island it has changed its form from age to age, it has lived through many storms, and it has withstood the attacks of many enemies, but it has never utterly died out. The continued national life of the people, not-withstanding foreign conquests and national revolutions, has remained unbroken for fourteen hundred years. At

type, and all spoke dialects of the Low German. From the earliest period in their insular history, these settlers knew themselves as ' the English kin '; and out of their union has arisen the English nation, which, through all the vicissitudes of internal growth and external influence, has preserved both its national character and its identity. In the course of its history it has received many infusions, it is true, — for the most part, however, from other branches of the Teutonic stock. No nation can claim absolute purity of blood; foreign elements are present in the veins of every people. But the national character is never lost so long as the paternal element is strong enough to absorb all other elements, and to impress upon the nation, as a whole, its own image and in-stincts." — *Origin and Growth of the English Constitution*, 86.

no moment has the tie between the present and the past been wholly rent asunder; at no moment have Englishmen sat down to put together a wholly new constitution in obedience to some dazzling theory. Each step in the growth has been the natural consequence of some earlier step; each change in the law and constitution has been not the bringing in of anything wholly new, but the development and improvement of something that was already old. The progress has in some ages been faster, in others slower; at moments it has seemed to stand still, or even to go back; but the great march of political development has never wholly stopped : it has never been permanently checked, since the day when the coming of the Teutonic conquerors first began to change Britain into England."[1]

The earliest legislative institutions of England after the coming of the Saxons bear internal evidence of Teutonic origin. Every freeman had, as in the ancient days of the race, a rightful place in the deliberative councils of his tribe or state. In the assemblies of the mark, the hundred, and the shire of the first kingdoms established there appears to have been no essential departure from ancient models. But as the petty kingdoms were slowly aggregated into the great heptarchic kingdoms, there grew up for each enlarged nationality a Witenagemot, or council of the chiefs — the witan or wise — and the folkmoot or old assembly of the freemen sank into a shiremoot, of which the new kingdom might

[1] *Growth of the English Constitution*, 18–20.

have many.   Possibly the shire represented the earlier
petty state, and came thus to retain the folkmoot.[1]   As

[1] " If each shire represented a complete kingdom, the shiremoot
would give a complete representative system existing in each kingdom.   But as the small kingdoms coalesced or were united by conquest, it does not seem to have been thought necessary to extend
the system; the council of the aggregated state is not a folkmoot,
but a witenagemot.   In those early kingdoms, which were identical
with the later shires, Kent, for instance, it might be expected
that we should find two central councils, the folkmoot or council
of the people of Kent, and the witenagemot or council of the
chiefs, answering to the greater and narrower assemblies of the
plebs and the *principes* in the *Germania*.   It is by no means im-
probable that such was the case; but as our knowledge on the
subject is derived from the charters attested by these assemblies,
or issued with their consent, and as the consent of the witan only
was necessary for the transfers of land, we have not the documentary
evidence that would suffice for proof.   We have many charters
issued in witenagemots under the kings of Kent; but the only
document issued by a folkmoot of Kent belongs to a date when
it had long been without a king.   The customs, however, of the
folkmoot are so common and so ancient, that they afford a strong
presumption of their universality; so that Kent and Sussex, and
perhaps Essex and East Anglia, may be fairly supposed to have had
the two regular assemblies in primitive simplicity as long as they
continued independent.   With regard to Wessex and Mercia, which
were aggregations of smaller states, no such hypothesis will hold
good.   There is no probability that a Mercian king would introduce a new constitution into the organization of his kingdom.   It
was enough that the Hwiccians, or Hecanians, or Magasætanians
had their folkmoot, without the Mercians [the United Kingdom]
having one too, and it was enough for the king, as ruler of Mercia,
to have his witenagemot without continuing to hold similar gatherings as overlord of Hwiccia and the associated districts.   The folkmoot was left to the shire, the witenagemot was gathered round
the king." — Stubbs, *Constitutional History of England*, I. 140,

the newer kingdom covered enlarged territory, its gemot was held in central or shifting localities, necessarily remote from the homes of most of the people, and could not be attended by all, or indeed by any considerable number of the humbler freemen, and thus its active membership became practically limited to persons of rank and to the great officers of the royal court. The folkmoot was left to the shire, the Witenagemot was gathered round the king.[1]

141. See Gneist, *Verwaltungsrecht*, I. 43, who seems to consider the folkmoot of the shire identical with the witenagemot.

[1] Stubbs, *Constitutional History of England*, I. 141. Kemble gives an admirable pointing to this subject: " In a country overrun with forests, intersected with deep streams or extensive marshes, and but ill provided with the means of internal communication, suit and service even at the county-court must have been a hardship to the cultivator; a duty performed not without danger, and often vexatiously interfering with agricultural processes on which the hopes of the year might depend. Much more keenly would this have been felt had every freeman been called upon to attend beyond the limits of his own shire, in places distant from, and totally unknown to him: how, for example, would a cultivator from Essex have been likely to look upon a journey into Gloucestershire at the severe season of Christmas, or the, to him, important farming period of Easter? [These were usual periods for holding the gemot.] What, moreover, could he care for general laws affecting many districts beside the one in which he lived, or for regulations applying to fractions of society in which he had no interest? For the Saxon cultivator was not then a politician; nor were general rules which embraced a whole kingdom of the same moment to him as those which might concern the little locality in which his alod lay. Or what benefit could be expected from his attendance at deliberations which concerned parts of the country with whose mode of life and necessities he was totally unacquainted? Lastly, what evil must have resulted to the republic by the withdrawal of whole

Folkmoots in the shape of shiremoots lingered, with
various changes, far down into the Middle Ages. And
so late as the reign of Athelstan they took part in agreeing to legislation, though not in originating it. Yet even
at sessions of the Witan, the freemen were not wholly
without voice ; for on the coming together of the military
host, some bodies of them, armed as of old, probably

populations from their usual places of employment, and the con-
gregating in a distant and unknown locality? If we consider these
facts, we shall find little difficulty in imagining that any scheme
which relieved him from this burthen and threw it upon stronger
shoulders, would be a welcome one, and the foundation of a representative system seems laid *a priori*, and in the nature of things
itself. To the rich and powerful neighbour, whose absence from
his farms was immaterial, while his bailiffs remained on the spot to
superintend their cultivation; to the scírgeréfa, the earldorman, the
royal reeve, or royal thane, familiar with the public business, and
having influence and interest with the king; to the bishop or abbot
distinguished for his wisdom as well as his station; to any or all of
these he would be ready to commit the defence of his small, private
interests, satisfied to be virtually represented, if he were not compelled to leave the business and the enjoyments of his daily life. On
the other hand, to whom could the king look with greater security,
than to the men whose sympathies were all those of the ruling
caste; many of whom were his own kinsmen by blood or marriage,
more of whom were his own officers; men, too, accustomed to
business, and practically acquainted with the wants of the several
localities? Or how, when the customs and conditions of widely
different social aggregations were to be considered and reconciled,
could he do better than advise with those who were most able to
point out and meet the difficulties of the task? Thus it appears
to me, by a natural process did the folkmoot, or meeting of the
nation, become converted into a witenagemot, or meeting of councillors." — *Saxons in England*, II. 191–194.

took part in the making of laws. On other occasions, also, there is trace of a larger gathering than that of the · magistrates and wisemen only; and it is not impossible that the right of all freemen to attend at the Witan, as at other councils, may have lingered in theory, even if fitfully and uncertainly put into practice.[1]

---

[1] "The Witan gave their *wed* to observe, and cause to be observed, the laws they had enacted. Eádgár says, 'I command my geréfan, upon my friendship, and by all they possess, to punish every one that will not perform this, and who, by any neglect, shall break the *wed* of any Witan.' This seems to imply that the people were generally bound by the acts of the Witan and their pledge or *wed;* and if so, it would naturally involve the theory of representation. But this deduction will not stand. The whole principle of Teutonic legislation is, and always was, that the law is made by the constitution of the king and the consent of the people: and . . . one way in which that consent was obtained was by sending the *capitula* down into the provinces or shires, and taking the *wed* in the shire-moot. The passage in the text seems to presuppose an interchange of oaths and pledges between the king and the witan themselves; and even those who had no standing of their own in the folcmót or scírgemót, were required to be bound by *personal* consent. The lord was just as much commanded to take oath and pledge of his several dependents (the hired men, *familiares,* or people of his household), as the sheriff was required to take them of the free shire-thanes. Of course this excludes all idea of representation in our modern sense of the word, because with us promulgation by the Parliament is sufficient, and the constituent is bound, without any further ceremony, by the act of him whom he has sent in his own place. But the Teutons certainly did not elect their representatives as we elect ours, with full power to judge, decide for, and bind us, and therefore it was right and necessary that the laws, when made, should be duly ratified and accepted by all the people." — Kemble, *Saxons in England,* II. 236, 237.

With the union of the heptarchy under the crown of
Egbert, the heptarchic Witenagemots were merged in a
single Witenagemot for united England. The earlier
character of this council remained essentially unchanged,
and its active membership consisted of the king, the earldormen, the king's thegns, the bishops and high ecclesiastics, and generally the wisemen, — with uncertain and
occasional presence of lower elements. Though in reality an aristocratic gathering, it stood for the Teutonic
assembly in substantially representing and acting for the
nation in all matters of national concern ; and it exercised
powers derived from that ancient body.

This national Witenagemot was not destroyed by the
Norman Conquest. Its continuity remained unbroken.
The name of Witan went on in English as long as the
Chronicle continued, and the new Latin name *Magnum
Concilium,* which grew up by its side, was simply a translation of *mycel gemot.*[1] Under the feudal system of the
Norman epoch, the Witan grew into the Curia Regis, the
court of the king's vassals, a body which, owing to the
then magnitude of the royal power, was scarcely more
than a ceremonial coming together of courtiers. Its
powers became nominal. Such as it was, however, this
court of bishops, abbots, earls, barons, and knights was
the council by whose advice and consent the kings con-
descended to act, or to declare that they acted.[2]

By the reign of Henry II. — perhaps earlier — all the

---

[1] Taylor, *Origin and Growth of the English Constitution,* 239.
[2] Stubbs, *Constitutional History of England,* I. 405.

king's tenants-in-chief had a right to be present in this great council when special taxation was needed, and possibly at other times. There came to be manifested a tendency also to admit the whole body of smaller land-owners to similar rights, — a tendency which may be described as towards the concentration of the representation of the counties in the national Parliament; the combination of the shiremoots with the Witenagemot of the kingdom. But as, through sub-division of tenancies, the minor tenants-in-chief steadily grew in numbers, and as they were comparatively poor, it must have been diffi-cult for them to put their rights into practice. However enlarged in theory, the national council remained, there-fore, little more than a gathering of the great ecclesiastics and nobles; and it eventually developed into the House of Lords.

"Of one House of Parliament we may say," observes Mr. Freeman, "not that it grew out of the ancient as-sembly, but that it absolutely is the same by personal identity. The House of Lords not only springs out of, it actually is the ancient Witenagemot. I can see no break between the two. . . . In the constitution of the House of Lords I can see nothing mysterious or wonder-ful. Its hereditary character came in, like other things, step by step, by accident rather than by design. And it should not be forgotten that as long as the bishops keep their seats in the House the hereditary character of the House does not extend to all its members. To me it seems simply that two classes of men, the two highest classes, the earls and the bishops, never lost or disused that right of attending the national assembly which was at first common to them with all other freemen. Besides these two classes the king summoned other men to an early Parliament, pretty much, it would seem, at his own pleasure. . . . The House of Lords, then, I do not hesitate to say, represents, or rather is, the Witenagemot. . . . But the special function of the body into which the old national assembly has changed, the function of the 'other house,' the upper house, the House of Lords as opposed to the House of Commons, could not show itself till a second house of a more popular constitution had arisen by its side." [1]

The introduction of elected representatives into the national legislature gave rise to the modern Parliament, and created a new force that has changed the political course of the world. This system, unknown to ancient civilization, rested in reality upon the Teutonic principle of legislation by the entire body of freemen. The principle had always proved inapplicable, save within limited territory. All attempts made without representative machinery, in Saxon and early mediæval times, to include in the active membership of the national council persons below the higher ranks, had failed of practical result. Yet the idea of election and representation in other than legislative forms, was anciently familiar to the English people. For the kingship itself was elective. Election was of immemorial usage in the

---

[1] *Growth of the English Constitution*, 62-65.

Church.   From very early Saxon days a reeve and four men attended in the court of the hundred, and in the shiremoot, as chosen representatives of the town.   And in judicial matters the principle bore a leading part. Under the Plantagenets it came to be applied to almost every kind of business, judicial, fiscal, and administrative. Not, however, until the time of John and Henry III. was it extended to the national Parliament.[1]   In 1213 King John held a council at St. Albans, which was attended, not only by the greater clergy and lords, but also by the representative reeve and four men from each town on the royal demesne, so long familiar to the folkmoot.   And four instances of summoning representatives of the shires

---

[1] " The political systems of the Teutonic nations, as they appear to us when written history begins, contained the germs of the representative principle, and in every one of the modern European states that have arisen out of the settlements made by the Teutonic nations on Roman soil, a serious attempt has at some time been made in the direction of representative government.   The remarkable fact is that in every continental state in which such an attempt was made, it ended at last in failure and disappointment.   By the sixteenth century, nearly every effort in the direction of representative government upon the continent of Europe had come to an end.   In England only, among the Teutonic nations, did the representative system survive; in England only has the representative principle — which has been called ' a Teutonic invention ' — been able to maintain a continuous existence.   In this way the English nation has been able to hand down the representative principle from the barbarian epoch to modern times.   In this way England has become the ' mother of parliaments,' — the teacher of the science of representative government to all the world." — *Origin and Growth of the English Constitution*, 428, 429.

to Parliament occurred before De Montfort's famous Parliament of 1265, to which Hallam mistakenly refers as the "origin of popular representation."[1]　Thus, in 1213, John summoned four knights out of each county to Oxford.　In 1254, forty years later, during the absence of Henry III. in Gascony, Queen Eleanor and the Earl of Cornwall, acting as regents, directed the sheriffs to cause "to come before the king's council at Westminster, two lawful and discreet knights from each county, whom the men of the county shall have chosen for this purpose, in the place of all and each of them, to consider, together with the knights of other counties, what aid they will grant to the king."[2]　The third instance was in 1261, during the Barons' War, when the confederate barons summoned to St. Albans three knights from each county, whom, however, Henry III. ordered to repair to himself at Windsor instead.　And the fourth instance occurred after the overthrow of the king at the battle of Lewes, May 14, 1264, when De Montfort, in the king's name, called his first Parliament at London, and summoned to it four knights from each shire.　The great Parliament

---

[1] "Almost all judicious inquirers seemed to have acquiesced in admitting this origin of popular representation." — Hallam, *Middle Ages*, III. 27.

[2] The original of the writ reads "quatuor legales et discretos milites de comitatibus praedictis [Bedeford et Bukingeham.] quos iidem comitatus ad hoc elegerint, vice omnium et singulorum eorundem comitatum, videlicet duos de uno comitatu et duos de alio." — *Lords' Report on the Dignity of a Peer*, I. 95, and App. I. 13; *Select Charters*, 367.

which has justly given to Simon De Montfort the title of Founder of the House of Commons,[1] met in 1265, when, in the name of the imprisoned king, he directed the sheriffs to return not only two knights from each shire, but also two citizens from each city, and two burgesses from each borough. This practically completed the constitution of the English Parliament, though for some years longer the meetings of the Great Council of nobles continued frequent, and representative gatherings were held but occasionally. In the parlance of the Middle Ages, De Montfort admitted the Third Estate to power. It was a return, under the new representative method, of the popular element in legislative affairs which was characteristic of Teutonic institutions.

The final settlement of the Parliament into two separate houses was accomplished during the thirteenth and fourteenth centuries. To a Parliament held by Edward I.[2] in 1295 there were summoned, in addition to the lay

[1] "Der Schöpfer des Hauses der Gemeinen." — Pauli, *Simon von Montfort.*

[2] "The materials of a parliamentary constitution were ready to his (Edward's) hand, yet it cannot be denied that it is to him we owe its regular and practical establishment. Without a single afterthought, or reservation of any kind, he at once accepted the limitation of his own powers. To the Parliament thus formed he submitted his legislative enactments. He requested their advice on the most important administrative measures, and even yielded to them, though not without some reluctance, the last remnant of his powers of arbitrary taxation. He had his reward. Great as were his achievements in peace and war, the Parliament of England was the noblest monument ever reared by mortal man." — S. R.

and spiritual lords, two knights from each shire, two citizens from each city, and two burgesses from each borough, and together with these, the prior of each cathedral and the archdeacons of each diocese in person, and elected proctors for the cathedral and parochial clergy. This great Parliament sat in three separate houses, each granting a different proportional tax. It was a recognition of the maxim that a tax required the consent of those who were expected to pay it. But the clergy had always been represented by the bishops and other members of their order in the national councils — as they still are by their bishops. Moreover, they had long voted taxes in their own ecclesiastical assemblies, the provincial convocations of Canterbury and York, and were very generally loth to take part in legislative action beyond that relating to subsidies. It came about, therefore, that though summoned to each Parliament succeeding that of 1295, their attendance, reluctant and irregular, finally ceased altogether in the fourteenth century. Convocation remaining a separate "legislature in ecclesiastical matters,"[1] maintained its right to vote taxes until long after the Reformation.[2] In this way England

---

Gardiner, *History of England*, I. 21. "It was by Edward I. that the bases were settled upon which the English Constitution rests. . . . There was work enough left for future generations to do, but their work would consist merely in filling in the details of the outline which had been drawn once for all by a steady hand." — *Ibid.* 1. 16.

[1] Hallam, *Middle Ages*, III. 137.

[2] The taxation of the clergy out of convocation was arranged between Lord Chancellor Clarendon and Archbishop Sheldon.

came to have a legislature of two houses instead of three. And such was the historical origin of the " bicameral system," which in modern times has spread from England over the Christian world.[1]

The actual date of the separation of the Lords and Commons is somewhat uncertain. Knights of the shire continued for a time to vote with the barons after the introduction into Parliament of city and borough members. The latter probably formed from the first a distinct house, though the earliest mention in the rolls of Parliament of a separate session is in 1332.[2] Two houses may be regarded as established usage by the year 1339, and by 1347 the knights of the shire had become associated in the membership of the House of Commons.[3]

Bishop Gibson pronounced it "the greatest alteration of the Constitution ever made without an express law." — See Hallam, *Constitutional History*, III. 240, 241.

[1] The philosophic advantages of a bicameral system have been ably discussed by Bentham and Bowyer in England, and by Kent, Story, and Lieber in America. See Creasy, *English Constitution*, 178; Sheldon Amos, *Science of Politics*, 236–246; *Quarterly Review*, No. 316, October 1884, etc.

[2] *Rot. Parl.*, II. 66.

[3] "The knights, who represented the landed property of the country, gave the House of Commons, from the first, stability, weight and permanence, and obtained for it a respect which the citizens and burgesses alone could not have commanded. . . . The commingling of the knights and burgesses in a single House was rendered possible by the existence in the English Constitution of a peculiarity which most prominently and honourably distinguished it from nearly every kindred constitution in Europe, — the absence of an exclusive noble caste. In most of the continental states the

The development of the organism of Parliament need
not be further followed. But before leaving the theme

nobles formed a distinct class, distinguished, by the privileges inherent in their blood, from ordinary freemen, and transmitting their
privileges, and in some countries their titles also, to *all* their descendants in perpetuity. The words 'nobleman' and 'gentleman'
were strictly synonymous; the estate of the nobles — wherever the
system of estates obtained — represented in the national assembly
not only the high nobility, but the class who, in England, formed
the 'landed gentry'; and the Commons, the *Tiers État*, consisted
almost exclusively of citizens and burgesses. In England, on the
contrary, the privileges of nobility have always, except, perhaps, in
the days of the ancient *Eorlas*, been confined to one only of the
family at a time, — the actual possessor of the peerage. The sons
of peers are commoners, and on a perfect equality, as regards legal
and political privileges, with the humblest citizen. . . . Had it
been otherwise, the House of Commons could scarcely have become
what it is at the present day." — Taswell-Langmead, *English Constitutional History*, 264, 265, 266. "On the same benches on which
sat the goldsmiths, drapers, and grocers, who had been returned to
Parliament by the commercial towns, sat also members who, in any
other country, would have been called noblemen, — hereditary lords
of manors, entitled to hold courts and to bear coat armour, and able
to trace back an honourable descent through many generations."
— Macaulay, *History of England*, I. 38. This fact has been often
referred to as a proof of the essential democracy of English institutions. But there is another side. Has not the success of the
so-called democratic institutions of England been due in part to
this blending of the highest elements of the nation with the common? It cannot be denied that the presence of the aristocratic
element gave a force and stability in the early days of the House of
Commons that would otherwise have been wanting. How far this
force has continued to the present time would be a study full of
suggestiveness. Certainly the House of Commons is the strongest
legislative body in the world, and at the same time the most
aristocratic democratic body known to history.

a word should be said regarding a nearly allied body, the Privy Council. From the period of the reign of Henry III. an inner or executive council — the Concilium Ordinarium — attained prominence in affairs of government. This consisted of the great court officers, the judges and a varying number of bishops, barons and prominent personages clerical and lay. It grew out of, and was at first a part of, the Witenagemot or Great Council; being in effect a permanent committee to look after state matters in the interval between sessions of the larger assembly. Whenever the Great Council met, this Ordinary Council was merged in that body for the time being. It bore a mixed relation to executive and judicial business ; and for occasions of temporary or minor importance it issued ordinances having the force of statute law ; thus taking to itself legislative powers. As the greater Council gradually changed by the development of the houses of Lords and Commons, the Ordinary Council became more and more an official body separate from either house, though composed, to considerable degree, of persons who were connected with Parliament also. Its membership, unlike that of the House of Lords, with which it remained most nearly associated, never partook of an hereditary character, but was constituted by appointment of the executive. It eventually grew into the Privy Council, the constitutional body of advisers of the king, whom he was bound by the laws and custom of the realm to consult.[1] And such it still

---

[1] Taswell-Langmead, *English Constitutional History*, 678.

remains, although the modern Cabinet has now largely absorbed its former functions.

The Senate of the United States is, in reality, a development from the House of Lords and the Privy Council, jointly; and as both these bodies came originally from the older legislative council of England, it is evolved, through them, from that ancient Great Council and the Witenagemot. In the British-American colonies, there could be, strictly speaking, no House of Lords, because there were no resident nobles. But the governor of each colony had a council of state, members of which were appointed by the executive or otherwise. It originally bore to him essentially the same relation that the Privy Council bore to the king.[1] When the second or lower house of the colonial legislature appeared, this council took on the functions of an upper house, though retaining its separate position as an executive, advisory body; and it thus had a double character. But the original idea of an executive council, distinct from that of an upper parliamentary chamber, lingered in the newly formed State Constitutions of Pennsylvania and Vermont until after the date of the Philadelphia Convention; these two States delegating executive powers to a governor and council, and having, for the time being, a legislature of one house only. The constitutions of all

[1] "The upper house usually consisted of from six to twenty men, summoned by the colonial governor, to serve for an indefinite time as advisers to the executive, just as many years ago was summoned the first body of nobles in England as advisers to the king." — Thorpe, *Story of the Constitution*, 16.

the other States of that period provided for the legislature of two houses which had gradually grown up
under colonial experience ; and the upper house of this
legislature in Maryland, Massachusetts, New York, North
Carolina, South Carolina, New Hampshire, and Virginia,
was called a "Senate." At the Philadelphia Convention
an attempt was made to engraft a privy council on the
Constitution of the United States, in addition to a Congress of two chambers, but the attempt failed.[1] Instead

[1] Referring to the method of the election of senators in the
Constitution, Campbell remarks: " For this novel feature in its
organization, we have, so far as America is concerned, to look
directly to Pennsylvania, in which colony it alone prevailed. When
Penn prepared his ' Frame of Government,' he provided for a council or upper house of the legislature, one-third of whose members
went out of office every year, and this system was continued in the
first State constitutions of Pennsylvania and Delaware. But Penn
merely borrowed this idea from the Netherland cities, where it was
well known. The people there had early learned the advantages
of combining experience with new blood, and so, in many of their
important bodies, they changed only a fraction at a time."— *Puritan in Holland, England, and America*, II. 423. See Motley,
Dutch Republic, I. 83, as to the senate of Antwerp; and Davies,
Holland, I. 79, as to Dutch cities. Campbell's conclusion from
this claim, and that of an age qualification, that " we find in the
Senate of the United States a body which derives most of the peculiarities of its organization from the Netherland republic, and not
from the House of Lords " (*Ibid.*), is so wide of truth as to need no
comment here. " Franklin's plan of government provided that the
members should go out in rotation. See *Select Journal of Congress*, I. 286. The members of the upper houses in New York,
Virginia, and Delaware were elected on this plan."— J. H.
Robinson, "*Publications of the American Academy of Political
and Social Science*," No. 9, p. 217, n. 4.

of establishing a council, the Convention gave certain powers of such an executive body to the national Senate. Indeed, although the Senate was created as a branch of the legislature, the early senators seem to have thought of it as being, first and foremost, a body with executive functions. And this it was at the beginning. For the first five years of its existence its sessions were held with closed doors, and its principal transactions related to the confidential executive business of treaties and the confirming of appointments. Its present position as a legislative chamber as powerful and as active as the lower house of Congress, has resulted only from a long process of development. It has wielded, in fact, the three elements of authority, — executive, legislative, and judicial. And notwithstanding changes of form and detail, it has undoubtedly done so in essential succession to the old combined council and upper house of colonial days, and through that, to the English Privy Council and the upper house of Parliament, and thus to the Witenagemot.[1]

[1] The question of the similarity of the Senate to the House of Lords is likely to be debated as long as minds differ. But the historical derivation of that body from the colonial senate or upper house, which in turn came from the commercial charter, and, by imitation and the continuity of many functions and relations, from the House of Lords, is simply an historical fact. The points of likeness are real. The points of difference are largely the result of the process of development, and are therefore historical. But an interesting light is thrown on the fact of conscious copying from the House of Lords, by the language used in the Constitutional Convention at Philadelphia by Dickinson, when the Senate was under discussion: " In the formation of the Senate," he said, " we ought to

The House of Representatives is confessedly evolved from the House of Commons, through the lower colonial house, and the lower house of the State legislature. Its name was copied from the State constitutions of Massachusetts, New Hampshire, South Carolina, Pennsylvania, and Vermont. In working operation it has shown itself to be somewhat dissimilar to its English original; the difference largely arising from the circumscribed nature of its legislative functions as defined and limited by Article I. of the Constitution. The American Congress lacks, indeed, the supreme power of Parliament; which is unchecked either by the influence of the sovereign, or by the law of a written constitution. But, as a matter of fact, this differentiation is but added proof of the true process of development through colonial forms. For the colonial legislature was a strictly limited body; it possessed no control over the colonial executive, and its law-making powers were modified by the terms of a written charter, as also by the very existence of the supreme power of crown and Parliament.

carry through such a refining process as will assimilate it, as nearly as may be, to the House of Lords of England." — Elliot's *Debates*, V. 163. Again, having moved, in committee of the whole, " that the members of the second branch [of Congress] ought to be chosen by the individual legislatures " — the principle which was incorporated in the Constitution — he said, that he introduced this motion, because, among other things, " he wished the Senate to consist of the most distinguished characters, bearing as strong a likeness to the British House of Lords as possible; and thought such characters more likely to be selected by the State legislatures than in any other mode." — *Ibid.* 166. See also *Ibid.* 178.

Singular evidence of the persistence in America of even accidental elements in the political usage of the mother-country, is afforded by the provision in the Constitution for the presiding officers. The president of the upper house of Parliament is not necessarily a member at all, but a person holding an entirely outside office, in connection with which he bears relation to the house. He is not chosen by the body over which he presides. Thus, also, the chairman of the Senate is the Vice-President of the United States, an outside officer not chosen by the Senators. He derives his office from that of deputy or lieutenant governor, as found in the royal charters and in colonial practice. As a possible successor to the national presidency in case of the President's death or disability, he is a substitute for the heir apparent in hereditary monarchies. Many of the new State constitutions made provision for the deputy governor to preside in the upper house of the legislature, and also to succeed to the governorship in case of vacancy. In four of the States the title applied to this officer was " Vice-President." The lower house of Parliament and the lower house of Congress has each its " Speaker," elected by the chamber itself from among its own members, — an office the origin of which dates back to the time when the elect of the House of Commons, representing that body, communicated its proceedings to the king for the latter's promulgation as law ; acting as speaker for the Commons to the king.[1]

[1] " In the use of the word which designates the presiding officer

"If we could conceive a political architect of the eighteenth century," observes Sir Henry Maine, "endeavouring to build a new constitution in ignorance of the existence of the British Parliament, or with the deliberate determination to neglect it, he might be supposed to construct his legislature with one chamber, or three, or four; he would have been in the highest degree unlikely to construct it with two. In the modern feudal world, the community naturally distributed itself into classes or Estates, and there are abundant traces of legislatures in which these classes were represented according to various principles. But the Estates of the realm were grouped in all sorts of ways. In France, the States General were composed of three orders, — the clergy, the nobility, and the rest of the nation as the *Tiers État.* There were three orders also in Spain. In Sweden, there

of [the House of Representatives] the Convention which framed the Constitution adopted, as it had done in so many other instances, the language of the law of England in regard to the presiding officer of the House of Commons. While there is in the Constitution no very definite description of the powers which may be exercised by the Speaker of the House, that office has become, by the practice and the rules of the House, the repository of more unrestricted power than any other officer of the government of the United States possesses." — Mr. Justice Miller, *Lectures on the Constitution of the United States*, 198. The editor of this work, Mr. J. C. Bancroft Davis, in referring in a note to the expansion of the Speaker's powers *since* the adoption of the Constitution, says: "The enormous power which the Speaker of the House of Representative wields over the legislation of Congress . . . is not enjoyed by the presiding officer of that great body in England *from whence the office and its title are derived.*" — *Ibid.* 219.

were four, — the clergy, the nobility, the burghers, and the peasants. The exceptional two houses of the British Constitution arose from special causes."[1]

Mr. Freeman, touching the same subject, remarks : "The form of government which political writers call *bicameral* — that is to say, where the legislative assembly consists of two chambers or houses — arose out of one of the accidents of English history. The merits of that form of government have often been discussed in our own times, but it is assumed on both sides that the only choice lies between one chamber and two ; no one proposes to have three or four. But most of the continental bodies of Estates consisted . . . of three houses ; in Sweden, where the peasants, the small freeholders, were important enough to be separately represented alongside of the nobles, clergy, and citizens, there were till lately four. The number two became the number of our houses of Parliament, not out of any conviction of the advantages of that number, but because it was found impossible to get the clergy of England habitually to act, as they did elsewhere, as a regular member of the parliamentary body. They shrank from the burthen, or they deemed secular legislation inconsistent with their profession. Thus instead of the clergy forming, as they did in France, a distinct Estate of the legislature, we got a Parliament of two houses, Lords and Commons."[2]

<hr>

[1] *Popular Government*, 224, 225.
[2] *Growth of the English Constitution*, 97.

When the question of two houses of Congress was under consideration in the Philadelphia Convention, the principle of a single chamber was in disrepute by reason of the recent failure of the Congress of the Confederation. Almost every State represented in the Convention possessed a legislature of two houses; and the colonial tendency from the beginning of settlement on the Western Continent had been, as we have seen, to follow the usage of the historic two houses of the mother-land. The proposal that the new constitution should provide for a national legislature of two branches was adopted by an all but unanimous vote of the members of the Convention; and Bancroft pertinently notes: " The decision was in harmony with the undisputed and unchanging conviction of the whole people of the United States." [1]

[1] *History of the Constitution.* Speaking of the adoption, by the Convention, of the bicameral system, Dr. J. H. Robinson asks: " Was the choice of the Convention then attributable to their admiration of the English Parliament? Not solely, certainly. There were, in 1787, no less than eleven practically independent communities, within 500 miles of Philadelphia, which had accepted the bicameral system of legislating. It had been known on this side of the Atlantic for more than a century, and was a simple and natural development of the colonial governments." — *Publications of the American Academy,* No. 9, p. 212.

" Since the beginning of the French Revolution, nearly all of the states of continental Europe have organized national assemblies, after the model of the English Parliament, in a spirit of conscious imitation. But the typical English national assembly, embodying what is generally known as the bicameral system, was not copied into the continental European constitutions until it had first been reproduced in a modified form by the founders of the federal republic of the United States.   In the several colonial commonwealths founded by English settlers upon American soil, the typical English national assembly reappeared in an embryonic form as the predestined product of a natural process of reproduction.   These assemblies ' were not formally instituted, but grew up by themselves, because it was in the nature of Englishmen to assemble.' " — Taylor, *Origin and Growth of the English Constitution,* 429; Seeley, *Expansion of England,* 67.

CHAPTER IV.

LEGISLATIVE POWERS.

WHAT glimpses we have of the earliest assemblies or gemots of England reveal the characteristic powers of ancient Teutonic assemblies, — the exercise of authority over tribal or national affairs, and the combining of judicial with legislative functions. Bede's account of the acceptance of Christianity by the Council of Northumbria, describes the king as consulting its members, each in turn, and giving final decision in agreement with the general voice.[1] The law of Wihtraed reads : "There the great men decreed, with the suffrages of all, these dooms, and added them to the lawful customs of the men of Kent."[2] The prologue of the laws of Ini recounts how "Ini, by the grace of God, king of the West Saxons, with the advice and by the teaching of Cénred my father, and of Hedde my bishop, and Ercenwold my bishop, with all my earldormen and the most eminent Witan of my people, and also with a great assembly of God's servants,[3] have been considering respecting our soul's heal and the stability of our realm, so that right law and right royal

[1] Bede, *Hist. Eccl.*, II. 13.   [2] Schmid, *Gesetze*, 15.
[3] Especially the clergy.

judgments might be settled and confirmed among our
people," [1] etc. Alfred, having compiled a body of laws
from old sources, declared in their promulgation, " I then,
Alfred, king of the West Saxons, showed these to all my
Witan, and they then said that it liked them well so to
hold them." [2] The judicial action of the assemblies
which banished and recalled Wilfrid is narrated by
Eddius as proceeding in regular order of accusation,
defence and sentence ; the bishops and earldormen
addressing the gathering, and the judgment being given
by the king or ruling earldorman. [3]

Mention of " counsel," " consent," and the like, to be
found in legal formularies from early times, indicates this
definite relation of the assemblies to legislation. Bede
tells how Ethelbert made, " with the advice of his Witan,
decrees and judgments." [4] Edmund begins his laws by
declaring them to have been established with the counsel
of his Witan, ecclesiastical and lay. [5] Edgar ordains
" with the counsel of his Witan." [6] Ethelred, in the
preamble of the code of 1008, exclaims : " This is the
ordinance which the king of the English, with his Witan,
both clerical and lay, have chosen and advised." [7]

---

[1] Schmid, *Gesetze*, 21.

[2] Alfred's *Dooms;* Thorpe, *Ancient Laws and Institutes*, I.
58, 59; Freeman, *Norman Conquest*, I. 53.

[3] Eddius, c. LIX (ed. Gale, 86).   [4] Bede, *Hist. Eccl.*, II. 5.

[5] Schmid, *Gesetze*, 172, 173, 177.   [6] *Ibid.* 184–187.

[7] Kemble, *Saxons in England*, II. 211. " The word *ceósan*, to
elect or choose, is the technical expression in Teutonic legislation
for ordinances which have been deliberated upon." — *Ibid.* 211, n. 7.

During the period from Egbert to Edward the Confessor, the powers of the national Witenagemot were very great. It elected kings, and on occasion deposed them. It adopted laws, levied taxes, made treaties of peace and alliance, raised military and naval forces, gave grants of folkland, appointed and removed bishops, earldormen, and other chief ecclesiastical and civil officers, and authorized the enforcement of decrees of the Church. It possessed also the functions of a supreme court of justice.[1] And yet, while exercising all these powers at intervals, the degree of its activity in public affairs varied with different reigns, increasing or diminishing according to the feebleness or the vigour of the sovereign for the time being. By the close of the Saxon epoch the crown

---

[1] "Of the manner of the deliberations or the forms of business we know little, but it is not unlikely that they were very complicated. We may conclude that the general outline of the proceedings was something of the following order. On common occasions the king summoned his Witan to attend him at some royal vill, at Christmas, or at Easter, for festive and ceremonial as well as business purposes. On extraordinary occasions he issued summonses, according to the nature of the exigency, appointing the time and place of meeting. When assembled, the Witan commenced their session by attending divine service and formally professing their adherence to the Catholic faith. The king then brought his propositions before them, in the Frankish manner, and after due deliberation they were accepted, modified, or rejected. The reeves, and perhaps on occasion officers specially designated for that service, carried the chapters down into the several counties, and there took a *wed*, or pledge, from the freemen that they would abide by what had been enacted." — Kemble, *Saxons in England*, II. 232, 233.

had absorbed many of its functions, though its right to advise and consent in the making of laws and in the levy of taxes was ever recognized.

As the Witenagemot survived the Norman Conquest, the same powers must be theoretically regarded as belonging to it after, as belonged to it before, that event.[1] Its feudalization, however, and the vigorous control exercised by the Conqueror and his immediate successors, reduced its efficiency almost to a shadow. Its meetings became infrequent, and the proceedings at them were, in general, devoid of reality. Yet, though minimizing its influence, the Norman kings carefully observed old forms, and professed to act by its " counsel and advice." [2]

With the accession of the Plantagenets, much that had been lost was regained. Henry II. habitually consulted his legislature, laying before it every matter of importance. Richard Cœur de Lion did the same. Even John, in the earlier half of his reign, made formal show of respect for his authorized advisers. And before

---

[1] "As no formal change took place in the constitution of the national assembly, so no formal change took place in its powers." — Freeman, *Norman Conquest*, V. 280. " It seems to be admitted that the Norman Conquest wrought no formal change in the constitution of the Witan; after the Conquest, the Great Council remains in possession of all the powers of the old Witenagemot. In legal theory, at least, what the Witan was in the days of King Edward, it seems to have remained in the days of King William. In the forms of legislation, change there was none." — *Origin and Growth of the English Constitution.* 240.

[2] "This immemorial counsel and consent descends from the earliest Teutonic legislation." — *Select Charters*, p. 18.

the time of Henry III., the Council, though still dominated by the royal will, succeeded in turning the nominal assent, that Norman sovereigns had taken for granted, into a genuine consultation, and secured the provision of Magna Charta,[1] that no tax, except three customary feudal aids, should be levied without its consent. Its old right to a share in making the laws became an actuality. Its judicial functions, at least in the case of high offenders, were put in exercise. It dealt with foreign alliances, with the organization of the national defence, and with questions of peace and war. During the absence of the sovereign it practically arranged the regency, and by a series of acts of electing and acknowledging kings, it reaffirmed its ancient privilege of regulating the royal succession. In the Barons' War high claims were made and exceptional powers enforced even against the throne.

Attaining under Edward I. its perfected organization of two houses, Parliament attained also, in principle, the essentials of authority which it has ever since claimed. But only by repeated alternations of ascendency over, and subordination to, the crown, did this authority gradually come to be recognized by the king and the nation as a really co-ordinate element in the government. Even Edward, though consulting his full Parliament on grave affairs, put in its place, for much of the ordinary work of administration, his inner or Privy Council, and was slow in admitting the new House of Commons to the rights conceded to the older assembly of the Lords.

[1] *M. C.* XIV.

The fourteenth century, covering the reigns of Edward II., Edward III., and Richard II., saw much alternation in the political balance. A height of parliamentary influence was reached in the earlier part of the reign of Richard II., when, the king being a minor, the whole executive government was transferred to the two houses.[1] But Richard's later years saw sharp reaction in the direction of uncontrolled royal power — a reaction that was followed in turn by that king's deposition, and the seating of Henry IV. upon the throne, with a parliament-given title. And legislative potency and privilege grew and flourished greatly under the House of Lancaster.

A succession of more serious alternations began with the ascension of the House of York. At first many causes combined to weaken Parliament, which dwindled to a mere instrument for registering the royal will. Its deepest abasement was reached in 1539, when a parliamentary act (13 Henry VIII. c. 8) accorded to individual proclamations of the sovereign all the force of legislative statutes.[2] Not till the reign of Elizabeth did

---

[1] Hallam, *Middle Ages*, III. 59.

[2] "A remarkable example of the way in which Henry VIII. contrived to unite the exercise of practically absolute power with respect for constitutional forms — to play the despot by the co-operation of Parliament — is afforded by the act giving the king's proclamations the force of law. The king having issued certain royal proclamations, the judges held that those who disobeyed them could not be punished by the Council. The king then appealed to Parliament to give his proclamations the force of statutes. This request was complied with, but not without 'many large words.'" — Taswell-Langmead, *English Constitutional History*, 385.

signs of parliamentary revival appear. But stubborn assertion of the old privileges confronted James I., and the
attempt of Charles I. to put an extreme royalist philosophy into practice in the teeth of an aggressive Puritan
House of Commons, resulted in the overthrow of the
throne and the House of Lords together; an overthrow
so disastrous, that neither has since fully recovered the
place once held in the fabric of the state. In creating a
commonwealth, however, the Commons went too far, and
at the Restoration the pendulum swung back once more,
and a revival of arbitrary executive rule ensued under
Charles II. and James II. Nevertheless, the fate of the
Stuarts was to promote parliamentary independence by
opposing it, and the Revolution of 1688 settled forever
the power of the legislature by establishing, beyond further question, the great parliamentary functions.

Thus it came about that under William and Mary, and
Queen Anne, the executive and legislative branches of
the government enjoyed a mutually independent relation.
And although the gradual rise of the Cabinet system into
political potency, together with the feebleness of the first
two sovereigns of the House of Hanover, prepared the
way for changes in the England of to-day by which
Parliament has come to control the crown, yet George
III. held his own by vigorous assertion of royal influence, and during his reign the balance was maintained
and a check given to final and complete parliamentary
supremacy. As this particular phase of the long constitutional development, with a distinct executive and legis-

lature, neither dominated by the other, was akin to the
theory and practice of executive and legislative relations
in the American colonies, and as it was contemporaneous
with the period of American independence, it naturally,
almost inevitably, left its impress upon the Constitution
of the United States.

Having thus briefly reviewed the process by which
parliamentary influence was evolved, it will be instructive
to take a nearer view of the chief points wherein the
American Congress derives its powers from this legislative
past.

We cannot do better than begin with a characteristic
point of procedure, by examining the origin of bills. In
Saxon times, and under the Norman and early Plantagenet kings, legislation was usually initiated by the sovereign, propositions being laid by him before the Council
with a view to its advice and consent. But as parliamentary organization approached completion, Parliament
itself came to take the initiative, and in the fourteenth
century nearly all legislation arose from its petitions
to the king.[1] The king's favourable answer gave to
petitions the force of statutes. But difficulty was early
experienced from evasive, delayed, and otherwise unsatis-
factory answers, and from the fact that laws were occasionally placed upon the roll, as acts of Parliament, which,

---

[1] "The statutes are made by the king with the advice and consent of the lords spiritual and temporal; the petitions are answered
'*le roi le veut*' or '*le roi s'avisera*' with the advice of the lords." —
Stubbs, *Constitutional History of England*, III. 500.

in being turned into statutes under the king's hand had been made to differ materially from the purport of petitions.[1]   Parliament put forth successive efforts to prevent such abuses ; and to complaints on the subject Henry V. returned answer in 1414 that "nothing be enacted to the petitions of his Commons that be contrary of their asking whereby they should be bound without their assent."[2]

[1] This was a grave matter, and affected the Records of Chancery. In 1404 the Commons complained that a Subsidy Act had been recorded on the Rolls of Chancery in a form contrary to their actual grant, and prayed that their intention in making the grant be declared, and that the Barons of the Exchequer be instructed not to levy the subsidy in its untrue form. — See Clifford, *History of Private Bill Legislation*, I. 325.

[2] *Rot. Parl.* IV. 22. This petition is interesting, as the first instance in which the English language was used in petitions by the House of Commons. After asserting the ancient Teutonic principle that no law could be made without their assent, the Commons go on to say : "Consideringe that the Comune of youre lond, the whiche that is, and ever hath be, a membre of youre Parlement, ben as well Assentirs as Peticioners, that fro this tyme foreward, by compleynte of the comune of eny myschief axkynge remedie by mouthe of their Speker for the Comune, other ellys by Petition writen, that ther never be no Lawe made theruppon, and engrosed as Statut and Lawe, nother by addicions, nother by diminucions, by no maner of terme or termes, the whiche that sholde chaunge the sentence, and the entente axked by the Speker mouthe, or the Petitions biforesaid yeven up yn writyng by the manere forsaid, withoute assent of the foresaid Comune. Consideringe oure soverain lord, that it is not in no wyse the entente of youre Comunes, zif hit be so that they axke you by spekying, or by writying, too thynges or three, or as manye as theym lust : but that ever it stande in the fredom of your hie Regalie, to graunte whiche of thoo that you luste, and to werune the remanent." The king, in replying, "of his grace

In the next reign a remedy was found in the introduction
of completely drawn statutes under the name of Bills —
petitiones formam actuum in se continientes.[1] This form
of procedure, used at first by the Commons in their
grants of money, was eventually applied to all varieties
of legislation — bills introduced in either house and
agreed to in the other, being sent to the king for his
approval or veto without alteration.

The Constitution of the United States perpetuates
this usage by providing for the initiation of laws by
either house in the form of bills, and by limiting the
executive to simple veto or approval. "Every bill
which shall have passed the House of Representatives
and the Senate, shall, before it becomes a law, be presented to the President of the United States," for his
approval or veto.[2]

especial graunteth that fro hensforth, no thyng be enacted to the
Peticions of his Comune, that be contrairie of hir askyng, wharby
they shuld be bounde withoute their assent. Savyng alwey to our
liege Lord his real Prerogatif, to graunte and denye what him lust
of their Petitions and askynges aforesaide."

[1] Ruffhead's *Statutes*, I. 16, *pref.*

[2] See *Constitution of the United States*, Art. I. Sec. 7. The
general procedure of the American Congress is based upon historical antecedents and the experience growing out of congressional
life. "The provision that each house may determine the rules
of its proceedings, has led to the adoption of two systems, differing widely from each other, in each of the bodies. The main
basis, however, on which those rules have been constructed, is
Jefferson's *Manual*, a work prepared by him mainly from the historical precedents in the English House of Commons. These rules
have become, by many changes and amendments, very numerous."

Each house of Parliament possesses certain privileges peculiar to itself. The chief of these which have made their way into the Constitution of the United States are the judicial rights of the Senate, and the right of impeachment and that of initiating money bills which belong to the House of Representatives. The judicial powers usual to ancient Teutonic assemblies were put in operation, as already stated, by the Witenagemot of England, and eventually descended to the House of Lords. The right of impeachment was employed by the House of Commons as early as 1376 (50 Edward III.) ; but the nearest approach to the exercise of judicial functions ever made by the lower house was under the form of bills of attainder, which were in reality a species of legislation.[1]   Impeachment became

---

— Miller, *Lectures on the Constitution of the United States*, 194, 195. "Parliamentary law" is so familiar in the United States, as governing all public assemblies, that its origin is seldom considered.

  [1] "The proceedings of Parliament in passing bills of attainder, and of pains and penalties, do not vary from those adopted in regard to other bills.   They may be introduced into either house, but ordinarily commence in the House of Lords.   They pass through the same stages, and when agreed to by both houses, they receive the royal assent in the usual form.   But the parties who are subjected to these proceedings are admitted to defend themselves by counsel and witnesses before both houses ; and the solemnity of the proceeding would cause measures to be taken to enforce the attendance of members upon their service in Parliament.   In evil times this summary power of Parliament to punish criminals by statute has been perverted and abused, and in the best of times it should be regarded with jealousy ; but, whenever a fitting occasion arises for its exercise, it is undoubtedly the highest form of parliamentary

an engine of great political power, and though fitfully employed, was never allowed to lapse; the last two cases being those of Warren Hastings in 1788, and of Melville in 1804.[1]   In strictly judicial procedure, the Commons were held to be accusers and advocates, and the Lords the judges of the case.   The judicial power which at one time lodged in the whole Parliament was declared in 1399, at the suggestion of the Commons themselves, to reside in the Lords only.[2]   The Constitution of the United States, following in this the State constitutions of Delaware, Massachusetts, New Hampshire, New York, Pennsylvania, South Carolina, Vermont, and Virginia, gives judicial powers to the upper, and the right of impeachment to the lower, house. "The Senate shall have the sole power to try impeachments.   When sitting for that purpose, they shall be

judicature." — May, *Parliamentary Practice*, ed. 1883, p. 744. "The nearest approach" of the House of Commons to participation in a trial "was made when, in 1283, they were summoned to Shrewsbury on the trial of David of Wales; but they attended merely as witnesses." — Stubbs, *Constitutional History of England*, II. 270, 271.

[1] From the impeachment of Sir Giles Mompesson and Lord Bacon in 1621, down to the Revolution of 1688, there were about forty cases of impeachment.   Among these were the notable impeachments of George Villers, Duke of Buckingham; Thomas Wentworth, Earl of Strafford; Archbishop Laud; and Edward Hyde, Earl of Clarendon.   Under William III., Queen Anne, and George I. there were fifteen impeachments; under George III. there was one only, that of Lord Lovat, 1746.

[2] See Rowland, *Manual of English Constitution*, 457; Hallam, *Constitutional History*, I. 487 *et seq.;* I. 508, etc.

on oath or affirmation. When the President of the
United States is tried, the Chief Justice shall preside,
and no person shall be convicted without the concurrence of two-thirds of the members present."[1]   "The
House of Representatives . . . shall have the sole power
of impeachment."[2]

The power to depose the executive himself was
claimed by the Witenagemot and by the later Parliament; and the exercise of such a power is attested by
several historical examples. By the terms of Article I.
of the Constitution, just quoted, the American executive
may likewise be removed from his official position by
act of the legislature, through a special process of trial.

---

[1] *Constitution of the United States,* Art. I. Sec. 3.

[2] *Ibid.* Art. I. Sec. 2. Though taken from State usage (see
Bryce, *American Commonwealth,* I. 47; Robinson, *Publications
of American Academy,* No. 9, p. 219), yet this part of the Constitution was taken also and consciously from the original English
usage, as is made evident by the *Federalist* (No. 65) : "It is not
disputed that the power of originating the inquiry, or in other words,
of preferring the impeachment, ought to be lodged in the hands of
one branch of the legislative body; will not the reasons which indicate the propriety of this arrangement strongly plead for an ad-
mission of the other branch of that body to a share of the inquiry?
*The model from which the idea of this institution has been borrowed,
pointed out that course to the Convention.   In Great Britain, it is
the province of the House of Commons to prefer the impeachment,
and the House of Lords to decide upon it.   Several of the State constitutions have followed the same example.*" Seven persons have
been impeached in the United States.   Of these, five have been ac-
quitted; one a President of the United States, one a Justice of the
Supreme Court, one a District Judge, one a Senator, and one a
Secretary of War.   Two District Judges have been convicted.

Another point of interest in the same connection concerns the pardoning power in cases of impeachment. At the trial of Thomas Osborne, Earl of Danby, in 1679, in the reign of Charles II., the defendant claimed the right to implead the king's pardon in bar of a parliamentary impeachment. But the Commons resolved, " that the pardon so impleaded was illegal and void, and ought not to be allowed in bar of the impeachment of the Commons of England." [1] Before the question could be settled, Parliament was prorogued by the king. But in the year following the Revolution of 1688 the Commons again voted, that "a pardon is not pleadable in bar of an impeachment." [2] Finally, it was decided by the Act of Settlement (12 and 13 William III., c. 2), "that no pardon under the Great Seal of England shall be pleadable to an impeachment by the Commons in Parliament." The crown's right to pardon after sentence remains, and has been exercised occasionally, with the effect of nullifying the action of Parliament.[3] But the Constitution of the United States, following the historical spirit, goes beyond the letter of the English usage, by restricting the pardoning power so as expressly

[1] *Commons Journal,* 28 April and 5 May, 1679.

[2] *Ibid.* 6 June, 1689.

[3] The sentence on Lord Chancellor Bacon was remitted by James I. Indirectly the Commons possess the power of pardoning, by declining to demand judgment after the Lords have found the accused guilty; for judgment cannot be pronounced by the Lords until it is demanded by the Commons. See May, *Parliamentary Practice,* 9th ed., 739.

to exclude impeached persons. The President " shall have power to grant reprieves and pardons for offences against the United States, *except in cases of impeachment.*"[1]

The right of the House of Commons to initiate money bills dates from 1407. A question on the subject having arisen between the houses, Henry IV. ordained in that year, that the Commons should "grant," and the Lords "assent to," votes of money, which should be reported to the king " by the mouth of the Speaker of the Commons."[2] Subsequent attempts of the House of Lords to encroach upon this privilege were energetically resisted by the lower house. The latter even held that money bills should not be so much as amended by the Lords; and whenever such amendments actually were made, and were thought desirable by the Commons, contest over the point of privilege was avoided by dropping the amended bill altogether, passing a fresh one embodying the purpose of the amendments, and sending it up for the simple assent of the upper chamber. However this might answer as a nominal protection of the privilege, it nevertheless gave force to the Lords' amendments. The right of the Lords " to pass all or reject all without diminution or alteration " was admitted by the Commons in 1671 and in 1689 ; but the peers seldom put the right into practice. At the period of the formation of the American Constitution it was

[1] *Constitution of the United States*, Art. II. Sec. 2.
[2] *Rot. Parl.* III. 611; see also *Lords' Report*, I. 358, 359.

matter of fresh parliamentary history, that although only
the lower house could originate money bills, the Lords
were not without practical voice regarding them. The
Constitution of the United States provides, in language
closely copied from the State constitutions of Massachusetts and New Hampshire, " that all bills for raising
revenue shall originate in the House of Representatives ;
but the Senate may propose and concur with amendments as on other bills." [1] Notwithstanding such specific
constitutional authorization, the English traditional spirit
of complete restriction as regards this privilege, has
manifested itself with singular force and persistency in

[1] *Constitution of the United States*, Art. I. Sec. 7. The debate
on this portion of the Constitution in the Philadelphia Convention
is full of references to English historical usage. Rutledge, referring in the course of the argument, to members of the Convention
who had taken part, says: "They tell us that we ought to be
guided by the long experience of Great Britain, and not our own
experience of eleven years. . . . The House of Commons not
only have the exclusive right of originating, but the Lords are not
allowed to alter or amend a money bill." — Elliot, *Debates*, V. 419.
The English usage was adopted, modified only by the distinct assertion of the right of the upper house to a voice in amendments.
Further light upon the action of the Convention in consciously following English examples is supplied by the *Federalist:* — "The
House of Representatives can not only refuse, but they alone can
propose, the supplies requisite for the support of government.
They, in a word, hold the purse; that powerful instrument by
which we behold, in the history of the British Constitution, an
infant and humble representation of the people gradually enlarging
the sphere of its activity and importance, and finally reducing, as far
as it seems to have wished, all the overgrown prerogatives of the
other branches of the government." — *Federalist*, No. 58.

the American lower house ; and the Senate has established the practice of amending money bills, only after great difficulty, and at cost of repeated contests with the Representatives.[1]

[1] " As we would understand the meaning of the term ' revenue ' at the present day, the expression ' bills for raising revenue ' would have reference to laws for the purpose of obtaining money by some form of taxation, or other means of raising the necessary funds to be used in supplying the wants of the government, paying its expenses, and discharging its debts. The appropriation of that money, which is always necessarily done by virtue of an act of Congress, would seem to be quite a different thing from the laws prescribing how the money shall be raised. In practice, however, the House of Representatives has insisted that, not only shall it originate all bills of ways and means for raising revenue, for which purpose there is a committee appointed in that body called the ' Committee of Ways and Means,' but it has also claimed that all the appropriation bills, and especially the annual appropriation bills, which are prepared each year to meet the current expenses of the government during the succeeding fiscal year, shall originate in that body; and it has, therefore, a standing ' Committee on Appropriations.' This has been the practice now for so long a time that it may be doubted whether it will be seriously questioned. The Senate, however, has never given its full consent to this proposition, but has, on the contrary, from time to time originated bills appropriating money for specific purposes; although it is not believed that it has for a great many years attempted to act upon any of the general appropriation bills until they have been sent to that body from the House. . . . It is difficult to see, under this clause of the Constitution, how it is, when no new law is necessary to raise revenue, that the act appropriating or directing how the revenue already raised . . . shall be appropriated can be properly called a bill for raising revenue. Undoubtedly the adoption of this article into the Constitution, and the construction which has been given to it, is the result of the practices of our English ancestors." — Miller, *Lectures on the Constitution of the United States*, 204, 205.

Privileges anciently possessed by both houses of Parliament equally, and common also to both houses of
Congress, are freedom of speech, freedom from arrest,
and the right of the chambers to decide contested membership.[1]

The Lords, being abundantly able to defend their rights
by force of arms, seem always to have exercised freedom
of speech in their own house, unchallenged. But during
the first three centuries of the existence of the House of
Commons, the Speaker and individual members were frequently proceeded against by the crown for utterances
in Parliament. Claims to freedom of speech were early
made by the Commons ; and the first of the Lancastrians, Henry IV., affirmed the privilege to belong to both
houses. In 1541 (33 Henry VIII.) it was named among
the rights and privileges claimed. from the sovereign
at the opening of Parliament.[2] Eighty years later, in
1621, the Commons declared, "that every member hath
freedom from all impeachment, imprisonment, or molestation other than censure of the House itself, for or
concerning any bill, speaking, reasoning, or declaring of
any matter or matters touching the Parliament, or Parliament business."[3] The last instance of the crown's open
violation of the right was in the famous prosecution of

[1] Sir Erskine May, in *Parliamentary Practice*, gives historical
and legal information as to the various branches of parliamentary
privileges. The phrase "privilege of Parliament" has much wider
meaning than formerly.

[2] *Rot. Parl.* 33 Hen. VIII.

[3] Hatsell, *Precedents*, I. 79.

Sir John Eliot and other members by Charles I., — one of the acts that hastened that monarch's overthrow. The privilege was finally confirmed by the Bill of Rights, the ninth article of which provides, "that the freedom of speech and debates or proceedings in Parliament ought not to be impeached or questioned in any court or place out of Parliament."[1]   And, very nearly in this language, it appears in the Constitution of the United States, as belonging to the members of Congress : "For any speech or debate in either house they shall not be questioned in any other place."[2]

The privilege of freedom from arrest and molestation probably dates from the earliest existence of legislative bodies in England.   Ethelbert, in a law of the Kingdom of Kent in the sixth century, ordained : "'That if the king call his leod (people) to him, and one there do them evil, let him compensate with a twofold bot and fifty shillings to the king."[3]   A law of King Canute provided : "That every man be entitled to girth [*i.e.* freedom from molestation] to the gemot and from the gemot, except he be a notorious thief."[4]   Members summoned to the

---

[1] 1 Will. and Mary, Sess. 2, c. 2.   See, on the general subject, May, *Parliamentary Practice,* 118–123.

[2] *Constitution of the United States,* Art. I. Sec. 6.

[3] Ethelbert, § 1; *Select Charters,* p. 61.

[4] Canute, § 83; cf. Edward Conf. § 2; *Select Charters,* 74; Thorpe, *Ancient Laws and Institutes.*

The same freedom to persons attending upon ecclesiastical synods was granted by Edward the Confessor. — Ll. Edward Conf. Art. 2, cl. 8.   The law provides, "ad synodos venientibus, sive summoniti sint, sive per se quid agendum habuerint, sit summa pax."

Parliament of later days by the sovereign were supposed
to be under his protection. During the reign of Edward
I. the legal principle was enunciated, that it was unbe-
coming for a member of the king's council to be dis-
trained in time of its session ;[1] and action of similar
purport was taken by Edward II.[2] A statute of 1432
required the punishment of any who should molest comers
to Parliament, giving, as in the ancient law of Ethelbert,
double damages to the party injured.[3] But notwithstanding the immemorial recognition of the privilege and
its repeated enactment in law, frequent contests took
place for its enforcement. Immunity was eventually
extended to the servants and to the property of members, — an abuse on the side of Parliament. But in 1770,
just before the period of American independence, the right
was restricted to its ancient limitations, giving freedom
from arrest to members only.[4] It has always been restricted to arrest due to civil causes, and has not interfered with the execution of criminal law in cases of
" treason, felony, or breach of the peace."[5]

This privilege in its ancient form is found in the
Constitution of the United States. "They [the senators
and representatives] shall in all cases except treason,

---

[1] *Rot. Parl.* I. 61.

[2] Hatsell, *Precedents,* I. 12.

[3] Stat. 11 Hen. VI. c. 11; *Statutes,* II. 286; *Rot. Parl.* IV. 453.

[4] 10 Geo. III. c. 50. Several previous statutes had restrained
the evil in part: 12 and 13 Will. III. c. 3; 2 and 3 Anne, c. 18;
11 Geo. II. c. 24.

[5] Taswell-Langmead, *English Constitutional History,* 328.

felony, and breach of the peace, be privileged from arrest at the session of their respective houses, and in going to and returning from the same."[1]

The right of the House of Commons to decide contested elections of members was not originally looked upon as a privilege of Parliament, and was not fully established as such until the time of Elizabeth.[2] Instances of contact of the Commons with disputed elections occurred in the reigns of Mary, Elizabeth, and James I.[3] The right was recognized by the Court of Exchequer Chamber, 1674;[4] by the House of Lords in 1689,[5] and by the law courts in 1680[6] and 1702.[7] It has been abandoned in our own day, an act having been passed so recently as 1868, providing for trial of election cases by judges of the superior courts of law.[8] But the Constitution of the United States shows the impress of the period of its formation, in the provision: "Each house shall be the judge of the elections and qualifications of its own members."[9]

---

[1] *Constitution of the United States*, Art. I. Sec. 6.

[2] D'Ewes, *Journal*, 393.

[3] *Com. Jour.*, I Mary, 27; Hallam, *Constitutional History*, 7th ed., I. 275; *Parliamentary History*, I. 967.

[4] *Barnardiston v. Soame*, 6 Howell, St. Tr. 1092.

[5] *Ibid.* 1119.

[6] *Onslow's Case*, 2 Ventris, 37.

[7] *Prideaux v. Morris*, 2 Salkeld, 502. The further act, 7 Will. III. c. 7, provided that "the last determination of the House of Commons concerning the right of election is to be pursued."

[8] 31 and 32 Vic. c. 125.

[9] *Constitution of the United States*, Art. I. Sec. 5. This is a sin-

Amid all the parliamentary privileges, that which has been most modified, and the practical abandonment of which has had the most far-reaching political results, concerns the secrecy of proceedings. The original motive for secrecy of debate was the anxiety of members to protect themselves against the disapproval of the sovereign ; but secrecy was found quite as convenient as a cover to hide proceedings from the constituencies. And not until after prolonged struggle, was the right of the electors, and of the public at large, to know what the representatives of the nation were doing in the Parliament virtually conceded.[1] Until recent times the business of legislation in England was conducted with secrecy. Provision for official publication dates from the issue of the " Diurnal Occurrences of Parliament," beginning in 1641, in the time of the Commonwealth. But this was a record of transactions only, and the making public of speeches, except by special leave, was prohibited under severe penalties.[2] After the Restoration, incorrect accounts of transactions having appeared, an act was passed (1680) which stipulated that, under the supervision of the

---

gular illustration of the fact, that some old English usages which have been abandoned in the mother-country, still survive in the United States.

[1] *English Constitutional History*, 149.

[2] Sir Edward Dering, of Surrenden Dering, printed a collection of his own speeches without leave, and for this offence was expelled from the House of Commons, and imprisoned in the Tower of London; and his book was ordered to be burnt by the common hangman. *Com. Jour.*, II. 411, February 2, 1641.

Speaker of the House of Commons, an authorized publication of votes and proceedings should be made, but still without the debates.[1] Nevertheless, what purported to be reports of speeches and discussions occasionally got into the press; and public opinion sided so strongly against Parliament in a contest which it undertook in 1771, that publication of debates, though never formally legalized, has not since been interfered with.[2] This settlement was recent history at the time of the adoption of the Constitution of the United States, which contains a provision on the subject similar in principle to that existing subsequently to 1680 as the law of Parliament, and relates only to congressional action, and not to debate. Since the adoption of the Constitution, however, debates have come to be published, — though the Senate habitually met in secret session during the first years of its existence, and still does so, with more or less frequency. The requirement of the Constitution reads : " Each house shall keep a journal of its proceedings, and from time to time publish the same, excepting such parts as may in their judgment require secrecy."[3]

In the Act of Settlement is a clause to the effect " that no person who has an office or place of profit under the king, or receives a pension from the crown, shall be capable of serving as a member of the House of Com-

---

[1] *Com. Jour.*, IX. 74.

[2] Cobbett, *Parliamentary History*, XVII. 59-163.

[3] *Constitution of the United States*, Art. I. Sec. 5.

mons."[1]   This was intended to check the corrupt
influence of the executive over Parliament.   But the
exclusion of all national officers soon came to be regarded
as too severe a measure, and the clause was repealed
before it came into actual operation.[2]   A modified enactment took its place in the reign of Queen Anne.[3]   But
the evil remained, the crown continuing to exert more
or less control by gifts of offices and pensions.   Thus,
in 1741 two hundred appointments were found in the
possession of members of the House of Commons.[4]
The Place Bill of 1742 excluded from the House a
large number of officials.[5]   In 1782, five years before
the date of the American Constitution, the Civil List Act
brought about further reform of the same character ; and
the modern system, by which an appointment to office
vacates membership in the Commons — with possibility
of re-election — may be said to date from the passage
of this law.[6]   The Constitution of the United States goes
somewhat beyond this final stage of English usage, and
corresponds more nearly with the spirit of the Act of Settlement.   " No senator or representative shall, during the
time for which he was elected, be appointed to any civil
office under the authority of the United States, which
shall have been created, or the emoluments whereof
shall have been increased, during such time ; and no

---

[1] 12 and 13 Will. III. c. 2., III. 6.   [3] 6 Anne, c. 7.

[2] 4 Anne, c. 8, s. 25   [4] *Lords' Protests*, 1741.

[5] 15 Geo. II. c. 22.

[6] Lord Rockingham's Civil List Act, 22 Geo. III. c. 82.

person holding any office under the United States shall
be a member of either house during his continuance in
office."[1]

It is needless to consider in detail the full list of
congressional powers enumerated in Article I., Section
8, of the Constitution, or to compare these powers with
those of Parliament and of the colonial legislatures from
which they have been mainly copied or derived.[2] It
will be interesting, however, in bringing this chapter to
a close, to review the historical development of such

---

[1] *Constitution of the United States*, Art. I. Sec. 6.

[2] Congress alone has the right to declare war; and seemingly
this is a departure from the usage of the English Parliament at the
time the Constitution was adopted. But the ninth article of the
ordinances of 1311 required that "the king henceforth shall not go
out of his realm, nor undertake against any one deed of war without
the common assent of his baronage, and that in Parliament." — *Statutes*, I. 59. "The right to be consulted in war and peace, which
the Commons had established under Edward III., and maintained
under Richard II., was extended under the Lancastrians, so as to
include all questions of national interest." — Taswell-Langmead,
English Constitutional History, 321. Any examination in detail
would reveal the fact that the powers of Congress are really a
modification or adaptation of those of the colonial legislatures and
of the English Parliament. Congress has not a supreme position,
such as Parliament has. But its construction as a legislature having
constitutional limitations is taken from the State legislatures, which
were limited by the State constitutions; and back of these, from
the colonial legislatures, which were limited by the colonial charters
and, to some extent, by the supremacy of the home Parliament.
Of course, the differences between national conditions in the United
States and in England have introduced many American peculiarities.

fundamental functions as those of supply and accounts, and with them, of the general subject of taxation.

The principle of appropriating the supplies, *i.e.* voting a sum for specific purposes only, instead of placing it without reserve in the hands of the king, certainly dates back as far as 1353. For a long period it was put into exercise only at rare intervals, but during the Commonwealth the House of Commons gained full control over expenditure, with apparent advantage to the nation. And after the Restoration, the House claimed, and Charles II. conceded, the right of appropriation in the Appropriation Act of 1665.[1] From that time it became an indisputable principle, recognized by frequent, and at length constant, practice, that supplies granted by Parliament are only to be expended for particular objects specified by itself.[2] Since the reign of William and Mary, a clause has been inserted in the annual Appropriation Act, forbidding, under heavy penalties, Lords of the Treasury to issue, and officers of the Exchequer to obey, any warrant for the expenditure of money in the national treasury, upon any other service than that to which it has been distinctly appropriated.

The right of Parliament to audit accounts followed, by natural consequence, the practice of appropriating supplies. So early as 1340 a parliamentary committee was appointed to examine into the manner in which the last subsidy had been expended.[3] Although Henry IV. re-

[1] 17 Car. II. c. 1.   [3] Rot. Parl. II. 130.

[2] Hallam, Constitutional History. II. 355, 356.

sisted a similar movement in 1406, he conceded the
right in the year following; and audit has since been
regarded a settled usage. The two principles are united
in a single clause of the American Constitution : "No
money shall be drawn from the treasury, but in consequence of appropriations made by law; and regular
statement and account of the receipts and expenditures
of all public money shall be published from time to time."[1]

Legislative control over taxation bears close relation
to the history of Parliament. Though the Witenagemot
possessed the undoubted right of consenting to taxes,
the right was rarely put in exercise, the royal needs
being well supplied in early days by income from royal
farms and from what had been the folkland, with such
commuted payments of fcorm fultum, or provision in
kind, as represented either the reserved rents from
ancient possessions of the crown, or the quasi-volun-
tary tribute paid by the nation to its chosen head.[2]
The Norman sovereigns exacted feudal aids and other
special varieties of taxation, retaining and adding to
the imposts of the Saxon kings. But we have scant
evidence as to what extent the consent of the national
council was asked by them. Although a tax of the
reign of Henry I. is described as the "aid which my
barons gave me,"[3] it would appear that until the time

---

[1] *Constitution of the United States*, Art. I. Sec. 9.

[2] Stubbs, *Constitutional History of England*, I. 317.

[3] "Auxilium quod barones mihi dederunt." — *Chron. Abingd.*,
II. 113.

of Richard I. the sovereign usually contented himself
with merely announcing in assembly the amounts needed,
and the reason for his imposing subsidies.

Nevertheless, by the feudal doctrine, the payer of a
tax made a voluntary gift for the relief of the wants of
his ruler; and under King John, a theory that the
promise to pay tax affected only the individual promis-
ing created serious complications in the collection of
the revenues.   Magna Charta provided that, with the
exception of three specified feudal aids, no tax should
be levied without the assent of a council duly convoked.
Increase in the burden of taxation, and its pressure
upon all classes of the nation, served to arouse attention
to the subject; and the establishment of the representative system in Parliament had its essential origin in the
supposed necessity for obtaining the consent, directly
or by recognized proxy, of all who were taxed.[1]

After the famous Act *Confirmatio Chartarum*, in the
reign of Edward I.,[2] the exclusive right of the nation
to tax itself, through its representatives, became an
established principle; though uniformity of practice
under it was but gradually attained.[3]   Hallam names as

[1] "The rudimentary form of the principle that representation
should accompany taxation, gained ground after the practice arose
of bringing personal property and income under contribution."
— Stubbs, *Constitutional History of England*, I. 648.

[2] 25 Edw. I., St. I. c. 6.   Although a statute, the *Confirmatio
Chartarum* is drawn up in the form of a charter.   It passed Parliament, October 10, 1297.

[3] For a time the Estates of the realm assented to taxes separately,
and each with a separate quota.   This custom gradually ceased.

one of the settled results of the protracted contest between the crown and the people during the Middle Ages, that " the king could levy no sort of new tax upon his people, except by the grant of his Parliament." [1] The Petition of Right of Charles I. emphatically asserts the principle, [2] and the Bill of Rights of the time of William and Mary finally declares, " that levying money for or to the use of the crown by pretence of prerogative without grant of Parliament for longer time, or in other manner than the same is or shall be granted, is illegal." [3]   It is not too much to say, that the principle lies at the foundation of all others in the English constitution, and is a chief source of modern liberties.

The last instance of it was in the eighteenth year of Edward III. " In later reports both houses are mentioned, in conjunction with the observation 'that they have advised in common.' " — Gneist, *English Parliament*, 137, Shee's trans.

[1] *Constitutional History*, I. 2.   " The dependence of supplies on the redress of grievances originated under Richard II.   It had previously been usual for the king not to answer petitions until the last day of the session, when the supplies had, of course, been granted.   The attempt to invert this order of proceeding had been declared by Richard II.'s judges to be high treason.   But in the 2d of Henry IV. the Commons again endeavoured to secure this important lever for the application of parliamentary power. The king resisted firmly, and the Commons gave way for the time, but the practice gradually gained ground." — Taswell-Langmead, *English Constitutional History*, 312.   As early as 1309, the Commons granted a subsidy " upon this condition, that the king should take advice and grant redress upon certain articles wherein they are aggrieved."—See Prynne, *2d Register*, 68.   For a case involving a similar principle of early date, see *Parliamentary Writs*, I. 105.

[2] 3 Car. c. 2, s. 1.   [3] 1 Will. and Mary, Sess. 2, c. 2.

It was the alleged violation of this constitutional principle of taxation by consent of the taxpayers, through their elected or acknowledged representatives, that led to the revolt of the colonies in America. The principle appears among the oldest assertions of privilege on the part of the colonists; and declarations on the subject occur in their earliest legislation.[1] The home Parliament had, before the American Revolution, claimed the right to tax the colonies; but the claim had never been admitted on their part, and it had never been carried into effect. Their opposition rested upon the fact, that they were without representatives in Parliament; and when George III. forced an issue, petitions were addressed to the crown, and protests put forth by successive intercolonial congresses, on this specific ground. The Declaration of Independence names, as one of the reasons justifying final separation from England, that of her " imposing taxes on us without our consent."

There is, then, a certain historic fitness in the fact, that first among the powers of Congress enumerated in the Constitution of the United States is the power " to lay and collect taxes."[2] That power finds its proper

---

[1] In Plymouth, Massachusetts Bay, Virginia, Maryland, New York, and generally. See Story, *Constitution*, I. 116.

[2] *Constitution of the United States*, Art. I. Sec. 8. A limitation as to appropriations occurs in this section of Article I.: " No appropriation of money " for the support of armies, " shall be for a longer term than two years." " The clause," as Robinson remarks, " bears an obvious analogy to the custom in England." — *Publications of the American Academy*, No. 9, p. 220. See also *Federalist*, No. 61.

mention there because of the long and eventually successful struggle in the mother-land over the principle of liberty, that the property of the individual cannot be taken from him in the shape of taxation without his consent, given through his representatives; and because of the further contest over the same principle, which ended in American independence.

CHAPTER V.

TO what extent and in what manner the executive of the United States is related to the ancient executive of England, can best be understood by tracing the development of the latter, and by comparing the status of the English executive in the reign of George III. with that of the American executive, as defined in the American Constitution. The task is difficult, because English royal prerogative is of a character well-nigh undefinable, and because the history of the royal prerogative is closely interwoven with the general history of the nation. But if followed in outline, the kingly office will be found rising step by step from a simple Teutonic original, until it attains to practical absolutism, and then as gradually losing power until, under modern sovereigns, slight vestige of active authority remains. During the colonial time the king of England was, as we have seen, the executive of America. He governed the colonies in his own person, and also through governors, or other representatives. The presidency is derived both directly and indirectly from the kingship, at a stage of the development of the royal office subsequent to the period of greatest strength and previous to that of greatest weakness.

In the early Teutonic tribes, executive functions, as we understand them, were in an ill-defined and formative condition. There were elective officers of various titles, some for civil, and some for military affairs. Among these officers in certain tribes kings are named.[1] But the Teutonic kingship, though held in high honour, had only limited and uncertain powers in time of peace, and was not necessarily chief in command in time of war; being quite different from the ideal created by later associations.[2] Like other officials, the king was elected; but unlike them, was chosen, with the thought of blood

---

[1] From the words of Cæsar it has been supposed that kings were the exception rather than the rule. His words are: "In pace, nullus est communis magistratus; sed principes regionum atque pagorum inter suos jus dicunt." — *De Bello Gallico*, VI. 23. Tacitus draws a clear distinction between tribes having kings, and tribes not having them. — *Germania*, cc. 25, 44. Commenting upon this, so great an authority as Kemble says: "Even in the dim twilight of Teutonic history, we find tribes and nations subject to kings; others again, acknowledged no such office, and Tacitus seems to regard this state as the more natural to our forefathers. I do not think this is clear; on the contrary, kingship, in a certain sense, seems to me rooted in the German mind and institutions, and universal among some particular tribes and confederacies." — *Saxons in England*, I. 137.

[2] Waitz considers that the king was the military head in monarchical tribes. See *Deutsche Verfassungs-Geschichte*, I. 310 *sq.* But Tacitus says: "Duces ex virtute sumunt . . . et duces exemplo potius quam imperio, si prompti, si conspicui, si ante aciem agant, admiratione praesunt." — *Germania*, c. 7. See also Tacitus, *Germania*, c. 11.

descent, from the fittest members of a single family,
though there was no essential succession from father to
son.[1]   In his hereditary character, he was the official
representative of the unity of his nation, and in such
sense, rather than in the sense of rulership, its acknowledged head.   His title of King, or Cyning, the derivation
and meaning of which have been much discussed, probably had to do with the idea of Cyn or Kin; kinship
being conceived as blood relationship between people of
one race.[2]   The word was used, perhaps, as conveying

[1] Waitz, *Das Alte Recht*, 203–214; and *Deutsche Verfassungs-
Geschichte*, II. 148–164, 353, etc.   Allen says: "Among the members of the royal family there seems to have been an absolute liberty
of choice, as favour, convenience, or accident determined.   The
son was preferred to the father, the brother to the son, and in one
noted instance, the line of the younger prevailed over the descendants of the elder brother, though the latter had worn his crown
with credit and ability."— *Inquiry into the Rise and Growth of
Royal Prerogative*, 46.

[2] The meaning sometimes given to the word *cyning*— "child
of the race," from *cyn*, race or kin, and *ing*, the well-known
patronymic, would seem to be doubtful.   Max Müller states it as
his opinion that "the old Norse *Konr* and *Konungr*, the old high
German *chuninc*, and the Anglo-Saxon *cyning*, were common
Aryan words, not formed out of German materials, and therefore not
to be explained as regular German derivatives. . . .   It corresponds
with the Sanscrit *ganaka*. . . .   It simply meant father of a
family."— *Lectures on Science of Language*, II. 282, 284.   This
seems to accord with the patriarchal thought which may be
remotely associated with Teutonic kingship.   For as the ancient
conception of nationality was a tribal one, the idea of the unity of
the tribe or race might easily be associated with the idea of father-
hood,— headship of a family.   The fact of an hereditary royal

the thought of official impersonation of a common nationality, based upon a common tribal or blood kinship.   It
would be an easy transition, as a tribal nation grew into
widened life, for the functions of a national executive to
become attached, little by little, to this elected representative of the race.   And without venturing to theorize in
detail on the rise of the kingly office of later time from
such beginnings, we may possibly surmise that some early
king gradually attained executive supremacy by absorbing
powers before divided among several officials ; or that an
officer who had acquired the attributes of national power
took on the dignity of the kingly title and relation to the
state.[1]

family may look in the same direction, and point to a patriarchal
source for the royal office, the royal family being the patriarchal
line of descent in the tribe.   Some tribes may have wholly substituted elective officers for the patriarchate, and others may have
modified the patriarchal principle by electing the *cyning*, and
sharing his powers with elective officers.   For differing opinions on
the meaning of *Cyning*, see Freeman, *Norman Conquest*, I. 583,
584; Schmid, *Gesetze*, 551; Allen, Grimm, Palgrave, etc.   Bishop
Stubbs says : " The Anglo-Saxon probably connected the *cyning*
with the *cyn* more closely than scientific etymology would permit."
— *Constitutional History of England*, I. 166.

[1] Kemble has an interesting chapter on the development of
kingship.   *Saxons in England*, I. Chap. vi.   Dr. Rudolph Gneist
says : " Actual kingship begins to exist, — first, so soon as the dignity of the chieftain appears not only in the leadership of the
army, but when it becomes a comprehensive, supreme power, including the office of magistrate, of protector of the peace, of defender
of the Church, with the highest control of the commonwealth in
every department; secondly, so soon as this highest dignity has
become recognized by the popular idea as the family right of a high-

However the office itself may be accounted for, the tribes that immigrated to Britain seem to have been among those that were without it. Yet the royal idea was probably familiar to all tribes, and perhaps, as Kemble thinks, inherent in the Teutonic mind ; for in every instance kings were set up by these tribesmen shortly after their landing.[1] According to old records, the first chieftains who came over bore the titles of Earldorman[2] and Heretoga,[3] the former designation expressing civil, and the latter military, functions. But when battles of conquest had been fought, and the chiefs found themselves at the head of a Teutonic body settled down on new soil, the title of king was assumed.[4] The fact of military leadership, combined with the stubbornness of the long struggle with the native Britons, rendered the position of these first English kings stronger from the outset than that of any officials in the older

born race. Directly both these conditions coexist, the new idea shows itself in its new name." — *History of the English Constitution*, I. 14.

[1] "But sprung as he was from war, the king was no mere war leader, nor was he chosen on the ground of warlike merit. His office was not military, but national; his creation marked the moment when the various groups of conquering warriors felt the need of a collective and national life." — Green, *Making of England*, 172.

[2] "Her comen twegen ealdormen on Brytene Cerdic and Cynric his sunu." — *E. Chron.*, a. 495.

[3] "Heora heretogan wæron twegen gebroðra, Hengest and Horsa." — *E. Chron.*, a. 449.

[4] "Her Cerdic and Cynric Westseaxena rice onfengon." — *E. Chron.*, 519.

land. But the new kingship, like its ancient original, was tribal, and not territorial.[1] The king was king of his people, not of the land occupied by them.[2] And

[1] "It is a consideration well worthy to be kept in view, that during a large part of what we usually term modern history no such conception was entertained as that of 'territorial sovereignty.' . . . Territorial sovereignty — the view which connects sovereignty with the possession of a limited portion of the earth's surface — was distinctly an offshoot, though a tardy one, of *feudalism*. This might have been expected *a priori*, for it was feudalism which for the first time linked personal duties, and by consequence personal rights, to the ownership of land." — Maine, *Ancient Law*, 76, 78. "Clear cases of the change are to be seen in the official style of kings. Of our own kings, King John was the first who always called himself king of England. His predecessors commonly or always called themselves kings of the English." — Maine, *Early History of Institutions*, 73.

[2] "For many centuries before the union of the Scottish with the English crown, the title of the king had been that of king of England. In ancient times it was otherwise. During the Heptarchy the petty kings who ruled over the different tribes of Anglo-Saxons were styled kings of the West Saxons, Mercians, Northumbrians, Kentishmen, East Angles, East Saxons, or South Saxons; and after the imperfect union of these states under the West Saxons, the title of the predominant prince continued to be taken from his subjects, and not from the territory they inhabited. There are exceptions, indeed, to this rule in some of the Latin charters, which the clergy were left to fabricate in their own way; but Canute, a conqueror, is the first prince that styles himself in his laws king of England. In the preamble to his collection of laws, he is called king of the Danes and Northmen, and of the whole land of the Angles. This territorial designation, however, was dropped by his successors. The Confessor is styled king and lord of the Angles; and, notwithstanding the continual progress of feudal notions, the Conqueror, his sons, Stephen, and the two first princes

in course of time the office became very common in England, every small tribe or clan having its own cyning.

It was only by the rise of some of these tribal kings into influence over others, that the national sovereignty gradually appeared. By the seventh century there were at least eight greater kingdoms in England, and, two hundred years afterward, all were welded into one. Thus the settlement made by Cerdic and Cynric on the southern coast slowly grew, by the incorporation of many small kingdoms and independent earldormanships, into the lordship of the whole isle of Britain, into the immediate rulership of all the English inhabitants. An earldorman of Hampshire in this manner gradually developed into the king of the West Saxons, the king of the Saxons, the king of England, the king of Great Britain and Ireland, and eventually the sovereign head of an empire extending to every quarter of the earth.

The Church proved from the first a potent factor in this higher development of kingship. The conversion of the English introduced respect for rulers as taught in Holy Writ, and also that for law and authority as

of the House of Plantagenet, continued to use on their great seal the appellation of *Rex Anglorum*, though in the preambles to their charters and other public instruments they sometimes call themselves kings of England. John was the first prince who had engraved on his great seal the title of *Rex Angliæ;* and in that innovation, which has its origin in the feudal fiction that the whole soil of England belonged originally to the king, he has been followed by all his successors."—Allen, *Royal Prerogative,* 52-54.

still lingering from the old Roman empire. Though it destroyed the heathen claims of royal descent from Woden, it surrounded the king with a new and greater sacredness; and the Christian service of coronation, with its memorials of Jewish chieftains and Christian emperors, made him the "Lord's Anointed." The universality of the one faith, as well as the progress of a new civilization, brought about contact with European ideas. Finally, the Church of England united all Englishmen even in the days of the Heptarchy, — the jurisdiction of the archepiscopal see of Canterbury being older than that of the national throne, for which, in many particulars, it prepared the way.

The royal office also grew in influence with every advance in social transformation and civil development that marked the progress toward a wider national life. As head of the state, the king came to be accorded many privileges, and to enjoy large income from personal estates and public revenues. The earldormen, of whose rank his ancestors had once been, came to receive delegation of their powers from him, and to share these with a variety of royal officials. The royal comitatus, or body of personal followers, gave rise, in time, to a new territorial nobility, created by and directly connected with the court.[1] And the great officers of

---

[1] Mr. Taylor admirably summarizes the facts relating to this ancient Teutonic institution of the *comitatus*, which Tacitus refers to in the *Germania*. "The *comitatus* consisted originally of bands of professional warriors, united to a leader of their choice in a close and

the royal household became political officers, — a standing council or ministry for the transaction of ordinary
civil business, and the reception of judicial appeals.
Gradually the king grew to be regarded as the personal

peculiar personal relation. . . . The leader of such a band was
a *princeps*, his warlike followers, the *comites ;* and it was no disgrace to any man to be seen among the followers of a chief. The
clanship or *comitatus* thus formed had its divisions of rank, which
were fixed by the *princeps*. There was great emulation among the
comites of every *princeps* as to who should hold the highest place
in his esteem; and among the *princeps* as to who should have the
most numerous and bravest following. To be always surrounded
by a band of chosen young men — in peace an ornament, in war a
bulwark — was the greatest dignity and power that a chief could
possess. Upon the battle-field it was a disgrace for the *princeps* to
be surpassed by his *comites*, and it was a disgrace for the *comites*
not to equal their leader in valour. To survive a battle in which
their chief had fallen was eternal infamy. To defend and protect
the *princeps*, to make even their own renown subservient to his,
was the highest and holiest duty of the *comites*. The chieftains
fought for victory, the *comites* for their chief. The *comitatus* could
only be kept together by violence and war, for the *comites* were
entirely dependent upon the bounty of their chief. . . . In the
bonds of this strange military association, the chief and his followers
were united by the closest ties of mutual interest and honour. . . .
In the structure of the *comitatus* was imbedded the germ of a great
aftergrowth. The relation of lord and vassal, the first outcome of
the *comitatus*, was a purely personal one. But in the process of
time, when the lord makes a grant of land to his vassal in consideration of past services and upon the further consideration that the
vassal will hold such land upon the tenure of military service, a new
relation becomes involved with the old one. . . . Each chieftain
by whom a war band was led to the conquest of Britain, came attended by his *comites*. . . . As kingship advanced in power and
privilege, kings were able, of course, to confer upon their depend-

lord of his people, and, to some extent, of the soil also. From the reign of Athelstan imperial titles were assumed, either in imitation of continental examples, or, more probably, in assertion of English independence of the German emperor.[1]

In the sovereignty as finally evolved, the king's powers were considerable. With the advice and consent of the Witenagemot, he made laws and regulated matters affecting the general welfare. He negotiated peace and alliance, and received and appointed ambassadors. Though justice was administered in the local courts, and also through the Witenagemot, he might dispense it when the

ents a status and emoluments such as no one else could bestow. And as the king grew in power and importance, the companion or gesith soon changed his original title for a new one that more clearly expressed his somewhat changed relation. He became the thegn or servant instead of the companion of his lord. In this way originated a new nobility by service, which grew and widened until it at last absorbed and superseded the older nobility of blood. . . . As a king stood above earldorman and bishop, so stood the king's thegns above their thegns. . . . The greatest boon, however, which such a thegn expected his lord to bestow, was a grant of land out of the public domain, which the king had the power to make with the consent of the Witan. Upon estates created in this way the thegns began to dwell, and thus ceased to be members of their master's household. And so the thegnhood grew into a territorial nobility." — *Origin and Growth of the English Constitution*, 110, 111, 131, 132. "The development of the *comitatus* into a territorial nobility seems to be a feature peculiar to English history." — Stubbs, *Constitutional History of England*, I. 152.

[1] On the nature of the imperial title and position held by the early kings, see Freeman, *Norman Conquest*, I. 148, and Palgrave, *English Commonwealth*, pp. 627, cccxlii–cccxliv.

issue had not elsewhere obtained settlement. His power of appointment and of conferring honours made its influence felt in all portions of the realm. As maintainer of the peace, he called out the police or militia when necessary to preserve order, and exercised the right of pardon. He was commander-in-chief of the national host in time of war.

Yet this Saxon monarchy was far from being absolute. If strong under a strong king, it was weak under a weak one. Its authority was strictly limited by that of the Witenagemot, which participated in every act of government. Many of its prerogatives were deduced from the fact expressed by its very title, that the king was the representative of his people. His election rested with the Witan, which might depose him. Coronation, as essential as election, partook of the nature of a ratification or second election, and was, in effect, a compact between king and people, as well as a consecration to the kingly functions by the Church.[1]

---

[1] See Maskell, *Monumenta Ritualia Ecclesiae Anglicanae*, III. " In its origin the kingship of the English was distinctly elective, but with a restriction of choice in all ordinary cases to the members of one royal house. At the Norman Conquest a new royal stock was substituted for the ancient one of Cerdic [though in truth the Conqueror was a descendant of Cerdic], but the elective character of the kingship continued unaltered. . . . The succession of Edward I. marks the earliest important innovation. He was the first king who reigned before his coronation. The doctrine of hereditary right, which gradually arose as the personal idea of kingship was superseded by the territorial idea, had now largely obscured the elective character of the kingship. . . . But this obscuration

Even while adding to their authority, the kings parted
more and more with its substantial exercise, governing through subordinate officers, or granting power away

was never total. . . . Edward I. had been recognized as king four
days after the death of his father. The accession of Edward II. on
the day following his father's decease marks a further advance in
the hereditary doctrine; an advance, however, which was more than
neutralized by the revival, against his person, of the right of the
national assembly to depose the king. By the unopposed succession
of Richard II., to the exclusion of his uncles, the right of representative primogeniture was for the first time asserted in the devolution
of the crown. But as in the case of Edward II., so in the case of
Richard, no sooner had the doctrine of strict hereditary descent
progressed another step than it was met by the reassertion of the
right of Parliament to depose the sovereign, and by the negation
of any indefeasible right of primogeniture through the election of
Henry of Lancaster. It was by the House of York . . . that the
doctrine of indefeasible hereditary right was first propounded in its
full force and significance. . . . Yet even Edward IV. sought and
obtained a parliamentary confirmation of his title, and when, a
quarter of a century later, the crown was settled by Parliament on
Henry VII. and his issue, to the exclusion of the whole House of
York, the kingship was replaced on its elective basis. The elective
right of Parliament, however, was now exercised, not periodically
on the death of each sovereign, . . . but whenever it became necessary to elect a new royal stock, as in the case of Henry IV. and
of Henry VII. . . . James I., coming to the throne without a legal
title, attempted to revive the Yorkist theory of hereditary right. . . .
But the theory of indefeasible hereditary right, fortified as it was by
the Stuart addition of a sanction *jure divino*, utterly failed to take
permanent root, and was finally extirpated by the Revolution of 1688
and the subsequent Act of Settlement, which entailed the crown on
the descendants of Sophia of Hanover. In that statute Parliament,
for the last time in our history, exercised its paramount right to
settle the succession to the crown." — Taswell-Langmead, *English
Constitutional History*, 222–224.

in delegated privileges to individual nobles. The royal resources were continually diminished by the alienation of royal lands, — general taxation being thus necessitated. And with taxation was, even in Saxon times, brought in the element, which was destined eventually to exert, through Parliament, popular control and direction of the entire policy of the crown.

A change came with the Conquest. Though William the Conqueror, claiming to reign as the lawful successor of the Saxon kings, had himself elected by the Witan and proposed to follow customary forms and usages, his imperious will created a despotism ; which was continued, though less wisely, by William Rufus. And Henry I. centralized the working of the government in such a manner as greatly to increase the royal authority. Indeed, the Norman conception of the kingship combined the powers of the Anglo-Saxon royalty at their highest with those of the contemporaneous feudal monarchies of Europe, but without the limitations of either. The Norman king was not only the elected head of the nation, but also lord paramount of all land. He was the source of justice, the administrator of the public finances, and, with the nominal assent of a feudalized and subservient national council, the supreme legislator. Practically, he was autocratic ; for however carefully the ancient forms might be retained, no force of his time was strong enough to curb him.

But in England arbitrary power could not be established permanently. Henry II., founder of the Plantagenet dynasty, carried forward the task of administrative organism which Henry I. had begun, and achieved the complete development of the monarchy on a feudalized yet national basis. But while strengthening the crown, he took pains to revive the efficiency of the legislature, by consulting it in all important affairs. The forces of the nation, also, gradually underwent transformation in the merging of Saxon and Norman — both of Teutonic blood — into a single people. King John's abuse of power found a Norman baronage ready to champion old English liberties;[1] and Magna Charta, though in the form of a royal grant, was really a constitutional treaty or compact between the king and the nation, in asser-

---

[1] "The Great Charter of liberties was the outcome of a movement of all the freemen of the realm, led by their natural leaders, the barons. Far from being a 'mere piece of class legislation,' extorted by the barons alone for their own special interests, it is in itself a noble and remarkable proof of the sympathy and union then existing between the aristocracy and all classes of the commonality. At least one-third of its provisions relate to promises and guarantees on behalf of the people in general, as contradistinguished from the baronage. But one fact is especially significant. The important and comprehensive clause (60), by which the customs and liberties granted to the king's tenants-in-chief are expressly extended to every sub-tenant in the kingdom, did not, like the similar provision in the Charter of Henry I., emanate from the king, but was spontaneously included by the barons themselves in the articles presented to John as a summary of their demands." — Taswell-Langmead, *English Constitutional History*, 102. See *Articles of the Barons*, c. 48; Blackstone's *Charters*, 1–9; *Select Charters*, 286; *Magna Charta*, c. 60.

tion of ancient limitations of the crown, and in protection of ancient private rights of the subject.[1]

The years that immediately followed the granting of Magna Charta were years of struggle between king and people over its principles, — a struggle marked by variation of fortune for one side and the other, but resulting, on the whole, in steady loss to the crown. Henry III. saw the Barons' War and the definite rise of parliamentary institutions. Parliament, fully matured under the great Edward, attained, in the early days of Richard II., as we have seen, the executive control of the nation. And Richard's later assertion of irresponsible authority was answered by his deposition, and the setting up of the Lancastrian dynasty by act of Parliament, —an act which marked the predominance of the legislature over the kingship.

But the Wars of the Roses created or signalized a genuine royalist reaction. Their sanguinary progress brought about the destruction of the ancient nobility. And with the destruction of the nobility, the power of

[1] M. Glasson says: " La Grande Charte est un Contrat, mais qui se rapproche du traité passé entre deux nations." — *Hist. du Dr. et des Inst. de l'Angl.*, III. 52. In commenting on the "Constitution Anglaise," M. Boutmy remarks: "Les pactes sont au nombre de trois: la grande charte (1215). . . . Le caractère de cet acte est aisé à définir. Ce n'est pas précisément un traité, puisqu'il n'y a pas ici deux souverainetés légitimes ni deux nations en présence ; ce n'est pas non plus une loi; elle serait entachée d'irrégularité et de violence; c'est un compromis ou un pacte." — *Études de Droit Constitutionnel*, 39, 41.

the Commons became insufficient to cope with the power of the crown. Under the House of Lancaster parliamentary principles had been prematurely asserted, and the House of York in ascending the throne, renewed and strengthened the arbitrary rule of the sovereign, and prepared the way for the Tudors and the Stuarts.

Indeed, during the Plantagenet period, which thus ended with the Yorkists, the royal powers had passed through a steadily formative process. The Plantagenet kings were at the head of the whole administrative system of the nation, and personally took part in all state business. They issued ordinances having much of the force of legislation. They personally heard cases and centralized judicature in their hands through national judges appointed by and representing them. They levied taxes in a variety of forms by their own will. When the parliamentary system was finally settled, they held an essential relation to its operation ; and parliamentary acts became law by passing from their hands to the statute book, or might be vetoed altogether. Their right of summoning sessions of Parliament was unquestioned, and with it the right of adjourning, proroguing and dissolving. They even moulded, in some degree, the internal constitution of Parliament, — the House of Lords being composed of members mediately or immediately constituted such by the crown ; the membership of the Commons also feeling their influence, by means of election writs and otherwise.[1]

---

[1] " In no part of the constitutional fabric was more authority left to the king, and in none was less interference attempted by

Nevertheless the kingship, which under the Conqueror had been absolute in fact without quite ignoring old constitutional limitations in theory, gradually became under the Plantagenets, limited in fact by the reassertion of the ancient rights of the legislature, though retaining much of absolutism in theory.

A royalist philosophy arose into formidable influence. Every successful affirmation of popular rights was accompanied by an advance of royal assumptions. Every assertion of the national will was met by a counter-assertion of royal privilege, the indefinite limit of prerogative being more and more indefinitely exaggerated. Clerical writers insisted upon the religious duty of obedience, and legal writers elaborated doctrines nearly akin to those of divine right, and surrounded them with theories of allegiance, and of treason, of oaths of fealty, and acts of homage. A sense of personal loyalty to the sovereign slowly arose. A claim of legitimacy — associated in men's minds with the thought of land-tenure — also came to the front; and out of it grew the idea that a

the Parliament, than in the constitution of Parliament itself. . . . The king retained the right of summoning the Estates whenever and wherever he chose; he could, without consulting the magnates, add such persons as he pleased to the permanent number of peers, and he might, no doubt, with very little trouble and with no sacrifice of popularity, have increased or diminished the number of members of the House of Commons by dealing with the sheriffs. On those points occasional contests turned, but they scarcely ever, as was the case in later reigns, came into the foreground as leading constitutional questions." — Stubbs, *Constitutional History of England*, II. 666.

kingdom is a king's personal heritage by primogeniture, by a right essentially the same as that of a lord to patrimonial estates. It was upon such an idea, notwithstanding the immemorial usage of election to the crown, that the House of York based its claim to reign.

Referring to this royalist philosophy and its results, Bishop Stubbs well remarks : "The ideal king could do all things, but without the counsel and consent of the Estates he could do nothing. The exaltation of the ideal king was the exaltation of the law that stood behind him, of the strength and majesty of the state which he impersonated. It could be no wonder if now and then a king should mistake the theory for the truth of fact, and, like Richard II., should attempt to put life in the splendid phantom. And when the king arose who had the will and the power, the nation had gone on so long believing in the theory, that they found no weapons to resist the fact, until the factitious theory of the Stuart's raised the ghost of mediæval absolutism, to be laid then and forever."[1]

---

[1] *Constitutional History of England*, III. 561. "The strength of the crown at the close of the Middle Ages lay in the permanence of the idea of royalty, the wealth of the king, the legal definitions and theory of the supreme power; its position was enhanced by the suicide of the baronage, the personal qualities of the new dynasty [the Tudor], the political weariness of the nation, and the altered position of the kings in the great states of Europe. The place of Henry VII. cannot be understood without reference to the events which, in France, Spain, and Germany, were consolidating great dynastic monarchies, in the activity of which the nations themselves had little independent participation." — *Ibid.* III. 562.

The reaction in favour of royal rule which began, as just stated, under the Yorkist dynasty, culminated under the Tudors, and in the reign of Henry VIII. At the Reformation, Henry possessed well-nigh resistless civil power, to which he added a new relationship to the national Church ; attempting control over the very minds and consciences of men. And though he conformed outwardly to constitutional usage, his Parliament was the merest tool for the execution of the royal wishes. Edward VI. and Mary, in matters of civil administration, followed in the steps of their father ; and Elizabeth, wisely exercising it for the good of the nation, held power as autocratic.

But the tide had reached a height, and needs must ebb. James I. experienced the beginnings of a counter-movement in the awakening of the spirit of parliamentary independence that had slumbered since the fall of the House of Lancaster. He met this movement by enunciating a most monstrous theory of divine right to absolute and irresponsible sovereignty, and forced into activity the old opposition to the crown in the new and dangerous form of political Puritanism. He was succeeded in his contest with Parliament by a son who surrendered life itself for the royalist doctrines, and saw the downfall of the throne, and of the ancient Constitution with it, in one common wreck. And a final reaffirmation of ultra-royal claims came in with the Restoration, — Charles II. and James II. erecting slowly, cautiously, and with professed respect for parliamentary institutions, the old structure of despotic government, only to bring about the expulsion of their dynasty, and the Revolution of 1688.

The Revolution "finally decided," remarks Lord Macaulay, "the great question whether the popular element which had, ever since the age of Fitz Walter and De Montfort, been found in the English polity, should be destroyed by the monarchical element, or should be suffered to develop itself freely, and to become dominant. The strife between the two principles had been long, fierce, and doubtful. . . . The king-at-arms who proclaimed William and Mary before Whitehall Gate did in truth announce that this great struggle was over; that there was an entire union between the throne and Parliament . . .; that the ancient laws by which the prerogative was bounded would henceforth be held as sacred as the prerogative itself, and would be followed out in their consequences; that the executive administration would be conducted in conformity with the sense of the representatives of the nation."[1]

Though the prerogatives of the monarchy suffered no legal diminution at the Revolution of 1688, but, as constitutional writers affirm, were after that event what they had been before, yet a code of unwritten law began to come into existence, that in many ways modified and neutralized the operation of the written law and of former constitutional usage. The English Constitution has since grown to be very largely a system of unconventional and political rules and theories. In

[1] *History of England*, II. 668.

outward appearance the Revolution of 1688 merely
transferred the sovereignty from James II. to William and
Mary. In reality it transferred the sovereignty from the
king to the House of Commons. For from the moment
when the sole right of the House to tax the nation
was established by the Bill of Rights, and when the
practice was settled of voting only annual supplies
to the crown, the Commons became the chief power in
the kingdom. It was impossible permanently to suspend
the sessions of Parliament, or to offer serious opposition
to its will, when either course must end in leaving the
government without money, in breaking up the military
and naval forces, and in rendering the public service
impossible.[1]

The personal influence of the king was weakened
at the Revolution, and has gone on declining since.
The deposition of a monarch who represented legitimist
descent, the election of an outsider in the person
of William of Orange, and the final seating of the
House of Hanover by act of Parliament, necessarily
put an end to much of the old philosophy. Disputed
succession, together with the lingering of a hostile legitimist party, forced the sovereigns whom Parliament had
set up, to rely upon parliamentary support, and compelled their acceptance of a great degree of parliamentary
control.

In a new and unexpected quarter arose the force
that was eventually to absorb what remained of the

---

[1] Green, *Short History of the English People*, 680.

sovereign power. During the reign of Charles II. the king's inner circle of advisers within the Privy Council came to be called the " Cabinet " ; and after the Revolution, through a suggestion of Lord Sunderland to William of Orange, the members of this Cabinet came to be selected from the political party in majority in the House of Commons.[1] The first George's ignorance of the English language, and his indifference to English political affairs, brought about a custom of holding Cabinet sessions without the presence of the king. In his reign, and that of George II., the Cabinet exercised, for the first time, the prerogatives of royalty, and the sovereign almost ceased to influence active government.

[1] "The Whigs, who had secured the crown to William III., expected that he would choose his ministers solely from their ranks. But the king was strongly opposed to government by party. He wished to retain the chief directing power himself and to secure the support of a united Parliament in carrying out his continental policy in opposition to Louis XIV. of France. Accordingly, down to the year 1693, he distributed the chief offices in the government about equally between the two parties. But this policy, while it maintained the chief efficient power in the hands of the king, not only failed to secure unanimity among the various ministers of the crown, but even allowed of open hostility between them, as well in the discharge of their executive duties as in the discussions in Parliament. The inconvenience of this state of things was so great that at length, between 1693 and 1696, acting on the advice of Robert, Earl of Sunderland, William abandoned the neutral position which he had hitherto maintained between the two parties, and entrusted all the chief administrative offices to the Whigs, who commanded a majority in the House of Commons." — Taswell-Langmead, *English Constitutional History*, 681.

"Ministers," exclaimed George II., "are the king in this country."[1]

Under this new system, the government was administered in all its departments by ministers responsible to Parliament for every act of official policy, without whose advice no act could be performed. These ministers might be dismissed for incapacity or failure, and impeached for political crimes; and they resigned when their advice was opposed by the crown, or their proceedings disapproved by Parliament. With his Cabinet thus responsible, "the king could do no wrong." The Stuarts had exercised power personally and had been held responsible in person. Their family had been driven altogether from the throne. But now, if the royal prerogative was stretched, the ministers were dealt with rather than the monarch. If a political crisis occurred, instead of a revolution there was only a change

---

[1] Lord Mahon, *History of England*, III. 280. "With George I. and George II. Hanoverian politics had occupied the first place in their thoughts and affections. Of English politics, English society, and even the English language, they knew little. The troublesome energies of Parliament were an enigma to them; and they cheerfully acquiesced in the ascendency of able ministers who had suppressed rebellions and crushed pretenders to their crown, — who had triumphed over parliamentary opposition and had borne all the burden of the government. Left to the indulgence of their personal tastes, occupied by frequent visits to the land of their birth, . . . they were not anxious to engage, more than was necessary, in the turbulent contests of a constitutional government. Having lent their name and authority to competent ministers, they acted upon their advice and aided them by all the means at the disposal of the court." — May, *Constitutional History of England*, I. 20.

of Cabinet. In the place of dangerous struggles between Parliament and the crown, there was only the contest between rival parties to obtain a parliamentary majority; and the party possessing the greater number of votes wielded all the power of the nation. Consequently, upon the ministry, for the time being, rested the entire burden of public affairs. The monarchy was relieved of its cares and perils by ministers, who appropriated nearly all its authority. The king reigned, but his ministers governed.[1]

George III. energetically opposed this form of encroachment, and reasserted the agency of the sovereign as a personal executive. But the new cabinet system was too far under way to be more than temporarily checked, and has attained in our day an undisputed ascendency. The power of the crown, as exercised by the Cabinet, has now greatly increased, but the personal influence of the wearer of the crown in matters of government has greatly diminished.[2] The power of

---

[1] May, *Constitutional History of England*, I. 19, 20. Mr. Bagehot describes the Cabinet as "a combining committee — a *hyphen* which joins, a *buckle* which fastens, the legislative part of the state to the executive part of the state. In its origin it belongs to the one, in its functions it belongs to the other." — *English Constitution*, 14.

[2] It would be a mistake to say, as many have said, that the personal influence of the monarch is practically gone. "There is not a doubt that the aggregate of direct influence nominally exercised by the sovereign upon the counsels and proceedings of her ministers is considerable in amount, tends to permanence and solidity of action, and confers much benefit on the country, without in the small-

Parliament has also increased, but is mainly directed by the ministry. English government has ceased to be, strictly speaking, either a royal or a parliamentary government, and has become a cabinet government, — blending the executive and legislative, by taking authority derived from the ancient representatives of each, and exercising it through a body having relation to both.

But although the interruption was only temporary, George III. did for an interval, and in some degree, break through this system ; or rather he succeeded in demonstrating that it was not complete, or fully established. He had been trained from youth in lofty conceptions of royal office. "George, be king," was the repeated admonition of his ambitious mother,[1] and her exultation at a triumph over popular opposition during the ministry of Lord Bute, found expression in the characteristic words, "Now my son *is* king of

est degree relieving the advisers of the crown from their undivided responsibility." — Gladstone. *Gleanings of Past Years*, I. 42. As these words apply to Queen Victoria, who is sometimes characterized, in a cabinet sense, as the most constitutional sovereign who has ever reigned over England, and as they proceed from a personage who has been in turn a member of both political parties in England, and has held a place in several cabinets and risen to the position of premier, they must be accorded historical weight. They are not, however, needed to establish recognition of the truth that the British sovereign is still a real factor in British administration and a most useful one. There are those who think that public interests would be better off if the personal influence of the monarch were greater, and the influence of mere party government less, than has come to be the case.

[1] Earl of Albemarle's *Rockingham Memoirs*, I. 3.

England." [1]   He was determined from the outset to reassert the personal power of the sovereign, which had almost disappeared from the sphere of government since the accession of the House of Hanover, and to rule freed from the trammels of ministers and parties, for the people, indeed, but not by the people. "The king desired," observes May, "to undertake personally the chief administration of public affairs, to direct the policy of his ministers, and himself to distribute the patronage of the crown. . . . His courtiers represented that he was enthralled by the dominant party, which had become superior to the throne itself, and that, in order to recover his just prerogative, it was necessary to break up the combination. But what was this in effect, but to assert that the king should now be his own minister? that ministers should be chosen, not because they had the confidence of Parliament and the country, but because they were agreeable to himself, and willing to carry out his policy? And this was the true object of the king. . . . When ministers not of his own choice were in office, he plotted against them and overthrew them, and when he had succeeded in establishing his friends in office, he en-

---

[1] Walpole, *Memoirs*, I. 233. George III. was the first *English* king of the House of Hanover, and gloried in the fact of his being English. With his own hand he placed in the draft of his first speech to Parliament, the words, "Born and educated in this country, I glory in the name of Briton." — Rose, *Correspondence*, II. 189. (Diary.) The traditions of the old English kingship before the days of George I. and George II. influenced him powerfully.

forced upon them the adoption of his own policy."[1]
And this writer approximately states the issue in saying
that His Majesty reverted "to a policy under which
kings had governed, and ministers had executed their
orders."[2]

It was in Lord North's ministry, from 1770 to 1782,
that the king attained his greatest personal power. And
this, let it be noted, was the period of the American
war, and ended just previous to the formation of the
Constitution of the United States. His personal government made a profound impression upon the Americans, and has left permanent trace in the constitutional
structure of the American executive. Lord North being
favourable to prerogative and warmly attached to his
sovereign, subordinated his own judgment to that of the
king, and steadily executed the royal will, instead of
enforcing his own and that of the ministry. Notably,
he continued the American war because George III.
would not consent to another course, although, as he
told the king in 1779, " he held in his heart, and had
held for three years past," that " it must end in the ruin

---

[1] May, *Constitutional History of England*, I. 23, 26.

[2] *Ibid.* I. 26. In debating the address at the opening of Parliament, Nov. 25th, 1779, Fox declared, that " he saw very early indeed,
in the present reign, the plan of government which had been laid
down, and had since been invariably pursued in every department.
It was not the mere rumour of the streets that the king was his own
minister; the fatal truth was evident, and had made itself evident
in every circumstance of the war carried on against America and
the West Indies." — *Parliamentary History*, XX. 1120.

of His Majesty and the country."[1]   The sovereign himself directed the minister in all important matters of foreign and domestic policy.

In 1780 the House of Commons adopted the famous resolution affirming "that the influence of the crown has increased, is increasing, and ought to be diminished."[2] But it was not until two years later, and after repeated motions of lack of confidence in the government, that Lord North resigned, and was succeeded first by Lord Rockingham and then by Lord Shelburne.[3]   The latter, in 1783, concluded the Peace of Versailles, by which the king acknowledged the independence of the United States.   In this latter year, the younger Pitt became Prime Minister; and under his able administration the ascendency of the crown was maintained for nearly half a century.

Such was the position of the English executive at the time of the assembling of the Constitutional Convention at Philadelphia.

---

[1] *Correspondence of George III. with Lord North,* 1768, 1783, ed. Donne.

[2] Cobbitt, *Parliamentary History,* XXI. 347.

[3] Lord Shelburne was in sympathy with the king's view of the royal office.   He would never consent, he said, "that the King of England should be a king of the Mahrattas; for among the Mahrattas the custom is, it seems, for a certain number of great lords to elect a Peishwah, who is thus the creature of the aristocracy, and is vested with the plenitude of power, while there is, in fact, nothing more than a royal pageant." — *Parliamentary History,* XXII. 1003.

CHAPTER VI.

THE AMERICAN EXECUTIVE.

THE derivation of the presidency from the old king-ship took place at a time and under conditions which assured the qualities of a personal executive, free from cabinet control. In our day, through the influence of political theory, an idea is very common that the English cabinet system, in the shape of parliamentary domination over the sovereign, has had continuous existence since the reign of William of Orange, except as momentarily interrupted by the aggression of George III. But contemporaries of the latter king had reason to entertain a very different idea. The continuity of the cabinet system from early germs was not apparent in the days of a monarch who, more or less successfully, set it at defiance. As the first really English sovereign of the House of Hanover, he undertook to exercise, as far as he was able, the powers of personal government, belonging from of old to English royalty. And he himself looked upon those powers as having been exercised by the kings continuously, except for a brief interval. That exception did not date from the reign of William III., or of Queen Anne — who, though possessing cabinets, had undoubtedly been personal executives — but from the reigns of the first Georges; and it was easily explained by the non-English singularities of those two monarchs. Nor was the cabinet system, even in their reigns, all that has been claimed. For the plain truth is, that the present parliamentary control through the cabinet rests upon no written law, but merely upon usage; and the usage upon which it rests became recognized and settled within living memory, and has had a duration of scarcely more than sixty years.

Mr. Bryce very fairly says of this modern English system: "We are prone to forget how recent it is. People commonly date it from the reign of William III., but it worked very irregularly till the Hanoverian kings came to the throne, and even then it at first worked by means of a monstrous system of bribery and place-mongering. In the days of George III., the personal power of the crown for awhile revived, and corruption declined. The executive head of the state was, during the latter decades of the century, a factor apart from its ministers. They were not then, as now, a mere committee of Parliament, but rather a compromise between the king's will and the will of the parliamentary majority. They deemed and declared themselves to owe a duty to the king, conflicting with, sometimes overriding, their duty to Parliament. Those phrases of abasement before the crown, which, when now employed by prime ministers, amuse us by their remoteness from the realities of the case, then expressed realities. In 1787, when the Constitutional

Convention met at Philadelphia, the cabinet system of government was in England still immature.   It was so immature that its true nature had not been perceived." [1]

Popular feeling among Americans at the close of the Revolution was opposed to kingship, — an opposition largely due to the fact that the struggle had been forced upon them by their sovereign in person.   The sense of loyalty which previously had so real an existence was forgotten in this new antipathy.[2]   One of the gravest

---

[1] *American Commonwealth,* I. 272, 273.   "It is not easy to say when the principle of the absolute dependence of ministers on a parliamentary majority, without regard to the wishes of the crown, passed into a settled doctrine.   Needless to say, that it has received no formally legal recognition, but is merely usage.   The long coincidence, during the dominance of Pitt and his Tory successors, down till 1827, of the wishes and interests of the crown with those of the parliamentary majority, prevented the question from arising in a practical shape." — *Ibid.* I. 273, n. 4.   He quotes Mr. Canning, who, even in 1827, writes to J. W. Croker : "Am I to understand, then, that you consider the king [George IV.] as completely in the hands of the Tory aristocracy as his father, or rather as George II. was in the hands of the Whigs?   If so, George III. reigned, and Mr. Pitt — both father and son — administered the government in vain.   I have a better opinion of the real vigour of the crown when it chooses to put forth its own strength, and I am not without some reliance on the body of the people ! " — *Croker Correspondence,* I. 368.

[2] Yet there was a considerable monarchical party in America. "The machinery of government under the Articles of Confederation was so defective, weak, and ineffectual that men, wise men, true and loyal Americans . . . demanded a government that would revive from prostration the public credit and faith of the nation, that would provide for the payment of interest on the public debt; they felt the need of a government with a strong arm, an elective monarchy." — Straus, *Republican Form of Government,* 132.   The move-

difficulties, therefore, which confronted the framers of
the Constitution, was the question of how to fill the
vacant place in the fabric of government occupied in
colonial times by the sovereign, and in such a way as
to secure headship for the nation and efficiency in
executive functions. It was admitted in debate during
the Convention, that the people would not endure the
setting up of a king. Yet, as by irresistible instinct,
they put much of the royal power back again in its

ment of the troops at Newburg, at the close of the war, to make
Washington a king, is in point. The words of the document presented by Colonel Nicola showed the need of settling a strong form
of government, and summed up by declaring that a republican
government was the most unstable and insecure, and a constitutional monarchy like that of England, the strongest and safest. It
concluded by saying: "Owing to the prejudices of the people it
might not at first be prudent to assume the title of royalty, but
if all other things were adjusted, we believe strong arguments
might be produced for admitting the title of king." Straus remarks: "This monarchical party spirit was so strong, that it survived even after the adoption of the Constitution until the election
of Jefferson as President, who refers to it in his inaugural address."
— *Ibid.* 134. Jefferson writes in the introduction of "Anas":
"The contests of that day were contests of principle between the
advocates of republican and those of kingly government." See
also the letter of James Monroe to Andrew Jackson, December,
1816, giving his recollections of the monarchical tendencies which
were shown by certain leaders of the Federal party both before
and after the Constitutional Convention. He says: "Many of the
circumstances on which my opinion is founded, took place in
debate and in society, and therefore find no place in any public
document. I am satisfied, however, that sufficient proof exists,
founded on facts and opinions of distinguished individuals, which
became public, to justify that which I had formed."

place at the apex of government, in the form of a colonial
governor or president made national. And as the people
were locally accustomed to this substitute for royalty,
they accepted the arrangement without resistance.[1]

[1] " When the subject was first considered in the Convention,
Wilson moved that a 'national executive, to consist of a single
person, be instituted.' But in so doing, he was not, he expressly
said, 'governed by the British model, which was inapplicable to the
situation in this country. . . .' Later, in answer, probably, to those
who saw in the single executive too close an approximation to the
King of England, he urged, that 'all the thirteen States, though
agreeing in scarcely any other instance, agree in placing a single
magistrate at the head of the government.' The fear was expressed
that the people also would immediately see the resemblance between a single executive and a king.—a person then in little
favour, and that such a feature might cause a summary rejection of
the whole proposed plan of union. The careful attempt in the *Federalist* [Nos. 67 and 69] to prove that no very close analogy did in
reality exist, shows that the fear was not without foundation.
Nevertheless, in spite of this and other objections, the question
whether or not the executive power should be intrusted to a single
person, was, after one postponement, settled in the affirmative by
a vote of seven to three. The question was never again seriously
opened. The unanimity on this important point is very striking,
in view of the prolonged discussion of many comparatively un-
important clauses. The reason for this exceptionally speedy
agreement is to be found partly in the obvious inconveniences of
a plural executive, the evil results of which had so palpably shown
themselves in the history of Holland. A more efficient cause,
however, than the experience of European states, is to be found
in the familiarity of the members with the single executive, not so
much of England as of the colonies. and more particularly of the
States." " The experience of Holland, which was cited in the Convention, probably had its influence in preventing the adoption of
a similar expedient in our case."—*American Academy Publications.*
No. 9, pp. 221, 222. and n. 4.

While it may be strange to contemplate the fact that thus, after all, the republican presidency is developed from a kingship, it will become apparent upon the slightest examination, that the President of to-day governs, in the main, with powers exercised before him by the colonial governors as the king's deputies, precisely because they were the very powers exercised at home by the king himself, — or, in other words, that identical powers of the historic executive of the English race are still put in operation by the American executive.[1] And as the presidential office comes from the ancient kingship indirectly, through the governorship, and also directly, it is hardly remarkable, when contemporaneous circumstances both in England and America are borne in mind, that it is that of an executive independent of the legislature, the director of his own cabinet, and the veritable administrator of the nation, --an executive more nearly resembling the old type of the kingship than, save in outward form and pageantry, the modern weakened royalty of England resembles it.

For Americans of a hundred years ago, when they

[1] " The governor of the independent State succeeded the governor of the dependent colony; and he, whether elected, or nominated, was essentially a reflected image of the kingship. The governor of the State retained the position of governor of the colony, with such changes as a republican system necessarily required." — Freeman, *History of the Federal Government*, I. 314, n. 1. Speaking of the President's office, Professor Johnson says: "The name itself had been familiar; Delaware, New Hampshire, Pennsylvania, and South Carolina had used the title of 'president' instead of 'governor.' " — *New Princeton Review*, September, 1887, p. 180.

thought of an executive at all, very naturally held to
the old conception of the nature and powers of English
royalty.   During their colonial experience, the sovereign's relation to affairs had been distinctly felt, and
was the chief political tie that bound them to the empire.   In that time no one was permitted to question,
nor seems to have desired to question, that the king
was king in America.   And notwithstanding the tendency to democratic opinion occasionally manifesting
itself, his supremacy was never lost sight of until independence came.   If it be remembered that among the
monarchs of the period were James I., Charles I., Charles
II., James II., and George III., it will be easy to understand how a strong sense of executive authority must
have been familiar to the American mind.   William
and Mary, and Queen Anne, though not despotic, were,
as just noted, personal rulers.   And the only exception
to the uniformity of this experience was, as already
pointed out, the contemptible one of the first two
Georges, — more than offset by the royal vigour of
George III.

The colonial governorship itself was of a personally
executive character.   For though the cabinet system is
generally found in the present colonies of England,
not one of the older colonies possessed it; their local
institutions having been copied from hers before its
invention.[1]   The governor's functions are thus described

[1] Dr. W. E. Griffis, in a pamphlet — *Influence of the Netherlands
in the Making of the English Commonwealth and the American*

by Mr. Justice Story: "The king had power to vest in the royal governors in the colonies, from time to time, such of his prerogatives as he should please ; such as the power to prorogue, adjourn, and dissolve the colonial assemblies ; to confirm acts and laws, to pardon offences, to act as captain general of the public forces, to appoint public officers, to act as chancellor and supreme ordinary, to sit in the highest court of appeals and errors, to exercise the duties of vice-admiral, and to grant commissions to privateers. These and some other prerogatives of the king were commonly exercised by the royal governors without objection."[1]

Republic, 40 — ventures, among many similar statements, the assertion that the State governors and the national President are the statholders of the States and the United States. As the governors were officials created by the charters granted to English colonies by English sovereigns, the calling them statholders, and implying that they had a Dutch beginning, is somewhat ludicrous. It is, however, a fair example of the excess to which writers go, who try too hard to discover a Dutch origin for American institutions.

[1] *On the Constitution*, I. 138. " In all the States the governor was commander-in-chief. . . . The President's pardoning power was drawn from the example of the States; they had granted it to the governors — in some cases with the advice of a council — in all the States except Connecticut, Rhode Island, and Georgia, where it was retained to the legislature, and in South Carolina, where it seems to have been forgotten in the constitution of 1778, but was given to the governor in 1790. The governor was elected directly by the people in Connecticut, Massachusetts, New Hampshire, New York, and Rhode Island, and indirectly, by the two houses in the other eight States; and in this nearly equal division we may, perhaps, find a reason for the Convention's hesitation to adopt either system, and for its futile attempt to introduce an electoral system as

To understand how the functions of the presidency
are derived from those of the kingship, it is only necessary to compare the actual provisions of the Constitution
with the royal powers as exercised in fact or in theory

a compromise. . . . Almost every State prescribed a form of oath
for its officers; the simple and impressive oath of the President
seems to have been taken from that of Pennsylvania, with a suggestion, much improved in language, from the oath of allegiance
of the same State." — Johnson, "First Century of the Constitution," *New Princeton Review*, September, 1887, pp. 180, 181.

Referring to the presidential electors, Robinson remarks : " The
fact that the election of the President is left to a body of men
chosen ' for the special purpose,' and ' at a particular conjuncture '
is the striking characteristic of the system. Two European poten-
tates, the German Emperor and the Pope, were at the time of the
Convention elected by small bodies of men, in one case even
called ' electors ' [*principes electores ;* Ger. *Kurfürsten*]. Sir Henry
Maine thinks that the members of the Convention ' were to a considerable extent guided' by the example of the Holy Roman
Empire. 'The American republican Electors,' he goes so far as
to say, ' are the German imperial Electors, except they are chosen
by the several States.' A glance at this feature of the Imperial
Constitution will, however, show that there is in reality almost no
similarity between it and our electoral colleges. The latter form a
numerous, ever-changing body, the members of which are chosen
for a single election only, whereas the imperial college was not only
small and *elastic,* but *permanent.* Further, the choice of the
Emperor was *direct;* that of the President, constitutionally at least,
is *indirect.* Had the choice of the President been left to the
governors of the States, as was suggested by Gerry, they would
have formed an electoral body somewhat resembling that of the
Empire. Although the plan of electing the President finds no
precedent in the Old World, we have already seen too much of the
variety of constitutional development on this side of the Atlantic,
hastily to declare it new. In the constitution of Maryland (1776)

at the time, or just prior to the time, of the Philadelphia Convention.[1]

The members of the Convention seem to have regarded the *Commentaries* of Sir William Blackstone as trustworthy authority on the subject of royal prerogative, and to have taken the book as, in some sense, a guide in their task of executive construction. For this they have been criticised. And the grounds of the criticism are thus stated by Mr. Bryce : "Their view was tinged not only by recollections of the influence exercised by King George III., an influence due to transitory causes, but which made

we find an *almost exact counterpart* of the electoral college chosen in each of the States on the occasion of a presidential election. The senators were selected by a body of electors, chosen every five years by the inhabitants of the State for *this particular purpose and occasion.*" — *Publications American Academy*, No. 9, pp. 228, 229. The correctness of Robinson's opinion as to this origin of the electoral system receives important confirmation from contemporaneous opinion of the constitutional period. In the Massachusetts Convention, Bowdoin expressed the view : " This method of choosing [the President] was probably taken from the manner of choosing senators under the constitution of Maryland." — Elliot's *Debates*, II. 128.

[1] Franklin's plan of union of the colonies submitted to the Congress at Albany, 1754, provided for a President General to govern the united colonies, who should be appointed and supported by the crown. This executive was to nominate military officers; commission all officers; manage, with the advice of a Grand Council, Indian affairs; have a veto upon all the acts of the Grand Council, and carry their acts into execution. See Frothingham, *Rise of the Republic of the United States*, 142, 143. Also Sparks, *Works of Franklin*, III. 51; Pownall, *Administration of the Colonies*, ed. 1768, App. IV.

them overrate its monarchical element, but also by the
presentation of it which they found in the work of Mr.
Justice Blackstone.   He, as was natural in a lawyer and
a man of letters, described rather its theory than its practice, and its theory was many years behind its practice."[1]
Nevertheless, if Blackstone represents the monarchical
powers as greater than they were in actual practice at
the moment of his writing, he yet represents what at one
time had been the powers of English kings.   In trusting
to him as a guide, the members of the Convention seem
to have committed, at worst, no greater fault than that
of modelling after an older and stronger form of the
English executive rather than a strictly contemporaneous
one.   The fact itself of the derivation of the powers of
the presidency from those of the kingship is not affected,
whether the point of touch between the two be at an
earlier or at a later period of the royal office.   The justice of the criticism, therefore, does not essentially concern the present inquiry.   And since, whether wisely or
unwisely, the members of the Convention did give the
Commentaries the consideration due to a standard, the
great law-book must be accorded a somewhat similar
place in comparing the results of their labour in the Constitution.

Following Blackstone's division, therefore, let us proceed to examine the threefold relation of the royal powers
(I.) to legislation, (II.) to foreign affairs, and (III.) to

---

[1] *American Commonwealth*, I. 26.

internal administration, — considering at the same time the presidential functions.[1]

I. As regards legislative relations, the sovereign of that period was, according to Blackstone, a constituent part of Parliament. As such, all bills required his approval, and he possessed, in theory at least, the right of veto.[2] He might address communications from time to time to Parliament, and he had the prerogative of convening, proroguing, adjourning, and dissolving that body.

Turning to the Constitution of the United States, we read : "Every bill which shall have passed the House of Representatives and the Senate shall, before it becomes a law, be presented to the President of the United States ; if he approve he shall sign it, but if not, he shall return it with his objections to that house in which it originated, who shall enter the objections at

[1] On this general theme, see Blackstone, *Commentaries*, Book I. Chap. VII.

[2] "Since the accession of the House of Hanover no sovereign [of England] has exercised the prerogative of refusing the royal assent to a bill which has passed both houses, but it is not surprising to find that George III. was prepared to do so. 'I hope,' he wrote to Lord North in 1774, 'the crown will always be able, in either house of Parliament, to throw out a bill; but I shall never consent to use any expression which tends to establish that at no time the right of the crown to dissent is to be used.'" — Taswell-Langmead, *English Constitutional History*, 706. See also Lord Brougham, *Works*, III. 85. It must be remembered, however, that in addition to the veto of parliamentary legislation, the sovereign, as also the governors, had the acknowledged right to veto colonial legislation. Thus, to Americans, veto power in the executive has ever been a reality.

large on their journal and proceed to reconsider it."[1]
The President's veto may be overridden, by a sufficient
majority in Congress, but that is rarely attempted, and
when attempted seldom accomplished; and therefore the
veto is potential in ordinary practice. While some political
writers at the present day have contended that the veto
power of the English sovereign has lapsed, as not having
been used since the reign of Queen Anne,[2] such lapse
was certainly not recognized in the days of George III.,
who expressly affirmed the right, though he did not

[1] *Constitution of the United States*, Art. I. Sec. 7.   Robinson thus
refers to the action of the Constitutional Convention on the veto
power: "The suggestion that the executive should have an absolute
veto on all legislation naturally met with little favour in the Convention, in spite of the influence of Wilson and Hamilton, who favoured
it on the ground that, like the veto of the English sovereign, although
seldom or never used, it would serve to prevent rash legislation.   A
motion to give the executive a suspensive veto was negatived by all
the States.   A motion of Gerry of Massachusetts, June 4th, giving
the executive the power to negative any legislative act which should
not afterwards be passed by two-thirds of each branch of the national
legislature, was passed by a vote of eight to two, and this important
point was once for all settled.   Not only was this idea of a qualified
veto taken directly from the constitution of Massachusetts (1780)
and New York (1777), but in the final draft the very words of the
Massachusetts constitution frequently occur." — *Publications American Academy*, No. 9, pp. 230, 231.   See also Elliot, *Debates*, V. 151,
155, and *Massachusetts Constitution* of 1780, Pt. II. Ch. I. Sec. I.
Art. II.

[2] The last occasions on which the royal veto power was exercised
in England were in 1692 and 1694, when William III. refused the
royal assent to the Bill for Triennial Parliaments and the Place
Bill, and in 1707, when Queen Anne refused assent to a Scotch
militia bill.

exercise it. And whatever the case in England, the practice of the veto power by the governors, and by the king in matters of colonial legislation in America, was a fully recognized legal right down to the outbreak of the American Revolution, and naturally passed into the constitutional law of the States and of the American nation.

In Article I. Section 3 of the Constitution it is provided : " He [the President] shall from time to time give to Congress information of the state of the Union, and recommend to their consideration such measures as he shall judge necessary and expedient ; he may on extraordinary occasions convene both houses, or either of them, and in case of disagreement between them, with respect to the time of adjournment, he may adjourn them to such time as he shall think proper."

The President's message is derived from the royal act of communicating with Parliament. The message is not a production of the Cabinet, like the modern speech from the throne, but a veritable communication of the executive in person. Washington was accustomed to deliver an oral address " like an English king, and drove in a coach and six to open Congress, with something of an English king's state." [1] Jefferson, however, filled with theories of democracy imbibed from France, introduced the practice of sending written messages, which has since been continued.[2]

---

[1] Bryce, *American Commonwealth*, I. 55.

[2] Burgess says: " The Constitution apparently vests in the President the power to initiate legislation, in the provision requiring

By royal theory, all laws proceed from the crown's authority. However they may be discussed and passed by Parliament, the sovereign gives them their force ; bills are turned into statutes by him. And although the theory has not been followed in the United States, the practice under it has. With rare exceptions, bills are turned into statutes by the President, and go forth directly from his hand to the statute book.

him to give information to the Congress of the 'state of the Union,' and to recommend such measures as he shall judge necessary and expedient. It does not appear to me that any further constitutional warrant is necessary to authorize the President to construct and present regular bills and projects of law to the Congress. The Constitution does not prescribe the form in which the President shall present the measures which he may recommend; nor does it vest the Congress with the power to do it, either by an express provision or by any reasonable implication. It leaves the determination of the form, therefore, to the President himself. We must look elsewhere for the explanation of the fact that the President does not present his recommendations to Congress in the form of regular bills or projects. It is to be found in the lack of any executive organs for presenting, explaining, defending, and, in general, managing such government bills in Congress. It cannot be predicted with certainty that the existence of such organs would strengthen the power of the executive in legislation. It might lessen his real influence." — *Political Science and Comparative Constitutional Law*, II. 254. It remains true, however, that though not having cabinet ministers with a seat in Congress, the President does initiate much legislation through contact informally with Congress. And at times these measures are discussed as carefully in Cabinet as if they were to be presented in the form of bills, and indeed are practically so presented. See notes of conversation with President Hayes, in present chapter.

II. In external relations of the nation the king was regarded, by Blackstone, the representative of his people, according to the idea of the Cyning dating from the earliest times. It was in that capacity that he dealt with other nationalities, sending ambassadors and ministers to foreign states, and receiving ambassadors and ministers from them ; making treaties, leagues, and alliances. He was commander-in-chief of the army and navy, with the executive powers of war, and the power to issue letters of marque and reprisal, and to grant safe-conducts and passports. He appointed and commissioned all military and naval officers.

Turning to the American Constitution, Article II., we find the President acting as the representative of the nation in relation to foreign affairs, on the same the lines. " He shall receive ambassadors and other ministers." [1] " He shall have power, by and with the advice and consent of the Senate, to make treaties, provided two-thirds of the senators present concur ; [2] and he shall nominate, and by and with the consent of the Senate shall appoint, ambassadors, other public ministers, and consuls." [3]

---

[1] *Constitution of the United States*, Art. II. Sec. 3.

[2] The President in practice first agrees with a foreign nation upon the terms of a treaty, and then submits the draft to the Senate for ratification. The Senate may ratify the treaty as it is presented, or may reject it, or may amend it. In the last case the amended treaty must be presented, of course, to the foreign power for agreement to its altered provisions.

[3] *Constitution of the United States*, Art. II. Sec. 2.

" The failure to establish an efficient council led the Convention

"The President shall be commander-in-chief of the army and navy of the United States, and of the militia of the several States when called into the actual service of the United States."[1] The President appoints, with the

to limit the President's power by giving the Senate control over some of his acts. The association of the Senate with the President in the exercise of the appointing power is strikingly similar to the system pursued in New York under the constitution of 1777. There the executive, free to act alone in all other respects, was bound to make appointments 'by and with the consent of a select committee of the Senate.' " — *Publications of the American Academy*, No. 9, p. 225. See *New York Constitution* (1777), Art. XXIII. For a different view of the origin of this relation of the Senate to the appointing power, see Campbell, *Puritan in Holland, England, and America*, II. 424.

The President's power of filling vacancies by commissions to expire at the end of the next session of the Senate, is taken in terms from the constitution of South Carolina.

[1] *Ibid.* "The power to declare war has not been confided to the President of the United States, but is conferred on Congress. The President, however, is by the same instrument made commander-in-chief of the army and navy, and it is possible for him, in the recess of Congress, if sufficiently reckless of consequences, to bring on a war with a foreign nation, by employing armed forces against it in a hostile manner. Those who opposed the action of the government in the case of the war with Mexico insisted that that war was brought on by the President wrongfully taking forcible possession of the territory in dispute; but Congress justified the President, and declared that war existed 'by the act of Mexico.' " — Cooley's Blackstone, *Commentaries*, Bk. I. 257, n. 14.

The "war powers" of the President are far beyond powers ordinarily exercised by constitutional monarchs. Lawrence says of them: " It was during the War of Secession that the powers of the President were exercised to an extent unprecedented in English history. Based on an insurrection in the several States therein

consent of the Senate, and commissions military and
naval officers. In time of war, he has all the powers

enumerated, and without awaiting a meeting of Congress convened
for the 4th of July, 1861, the President proclaimed, on the 19th
and 27th of April, the blockade of the ports of these States. By
his proclamation of May 3, 1861, he called into service upward of
42,000 volunteers to serve for three years, increased the regular
army by 22,000 men, and added 18,000 seamen to the naval service.
. . . These acts were sustained by the Supreme Court on the first
occasion on which the question came regularly before it, in the case
of the validity of the prizes made for violation of the President's
blockade. . . . President Lincoln's attorney-general had advised
him, in 1861, that it was for the President alone to pronounce upon
the political considerations which determine in what cases a sus-
pension of the privilege of *habeas corpus* might take place, and that
the authority conferred on him by the Constitution was in nowise
affected by the powers with which the act of 1789 had invested the
judges with regard to the writ of *habeas corpus.*

"Immediately after the secession of the South, a direct conflict
arose between the executive and judicial power in consequence
of the refusal, by order of the President, of a military commander
to obey a writ of *habeas corpus* issued by the Chief Justice of the
United States. Chief Justice Taney, after declaring that a military
government had been substituted for the government of the Constitution, says that nothing remains for him to do but to order all
the proceedings in the case, with his opinion, to be filed and recorded in the appropriate court, and direct the clerk to transmit a
copy under seal to the President of the United States. 'It will then
remain for that high officer, in fulfilment of his constitutional obligations to take care that the laws be faithfully executed, to determine what course he will take to cause the civil process of the
United States to be respected and enforced.' Perhaps a summary
of what were the pretensions of the executive as regards personal
liberty may be best found in a note addressed by Mr. Seward to
Lord Lyons in October, 1861 : 'It seems necessary to state, for the
information of that government, that Congress is by the Constitution

recognized by the laws and usages of war.   The right to declare war being confined to Congress, he can only

invested with no executive power or responsibility whatever, but on the contrary, that the President of the United States is, by the Constitution and laws, invested with the whole executive power of the government, and charged with the supreme direction of all municipal and ministerial civil agents, as well as of the whole land and naval forces of the United States, and that, invested with these ample powers, he is charged by the Constitution and laws with the absolute duty of suppressing insurrection, as well as of preventing and repelling invasion, and that for these purposes he constitutionally exercises the right of suspending the writ of *habeas corpus* whenever and wheresoever and in whatsoever extent the public safety, endangered by treason or invasion in arms, in his judgment requires.'

"At the date of Mr. Seward's note no proclamation, in the sense of his communication, had been issued, and no intimation of any such intention had been in any way given.   On the 24th of September a proclamation establishing martial law was issued, and by an order of the Department of War, of September 26, 1862, a national police was established in all the States to watch over the execution of the proclamation." — *North American Review*, November, 1880, pp. 395, 396.

Mr. Bryce, in speaking of the presidential power, says that in war time "it expands with portentous speed.   Both as commander-in-chief of the army and navy and as charged with the 'faithful execution of the laws,' the President is likely to be led to assume all the powers which the emergency requires.   How much he can legally do without the aid of statutes is disputed, for the acts of President Lincoln during the earlier part of the War of Secession, including his proclamation suspending the writ of *habeas corpus*, were subsequently legalized by Congress; but it is at least clear that Congress can make him, as it did make Lincoln, almost a dictator. And how much the war power may include appears in this, that, by virtue of it and without any previous legislative sanction, President Lincoln issued his emancipation proclamations of 1862 and 1863." — *American Commonwealth*, I. 50, 51.

proclaim it when Congress has acted. But in advance of any congressional enactment he may employ the army and navy to put down insurrection and repel invasion.

III. In internal affairs the king had, according to Blackstone, undefined powers in the execution of the laws. By his prerogative as Fountain of Honour he appointed officials and conferred honours. As Fountain of Justice, he was assumed to possess rights derived from the old judicial functions of the crown, — but exercised them by proxy, through judges of the law courts whom he appointed and commissioned.[1] As supreme conservator of the peace, he was in theory held to be

[1] Blackstone says: " From the same original, of the king's being the Fountain of Justice, we may also deduce the prerogative of issuing proclamations, which is vested in the king alone. The proclamations have then a binding force, when (as Sir Edward Coke observes) they are grounded upon or enforce the laws of the realm." — *Commentaries,* Bk. I. 269. The proclamations of the President follow this usage. But a proclamation may introduce a practically new condition of affairs, as did the celebrated Emancipation Proclamation of President Lincoln. Landon remarks: " There were many who regarded this proclamation as a violation of the Constitution, but the loyal answer was, that while the war lasted it was disloyalty to stickle over the Constitution, since unless the war could be victoriously ended, the Constitution itself would be of no value. But the true answer is, that as commander-in-chief of the army and navy, the President has the constitutional power to employ the means recognized by the laws of war as necessary to conquer the enemy. Congress can pass no law which can deprive the President of the power which the Constitution confers, in creating him commander-in-chief." — *Constitutional History and Government of the United States,* 205.

the prosecutor of crimes ; and in this capacity he granted reprieves and pardons.

Comparing the Constitution of the United States, Section 1 of Article II. is noted for its great width and flexibility, — "The executive power shall be vested in a President of the United States of America." And so is Section 2 of the same article, — "He shall take care that the laws be faithfully executed, and shall commission all officers of the United States."[1] The President appoints, with the consent of the Senate, all chief civil officers of the nation, and commissions all national officials. And though the English theory of relation to judicial matters is ignored, he has the royal power of appointing judges ; and the Chief Justice and Justices of the Supreme Court, and all judges of the national courts are commissioned by him. As preserver of the peace,

[1] In his discourse on *The Jubilee of the Constitution*, John Quincy Adams says : "It has perhaps never been duly remarked that, under the Constitution of the United States, the powers of the executive department, explicitly and emphatically concentrated in one person, are vastly more extensive and complicated than those of the legislative. The language of the instrument in conferring legislative authority is, '*All* legislative power, *herein granted*, shall be vested in a Congress of the United States, which shall consist of a Senate and House of Representatives.' But the executive authority is unreserved in terms, — ' *The* executive power shall be vested in a President of the United States of America.'"

Upshur says: "We have heard it gravely asserted in Congress, that, whatever power is neither legislative nor judiciary, is of course executive, and as such belongs to the President under the Constitution." — *Nature and Character of our Federal Government.*

he grants reprieves and pardons to breakers of the
peace.[1]

The relation of the President to his Cabinet has already
been referred to. When Article II. Section 2 of the
Constitution was in formation at Philadelphia, a proposition was made to give the executive a Privy Council
similar to that of the English king; and a draft was
offered to the effect, that " the President may from time
to time submit any matter to the discussion of the council
of state, and he may require the written opinions of any
one or more of the members. But he shall in all cases
exercise his own judgment, and either conform to such
opinions or not, as he may think proper."[2] This draft
was referred to a committee, which reported it in the
somewhat altered form, that " the President shall have a
Privy Council . . . whose duty it shall be to advise in
matters respecting the execution of his office, which he
shall think proper to lay before them; but their advice
shall not conclude him, nor affect his responsibility for
the measures which he shall adopt."[3] This was again

---

[1] "One of the powers intrusted to the President . . . is that of
granting reprieves and pardons. . . . It is derived from the history
of our British ancestors, and in the absence of any more particular
definition of it than is found in this short sentence of the Constitution, so far as it has become the subject of public discussion, or of
judicial decision, reliance has been had mainly upon the nature and
character of the power as exercised by the crown of Great Britain."
— Mr. Justice Miller, of the Supreme Court, *Lectures on Constitution
of the United States*, 164, 165.

[2] Elliot, *Debates*, V. 446.

[3] *Ibid.* V. 462.

referred to committee, and finally was adopted in the shape in which it appears in the Constitution, — providing simply that the President "may require the opinion, in writing, of the principal officer in each of the executive departments, upon any subject relating to the duties of their respective offices."[1]

Thus, a Privy Council was not established; and the President was left to advise with his own heads of departments, if he desired and in so far as he desired, or to act entirely without their advice and in accordance with his own will.[2]

[1] *Constitution of the United States*, Art. II. Sec. 2.

[2] " Jefferson, who certainly had as much confidence in his official advisers, among whom were Madison and Gallatin, as any other President, did not ask, I was assured by one of its most trusted members, the advice of his Cabinet on, perhaps, the two most important measures of his administration, — the purchase of Louisiana and the rejection of the treaty concluded by Monroe and Pinckney in 1806. The former of these measures, as involving the acquisition of foreign territory, was ever regarded as the great constitutional question of the day. President Lincoln, it is understood, seldom or never had any cabinet meetings." — W. B. Lawrence, LL.D., *North American Review*, November, 1880, p. 394.

The author once had a conversation with President Rutherford B. Hayes regarding the practical operation of the presidency. By his permission I made notes of the conversation at the time, for publication in this book. Asking about the action of a President independently of the advice of his Cabinet, " he told me that he himself and other Presidents had so acted occasionally. As to the general relations of the Cabinet, he said that Presidents were masters of the situation, not only by law, but by the fact that Cabinet officers were appointed by and dependent upon the executive. He said the custom of the past had varied; that some Presidents had

This intention to make the President a personal executive, free from cabinet or council control, receives further

been more influenced by their cabinets than others; that President
Buchanan was much worried by his Cabinet, because not strong
enough to insist on his own will.   On the other hand, President
Lincoln had decided on his emancipation proclamation without consulting his Cabinet, to whom he read it over merely for suggestion
and amendment.   He (President Hayes) had once decided a measure,
overruling his Cabinet.   He knew them to be opposed to it and did
not ask their views, but announced his own policy, and carried it
out.   In matters of a department, he gave greater weight to the
opinion of the secretary of that department, if the secretary opposed
his own views; but on two occasions, at least, he had decided and
carried out matters against the wishes of the secretary of the department affected.   He had done so in the case of his Secretary of the
Treasury, whose opinion he usually valued.   In each case, knowing
the certainty of diverse views from the secretary, he had not asked
those views, but had announced to the secretary his own policy and
decision.   In answer to a question of mine, as to whether the
President or the secretaries usually *initiated* business at meetings of
the Cabinet, he said that there was no uniform practice; but that
every secretary was full of ideas as to his own department.   When
wishing to introduce a measure, the secretary usually consulted the
President privately.   If the President disfavoured the proposed
measure, it was, of course, dropped.   In fact, no measures could
succeed except by the President's own act in either introducing
them or approving them.

   " He remarked, that few writers or public persons understood
the real power of the American executive.   Practically, the President had the nation in his hand.   He was commander-in-chief of
the army and navy, and had control of foreign affairs.   He could
at any time force Congress into war with foreign powers.   The
complicate relations with foreign powers rendered this always easy.
By law, Congress had the power to declare war, but the real power
was with the executive.   He detailed some of his own experience
with foreign affairs in proof of the constant delicacy of such mat-

light from the law of 1789, which created cabinet ministers or heads of executive departments. The law enacts

ters. But, said he, if once war exists, the President has the 'war
powers'; and no man has defined what those are, or placed a
limit on them. The executive power is large because not defined
in the Constitution. The real test has never come, because the
Presidents have, down to the present, been conservative, or what
might be called conscientious, men, and have kept within limited
range. And there is an unwritten law of usage that has come to
regulate an average administration. But if a Napoleon ever became
President, he could make the executive almost what he wished to
make it. The war power of President Lincoln went to lengths
which could scarcely be surpassed in despotic principle.

" I reminded him that Mr. Bryce characterized this power of
Lincoln as practically that of a dictator. President Hayes agreed
with the description. He said the scope of this executive power
had never been really realized, and that the practical use of
power, even by an ordinarily strong President, was greater than the
books ever described.

" He said that much of the legislation of Congress was ordinarily
initiated by the President. The Constitution did not provide for
this, but in practice it was done. A large part of legislation was
first considered in Cabinet, and then started in Congress by contact
privately between the secretaries and the committees of Congress.
I remarked that Mr. Bryce had enlarged on the weakness of the
contact between the President and Congress in the initiation of
legislation, and had especially pointed out that the presidential
message had no necessary influence. He replied that the message
was without legal force, and that Congress could be influenced by
it or not as it saw fit; but that if one were to compare the messages
with legislation, it would be found that legislation largely resulted
from the suggestions of messages. Really, the message made a
public statement of matters, which, less officially, were pressed upon
Congress by cabinet ministers as already mentioned. While it was
a fact that no regular channel of necessary legislative initiative was
possessed by the President, he, nevertheless, did initiate a large

that the Secretary of State "shall conduct the business of the said department [foreign affairs] in such manner as the President of the United States shall, from time to time, order and instruct."[1]   And the same principle was applied to the heads of other departments.[2]   The ministers were thus designed, in their very creation, to be merely the agents of the executive, and to carry out his will, rather than their own ; having precisely the relation that Lord North bore to George III.[3]   Washington

proportion of, sometimes the leading, legislation of his administration.   He had also a certain amount of influence in preventing in advance legislation that was distasteful to him, or even in shaping and amending bills in Congress, by intimating unofficially his disapproval and possible veto." — *Notes of Conversation of the Author with President Hayes*, September 30, 1889.

[1] *Act of July* 27, 1789.

[2] See 1 *Statutes at Large*, 49.   In addition to the words above, the law requires the Secretary of State or the Secretary of War to "perform and execute such duties as shall, from time to time, be enjoined on, or intrusted to him by the President of the United States, agreeably to the Constitution."   In like manner, the duty of the Secretary of the Navy "shall be to execute such orders as he shall receive from the President of the United States" relative to his department. — 1 *Statutes at Large*, 553.   These laws, with immaterial changes, are in force at the present day.   See *Revised Statutes of the United States*, passed by 1st session of 43d Congress, 1873–1874, etc.; 2d ed., p. 32, Sec. 202; p. 35, Sec. 216; p. 71, Sec. 417.

[3] "There can be no doubt that the President, in the exercise of his executive power under the Constitution, may act through the head of the appropriate department.   The heads of departments are his assistants in the performance of his executive duties, and their official acts, promulgated in the regular course of business, are presumptively his acts.   That has been many times decided by this [the Supreme] Court." — *Runkle v. United States*, 122 U. S. 543, 557.

originated the practice of consulting all the heads of departments on important measures. But although "cabinet
meetings" eventually became customary, the Presidents
have never hesitated to act independently of advice when
they thought fit, and it is said that Abraham Lincoln.
wielding greater power than any of his predecessors.
seldom held such meetings at all.

"The Cabinet, as a body of councillors," remarks Judge
Cooley, "has no necessary place in our constitutional
system, and each President will accord to it such weight
and influence in his administration as he shall see fit.
The President — not the Cabinet — is responsible for all
the measures of the administration, and whatever is done
by one of the heads of department is considered as done
by the President, through the proper executive agent.
In this fact consists one important difference between
the executive of Great Britain and of the United States ;
the acts of the former being considered as those of his
advisers, who alone are responsible therefor, while the
acts of the advisers of the American executive are considered as directed and controlled by him."[1] The President appoints as members of his Cabinet persons who
agree in his own political views, and they are not expected to resign merely because the opposition party is
in majority in Congress. It has frequently occurred
that the President's "friends" in one or both houses
of Congress have been in a minority for a considerable
period.

[1] Cooley's Blackstone, *Commentaries*, Bk. I. 231, n. 6.

It is noteworthy that while the English sovereign has lost influence in consequence of cabinet control, the President of the United States has not only maintained his power in time of peace, but demonstrated in time of war that it can rise, as it did in the administration of Lincoln, to a height approaching dictatorship.

Some English writers, notably Mr. Walter Bagehot, have criticised this want of a true cabinet system in the Constitution of the United States. Mr. Bagehot remarks: "The ancient theory holds, that the queen is the executive. The American Constitution was made upon a most careful argument, and most of that argument assumes the king to be the administrator of the English Constitution, and an unhereditary substitute for him, viz. a President, to be peremptorily necessary. Living across the Atlantic and misled by accepted doctrines, the acute framers of the Federal Constitution, even after the keenest attention, did not perceive the prime minister to be the principal executive of the British Constitution, and the sovereign a cog in the mechanism. There is, indeed, much excuse for the American legislators in the history of the time. They took their idea of our Constitution from the time they encountered it. But in the so-called government of Lord North, George III. was the government. Lord North was not only his appointee and his agent; the minister carried on a war which he disapproved and hated, because it was a war which his sovereign approved and liked. Inevitably, therefore, the American Convention believed the king, from whom they had suffered, to be the real executive, and not the minister, from whom they had not suffered." [1]

There are undoubted evils in the American system, with its possibility — which more than once has become fact — of detriment to public interests through conflict between the executive and the legislature. But on the whole, Americans, with their democratic tendencies, owe very much of the stability of their government to the weakness of their legislature and the strength of their executive. Had Congress possessed the power of Parliament to alter constitutional principle itself, by a majority vote at any session, and had the Cabinet controlled the President as the English Cabinet does the sovereign, the American commonwealth very probably might have been wrecked in its constructive period, or in passing through the storms of later time. The presidency is justly regarded by Americans as one of the most valuable creations of the Constitution of 1787. And the fact that the office is rooted in the past institutions of the race is not only the explanation of its existence, but a real, even though unrecognized, cause of its hold on the national heart.

The observations of Sir Henry Maine in this connection form too fitting a conclusion of the consideration of the subject to be omitted. "On the face of the Constitution of the United States the resemblance of the President of the United States to the European king, and especially to the King of Great Britain, is too obvi-

[1] *English Constitution*, 126.

ous for mistake. The President has, in various degrees, a number of powers which those who know something of kingship in its general history recognize at once as peculiarly associated with it, and with no other institution. The whole executive power is vested in him. He is commander of the army and navy. He makes treaties with the advice and consent of the Senate, and with the same advice and consent, he appoints ambassadors, ministers, judges, and all high functionaries. He has a qualified veto on legislation. He convenes Congress when no special time of meeting has been fixed. It is conceded in the *Federalist* that the similarity of the new presidential office to the functions of the British king was one of the points on which the opponents of the Constitution fastened. Hamilton replies to their arguments sometimes with cogency, sometimes, it must be avowed, a little captiously. . . . But he mainly relies on the points in which the President differs from the king on the terminability of the office,[1] on the participa-

---

[1] The Duc de la Rochefoucauld in a letter to Franklin, in 1789, expresses surprise that, having in mind the efforts to restrain the powers of the French monarch, Americans should have given such great scope to the functions of the President, especially to one whose re-election for life was possible. It is true that the unwritten constitution has now come to limit the President to a single re-election. But as the unwritten constitution is the result of custom merely, custom can change it. In fact, the custom was questioned so recently as the time of Grant, when a strong effort was made to give him a " third term." The only real limit to the continuation of a given President in power is the will of the people. And history shows that nations undergo changes in funda-

tion of the Senate in the exercise of several of his powers, on the limited nature of his veto of bills passed by Congress.   It is, however, tolerably clear that the mental operation through which the framers of the American Constitution passed was this : they took the King of Great Britain, went through his powers, and restrained them whenever they appeared to be excessive, or un-suited to the circumstances of the United States.   It is remarkable that the figure they had before them was not a generalized English king, nor an abstract constitutional monarch ; it was no anticipation of Queen Victoria, but George III. himself, whom they took for their model. Fifty years earlier, or a hundred years later, the English king would have struck them as in quite a different light. . . . Now the original of the President of the United States is manifestly a treaty-making king actively influencing the executive government.   Mr. Bagehot insisted

mental opinion in the course of ages.   Already a most intelligent portion of the community advocate a constitutional amendment to make the presidential term of office longer than four years. Length of term has so many arguments in its favour that, if the danger of it is not keenly feared, public opinion is likely, sooner or later, to move in such a direction.   The Americans are a practical people, and mere fear of danger will not be sufficient to keep them from whatever they come to regard as a practical good.   They apparently feel that they are able to cope with dangers, when dangers really come.   There can be small doubt that had Washington not declined, his "re-election for life," to which Rochefoucauld refers, would have been "possible."   And should another arise like him — some great hero such as history occasionally gives to nations — there is nothing to prevent his "re-election for life," so far as the Constitution is concerned.

that the great neglected fact in the English political system was the government of England by a committee of the legislature, calling themselves the Cabinet. This is exactly the method of government to which George III. refused to submit, and the framers of the American Constitution take George III.'s view of the kingly office for granted. They give the whole of the executive government to the President, and they do not permit his ministers to have a seat or speech in either branch of the legislature. They limit his power, and this not, however, by any contrivance known to modern constitutionalism, but by making the office of President terminable at intervals of four years. If Hamilton had lived a hundred years later, his comparison of the President with the king would have turned on very different points. He must have conceded that the republican functionary was the more powerful of the two." [1]

[1] Maine, *Popular Government*, 211–214.

"The President is, beyond doubt, the English king, modified by the necessities of a state of things in which hereditary succession was out of the question, and in which even a life term of office would have awakened the greatest jealousy." — Freeman, *The English People in its Three Homes*, 375.

"The organization of the executive department of the new government was attended with great difficulty. In the teeth of the prevailing prejudice against monarchy, it was no easy task to devise an acceptable scheme through which the federal chief magistrate could be clothed with the constitutional attributes of an English king. And yet that result was substantially accomplished. Although the President was simply a magistrate to be obeyed within the range of his powers, and personally liable to impeachment if he overstepped them, still he was endowed with as much, if not more,

The foregoing may appear strong language. But the essential truth must be admitted. It will not do to contend in opposition to this truth, that certain powers of the American executive are common to the executives of many nationalities, for the American has developed from its original through distinctly traceable channels. Nor will it be sufficient to insist upon the many differences between the English and American executives, for the points of agreement are none the less real. Though the President lacks the distinguishing heredity and pageantry of royalty, yet the characteristic powers he holds were held before him by the executive of the colonies, and of the home land.   "Assuming that there was to be such a magistrate, the statesmen of the Convention, like the solid, practical men they were, did not try to construct him out of their own brains, but looked to some existing models. They therefore made an enlarged copy of the State governor, or, to put the same thing differently, a reduced and improved copy of the English king." [1]

real power than was possessed even then by that dreaded original. The elective principle, it is true, was substituted for hereditary right, a definite term of office was prescribed, and all the pomp and pageantry of power was sternly cut off, and yet the real resemblance which remained between the two national chiefs was too close to escape the enemies of the Constitution, who bitterly assailed it on that ground." — Taylor, *Origin and Growth of English Constitution*, 69.

[1] Bryce, *American Commonwealth*, I. 36.

CHAPTER VII.

THE JUDICIARY.

THE English sovereign anciently exercised judicial functions which, by an evolutionary process, have gradually come to be separated from his executive functions, and deputed to a permanent body of judges, appointed by him, but independent of his direction. During the Saxon period, the kings decided cases which otherwise had failed in obtaining settlement, and after the Norman Conquest they continued to administer justice in person.[1] William the Conqueror, whenever present in England, held great courts of justice at Christmas, Easter, and Whitsuntide. To William Rufus, the barons recommended mercy in the sentence of minor criminals in 1096. Henry I. summoned Robert of Beleseme before his court, charged with treason under forty-five articles; and other cases, criminal and civil, are recorded of him. Some of the sayings of Henry II.

[1] Even queens sat in court in early Norman times. Queen Matilda, consort of the Conqueror, Queen Maud, consort of Henry I., and the queen consort of Henry III., are recorded as having done so. Heming, 512; *Hist. Mon. Abingd.*, II. 116, Rolls Ser.; Biglow, *Placita Anglo-Normannica*, 99; Spence, *Equit. Jurisdiction*, 101, n.

on the seat of judgment have come down to us.[1] Instances of personal decisions are narrated of John, Henry
III., Edward I., and Edward II. But royal hearings,
always and necessarily rare, gradually ceased. Edward
IV. visited the Court of King's Bench in person to
observe its procedure; in which, however, he did not
share.[2] When James I. attended a trial, and desired
to take part, he was informed by the judges, that he
could not deliver an opinion.[3] And the constitutional
principle has long since been recognized, that the sovereign, even though present, is not entitled to "determine
any case, but by the mouths of his judges, to whom he
has committed the whole of his judicial authority."[4]

---

[1] A defendant alleged, in a case tried before him in 1454, soon
after his obtaining the crown, that a charter of Henry I., placed in
evidence, had been improperly gotten. "*Per oculos Dei,*" exclaimed the king, taking the charter into his own hands, "*si cartam
hanc falsam comprobare possess, lucrum mille librarum mihi in
Anglia conferres.*" *Walter, Abbott of St. Martin of Battle v.
Gilbert de Balliol: Chron. Monasterii de Bello,* 106; Biglow, *Placita
Anglo-Normannica,* 175. In a case over a land franchise between
Baldwin, Archbishop of Canterbury, and the Abbot of St. Edmund,
conflicting charters were presented; upon which the puzzled monarch exclaimed, "*Nescio quid dicam: nisi ut cartae ad invicem
pugnent.*" The abbot offering to submit the contention to the
verdict of the counties of Norfolk and Suffolk, and the archbishop
declining the offer, the king arose in indignation, and left the court.
with the words: "*Qui potest capere capiat.*" *Archbishop of Canterbury v. Abbot of St. Edmund,* circ. 1186; *Chron. Jocelin de
Brakelonda,* 37, pub. Camden Soc.; Biglow, *Placita Anglo-Nor-
manica,* 238.

[2] Stow, *Chronicles,* 416.

[3] Blackstone, *Commentaries,* III. 41. [4] Coke, *4th Inst.,* 73.

The national legislature of England also, as we have seen, possessed judicial powers.[1] And by the changes of centuries it has come to share these with a variety of courts, though preserving the supreme jurisdiction pertaining to the House of Lords. The Witenagemot transmitted its judicial functions to the Norman Great Council, the Curia Regis. But at least from the time of Henry I., an inner body — an offshoot from the larger, yet taking to itself the name Curia Regis [2] — administered judicial and financial affairs, under the king or his deputy, the chief justiciar.[3] Judges made circuits

[1] The *Codex Diplomaticus* prints a very extended list of charters recording the results of trials by the Witenagemot. The documents give very minute information as to the nature, process, parties, and causes, with place and date of the gemot at which each trial was held and the names of those who presided.

[2] Hallam (*Middle Ages*, II. 423) refers to the confusing application of the term *Curia Regis*. It was used to designate (1) The *Commune Concilium*, or National Council of the realm, the Witenagemot in a feudalized form. (2) The *Ordinarium Concilium*, the perpetual or select council for judicial and administrative purposes. (3) The *Court of King's Bench*, growing out of the limited tribunal separated from this last by Henry II., in 1178, and soon after acquiring exclusively the denomination " Curia Regis."

[3] " As the highest judicial tribunal in the realm, the Curia Regis consisted of the king, sitting to administer justice in person, with the advice and counsel of those vassals who were members of the royal household and of such others as were, on account of their knowledge of law, specially appointed as judges. In the absence of the king his court was presided over by the justiciar, who was at all times the supreme administrator of law and finance. . . . By virtue of special writs, and as a special favour, the king could at his pleasure

of the kingdom, principally for fiscal, but also for judicial, purposes; and the local courts of each county — themselves outgrowths of the old folkmoots — were thus brought into connection with the national tribunals.[1]

call up causes from the local courts to be heard in his own court according to such new methods as his advisers might invent. Through the issuance of these special writs, the king became practically the fountain of justice; and through their agency the new system of royal law, which finds its source in the person of the king, was brought in to remedy the defects of the old, unelastic system of customary law which prevailed in the provincial courts of the people." — *Origin and Growth of English Constitution,* 245, 246. See Biglow, *History of Procedure in England;* Reeves, *History of English Law,* etc.

[1] Taylor has admirably condensed the facts. " In the course of the assessment and collection of the revenue, which was the chief work of the Curia as a financial body, local disputes so constantly arose that it became necessary to send detachments of justices to adjust the business of the exchequer in each shire. As early as the reign of Henry I., officers of the exchequer were frequently sent through the country to assess the revenue; and in the reign of his grandson, Henry II., this custom was enforced with systematic regularity. The justices while thus engaged in provincial business sat in the shiremoots, where judicial work soon followed in the path of their fiscal duties. In 1176 the kingdom was divided into six circuits, to each of which were assigned three justices, who are now for the first time given in the Pipe Rolls the name of *Justitiarii Itinerantes.* After several intermediate changes in the number of the circuits, it was at last provided by Magna Charta that two justices should be sent four times each year into each shire to take the assizes of *novel disseisin, mort d'ancester,* and *darrien presentment.* The provincial visitations of the justices from the exchequer, whose primary object was financial, thus led to the establishment of those judicial visitations which have ever remained an abiding feature in English judicature. Through these visitations was established that

This lesser Curia Regis in time became divided into three sections, which, in the latter part of the reign of Henry III., emerged as the distinctive courts of Exchequer, Common Pleas, and King's Bench, each charged with its own portion of business. The hearing of exceptional cases was still reserved to the inner council, and through the chancellor's relation to such cases eventually arose the Court of Chancery.[1] The council passed its

vitally important connection between the strong central system of administration embodied in the Norman Curia and the ancient system of local freedom embodied in the Old English shiremoots." — *Origin and Growth of the English Constitution,* 247, 248.

Stubbs says: "The visits of the itinerant justices form the link between the Curia Regis and the shiremoot, between royal and popular justice, between the old system and the new. The courts in which they preside are the ancient county courts, under new conditions, but substantially identical with those of the Anglo-Saxon times." — *Constitutional History of England,* I. 678.

The itinerant justices were for a long time active in extorting money from the people for the king's use. In 1242, at a great council assembled by Henry III., the barons complained, "Non cassaverunt justitiarii itinerantes itinerare per omnes partes. Angliae tam de placitis forestae quam de omnibus aliis placitis, ita quod omnes comitatus Angliae et omnia hundreda civitates et burgi, et fere omnes villae graviter amercientur; unde solummodo de illo itinere habet dominus rex vel habere debet maximam summam pecuniae, si persolvatur et bene colligatur. Unde bene dicunt quod per illa amerciamenta et per alia auxilia prius data, omnes de regno ita gravantur et depauperantur quod parum aut nihil habent in bonis." — Matt. Paris, 582.

[1] "The chancellor, who at a later period entered into many of the rights and dignities of the justiciar, appears in history very much earlier. The name, derived probably from the *cancelli,* or screen behind which the secretarial work of the royal household

powers on to the Privy Council, which continues its higher jurisdiction.[1] And thus judicial functions of the legislature, actively exercised by what was at first a sort of standing committee, came to be subdivided and put in operation through a gradually evolved system of courts, — the legislature itself continuing to exercise justice in what is now the House of Lords, successor to the Witan.[2] The judicial action of both the Privy Council and the House of Lords is taken in our

was carried on, claims a considerable antiquity; and the offices which it denotes are various in proportion. The chancellor of the Carolingian sovereigns, succeeding to the place of the more ancient *referendarius*, is simply the royal notary; the *archi-cancellarius* is the chief of a large body of such officers associated under the name of the chancery, and is the official keeper of the royal seal. It is from this minister that the English chancellor derives his name and function." — Stubbs, *Constitutional History of England*, 1. 398, 399. See also Waitz, *Deutsche Verfassungs-Geschichte*, 11. 409. For etymology of the word " chancellor," see Campbell, *Lives of the Lord Chancellors*, I. 1, 2.

[1] " The original tribunal, the king's ordinary council, retained its undiminished powers throughout, changing at various times and throwing off new offshoots, such as the Court of Star Chamber, until it has reached our own time in the form of the Judicial Committee of the Privy Council." — *Select Charters*, 24.

[2] " We must not forget," says Freeman, " that our judicial and parliamentary institutions are closely connected, that both spring out of the primitive assemblies, that things which now seem so unlike as our popular juries and the judicial powers of the House of Lords are in truth both of them fragments of the judicial powers which Tacitus speaks of as being vested in those primitive assemblies. It was only step by step that the functions of judge, juror, witness, and legislator became the utterly distinct functions which they are now." — *Growth of English Constitution*, 84.

day, not by those bodies as a whole, but by special judicial personages, — in the former by the "Judicial Committee," composed of judges of the several courts, and in the latter by the "law lords," *i.e.* peers who are or have been on the bench.

Thus by slow transfer of power originally belonging to both the executive and the legislature, the national judiciary finally emerged into definite being, and became a characteristic feature of the English Constitution. The system, at least in its leading and essential elements, concerns the present inquiry. For from it the American judicial system — with differences of detail — has directly come. The process of derivation has been first through the creation and action of the colonial courts and judges, and the application of English law and procedure on American soil; secondly, through the direct contact of the colonies with the English tribunals, and especially with the Privy Council as an imperial supreme court for all Americans down to 1776; thirdly, through the legal literature of England, which has ever been regarded and utilized by the American bar as its own; and lastly, through adaptation from English models, begun in the Philadelphia Convention, and since continued by Congress in dealing with Article III. of the Constitution.[1]

[1] Taylor notes this well-known identity of the American and English judicial systems. "So far as [the American] judicial organization is concerned, there has been but a slight departure from the ancient original. Such differences as do exist are rather differences of detail than of organic structure. In both systems the unit of local judicial administration is the county, where all causes,

Not only is the judiciary system of the United States derived from that of England, but even the co-ordinate and independent place accorded to it in the threefold division of government, and so often thought a novelty, is taken from English and colonial antecedents. Referring to this, Sir Henry Maine observes: " It may be confidently laid down that neither the institution of a Supreme Court, nor the entire structure of the Constitution of the United States, were the least likely to occur to anybody's mind before the publication of the *Esprit des Lois.* . . . The *Federalist* regards the opinions of Montesquieu as of paramount authority, and no opinion had more weight with its writers than that which affirmed the essential separation of the executive, legislative, and judicial powers. The distinction is so familiar to us, except equity and probate causes, are tried in the first instance according to the course of English customary law, subject to review in a central appellate court modelled after the great courts at Westminster. It is not the ancient county court, however, that is the local centre of judicial administration. In America, as in England, the ancient county court is overshadowed by the itinerant, or circuit court, held periodically in every county by the itinerant or circuit judge sent to preside in local tribunals by State authority. In every assize or circuit court held where English law prevails, the jury of presentment and the trial jury enter as component parts into the structure of a tribunal which, in its modern form, is the special possession of the English race. Each colony started out by adopting the whole body of English statutory and customary law, so far as its principles could be adapted to their changed social and political conditions. By a perusal of the colonial codes, it is possible to trace the beginnings of the great work of adaptation, which has not yet eliminated all the obsolete elements of the ancient system." — *Origin and Growth of the English Constitution,* 47, 48.

that we find it hard to believe that even the different
nature of the executive and legislative powers was
not recognized till the fourteenth century; but it
was not till the eighteenth that the *Esprit des Lois*
made the analysis of the various powers of the state
part of the accepted political doctrine of the civilized
world. Yet, as Madison saw, Montesquieu was really
writing of England, and contrasting it with France. . . .
The fact was, that in the middle of the eighteenth century
it was quite impossible to say where the respective provinces of the French king, and of the French parliament
in legislature, and still more of the same authorities in
judicature, began and ended. To this indistinctness of
boundary Montesquieu opposed the considerable, but
yet incomplete, separation of the executive, legislative,
and the judicial powers in England, and he founded on
the contrast his famous generalization."[1]

But although this influence of Montesquieu in promot-
ing the independent relation of the judiciary in the
American Constitution is unquestionable, the Philadelphia Convention had before its eyes in this, as in other
matters, the colonial adaptation of English usage then existing in the States of which the new nation was composed.
And the testimony of the *Federalist* is exceedingly explicit on this point. For after stating reasons for an
independent judiciary, it continues : "These considerations teach us to applaud the wisdom of those States
which have committed the judicial power in the last

[1] *Popular Government*, 218–220.

resort, not to a part of the legislature, but to distinct and independent bodies of men. Contrary to the supposition of those who have represented the plan of the Convention in this respect as novel and unprecedented, it is but a copy of the constitutions of New Hampshire, Massachusetts, Pennsylvania, Delaware, Maryland, Virginia, North Carolina, South Carolina, and Georgia, and the preference which has been given to these models is highly to be commended." [1]

When the Convention assembled in Philadelphia, State courts were in vigorous operation, but nothing had yet been done to supply the place formerly occupied by the English Privy Council as a supreme court of appeal common to all the colonies. Under any truly national constitution a national judicature was a necessity, not only for ordinary affairs, but also for those national matters which in the days of colonial dependence had been dealt with by the courts of England.

What the Convention did, was to add to the State courts one national supreme tribunal, and there it stopped. Other classes of national courts were contemplated, but the creation of them was left to Congress. Article III. of the Constitution reads: "The judicial power of the United States shall be vested in one Supreme Court, and in such minor courts as the Congress may, from time to time, ordain and establish." [2]

---

[1] *Federalist*, No. 81.

[2] *Constitution of the United States*, Art. III. Sec. 1. Without discussion, the committee of the whole, in the Philadelphia Conven-

The present national courts of the United States are, therefore, the creation of the Constitution directly, in the instance of the Supreme Court, and indirectly, in that of the minor courts established under the provisions of Article III. These minor courts may be changed or added to by Congress as need arises. They consist at present of the circuit courts of appeal, the circuit and district courts, and the Court of Claims, as national tribunals, and the courts of the District of Columbia and of the territories as local courts under national control. The State courts are also employed for such national cases as they are capable of dealing with. By the present condition of the law, many cases within reach of the national judicial power are left wholly to the State courts, while in other cases, the State courts are allowed a jurisdiction concurrent with that of the Federal courts; their judgments on questions of Federal law being subject to final review in the national Supreme Court. The full purpose of the Federal jurisdiction is met, if the case,

tion, voted for a national judiciary to be composed of one Supreme Court and inferior courts. Later on, dissatisfaction was expressed, that in view of the fact that the States already possessed a full system of inferior courts, there should be forced upon them, in addition, a body of national inferior tribunals. Madison urged, however, that an effective judiciary establishment for the nation, commensurate with the national legislative authority, was essential. In this position he was sustained by Wilson and Dickinson. But the original motion was stricken out by a vote of six States to four. A compromise suggested by Dickinson was then agreed to, providing for the establishment of such minor courts as Congress should decide upon. —See Elliot, *Debates*, V. 155, 159, 160.

though heard first in a State court, may be removed, at
the option of the parties, for final decision in the Federal
courts.   Congress has consequently left the parties at
liberty, with few exceptions, to bring their suits in the
State courts, no matter what the questions involved.
But at the same time, it has protected the Federal
authority, by providing for a transfer to the Federal
courts, either before or after judgment, of all cases to
which the Federal judicial power extends.[1]

Not only do the State courts — successors of the
colonial courts — thus share in the national judicature,
but the national courts apply State law whenever applicable to cases coming before them.   And though the
nation itself has no common law, its courts constantly
administer the English common law of the States where
it is proper to do so.   In this way the law applied by
the national courts is, first of all, that of the Constitution and of enactments of Congress, and secondly
that which has grown up from English antecedents in
the original thirteen States, or which has been adopted
in the later States, formed more or less closely upon
the older models.   The jurisprudence regulating the

---

[1] As Robinson expresses it, " There is no hard and fast line divid-
ing the jurisdiction of the Federal courts from that of the State
courts." — *Publications of the American Academy of Political and
Social Science*, No. 9, p. 236.   This striking peculiarity of the
American judicial system — its *flexibility* — seems to have been
wholly missed by De Tocqueville.   He admits " ce qu'un étranger
comprend avec le plus de peine aux États-Unis, c'est l'organisa-
tion judiciare." — *Démocratie en Amérique* I. 163.

procedure and moulding the decrees of the American Supreme Court is English jurisprudence, and it has thus become a new source of both American and English law. The system of inferior Federal courts is essentially a reproduction of the English itinerant system of judicature. In both civil and criminal cases the Federal courts proceed according to the English customary law, while in equity and admiralty causes they cling with like tenacity to the general body of English jurisprudence.[1]

An impression that the Supreme Court was created to be the "guardian" of the Constitution, by interpreting it, has often called forth admiration for what has been regarded a most novel contrivance of the Philadelphia Convention. Even so acute a writer as Sir Henry Maine assures us, that "there is no exact precedent for it either in the ancient or in the modern world."[2] Yet words describing such a function of the court are not to be found in the Constitution itself, and the procedure which really exists is neither of recent date nor without historical precedent. In deciding constitutional questions, the Supreme Court interprets the law in accordance with principles that have long governed the courts of England. For when an English judge finds conflict between an act of Parliament and a judicial decision, he sets aside the decision, as of an authority inferior to that of the act; and if two parliamentary

[1] See *Origin and Growth of the English Constitution*, **74.**
[2] *Popular Government*, 218.

acts conflict, the earlier is set aside as superseded by
the later one, — the court interpreting the law, simply
by determining what *is* law as distinguished from what
is not.   The range of this English usage was somewhat
amplified in the colonies, owing to the fact, that instead
of Parliament, the colonial courts had legislatures to deal
with, which acted, in most instances, under written charters
limiting their powers, — as also under the general domination of the home government.   The colonial judiciary
did not hesitate to adjudge a local statute invalid, if
its enactment could be shown to have exceeded powers
conferred by charter, — and the Privy Council, in the
capacity of a supreme court for the colonies, decided
in like manner conflicts between laws.   When State
constitutions succeeded to the charters, the process
was continued by the State courts in cases showing conflict between statutes and the new constitutions judi-
cially interpreted.[1]   The national government, with a
constitution of its own, created an element of superior
law, in conflict with which not only State but national

---

[1] The first cases after the Revolution, in which legislative enactments were declared unconstitutional were those of *Trevett* v.
Weeden, in 1786, and *Bayard* v. *Singleton*, in 1789.   The first
mentioned was decided in Rhode Island, where the colonial charter still did service as the State constitution.   Cooley observes,
regarding it, that it "is worthy of note that the first case in which
a legislative enactment was declared unconstitutional and void, on
the ground of incompatibility with the constitution of the State,
was decided under one of these royal charters." — *Constitutional
Limitations*, 36, n. 1.

enactments of lesser authority are nullified.[1]   All that the judiciary does in England, and all that it does in the States, and in the courts of the United States, is to uphold the authority of what it decides to be the higher law, as against all lesser laws or judicial decisions.   What therefore has been supposed to be the most unique feature of the American Supreme Court is really only another adaptation from the past, and rests upon colonial and English precedents.[2]

[1] " Sir Henry Maine speaks of the Supreme Court as a ' virtually unique creation of the founders of the Constitution.'   But it is . . . unique rather in position than in form.   There were supreme courts in many of the States, forming a separate branch of government, with judges chosen for good behaviour, and, in one State at least, in the manner prescribed by the Federal Constitution. Even in respect to constitutional importance, we find a precedent in the State courts; for Gerry, in maintaining that ' the judiciary would have a sufficient check against encroachments on their own department by their exposition of the laws, which involved a power of deciding on their constitutionality,' reminded the Convention that ' in some States the judges had actually set aside laws as being against the constitution.' " — *Publications of the American Academy*, No. 9, p. 241.

[2] " There is a story told of an intelligent Englishman who, having heard that the Supreme Federal Court was created to protect the Constitution, and had authority given it to annul bad laws, spent two days in hunting up and down the Federal Constitution for the provisions he had been told to admire.   No wonder he did not find them, for there is not a word in the Constitution on the subject. . . .   The so-called ' power of annulling an unconstitutional statute ' is a duty rather than a power, and a duty incumbent on the humblest State court, when a case raising the point comes before it, no less than on the Supreme Federal Court at Washington. When, therefore, people talk, as they sometimes do, even in the

The judges of England receive their appointment from the sovereign. Judges of the Supreme Court of the United States are appointed by the President, with consent of the Senate, under the provisions of Article II. Section 2, and judges of inferior national courts in like manner, under the general clause of the same article, which empowers the executive to name " all other officers of the United States whose appointments are not herein otherwise provided for." [1]   In the Philadelphia Convention a proposition at first prevailed that the Supreme Court judges should be appointed by the Senate, but at a later session, upon the report of a committee, the present provision was adopted by unanimous vote.[2] The States, in more recent times, have made the

United States, of the Supreme Court, as 'the guardian of the Constitution,' they mean nothing more than that it is the final court of appeal, before which suits involving constitutional questions may be brought up by the parties for decision. In so far the phrase is legitimate. But the functions of the Supreme Court are the same in kind as those of all other courts, State as well as Federal. Its duty and theirs is simply to declare and apply the law; and where any court, be it a State court of first instance, or the Federal court of last instance, finds a law of lower authority clashing with a law of higher authority, it must reject the former, as being really no law, and enforce the latter." — *American Commonwealth*, I. 246, 247.

[1] *Constitution of the United States*, Art. II. Sec. 2.

[2] After the discussion in the Philadelphia Convention over the mode of appointing judges, and a preliminary decision that the Senate should have the power (see Elliot, *Debates*, V. 188), Mr. Gorham " suggested that the judges be appointed by the executive, with the advice and consent of the second branch, in the mode

office of judge depend very generally upon election by the legislature, or even by the people. But the national judges are still appointed by the executive.

By legal theory, as we have seen, English judges represent the sovereign in the dispensation of justice, and accordingly their commissions were formerly limited to such terms of office as the crown might prescribe. This control of tenure proved to be dangerous to public liberties, through liability of miscarriage of justice from political interest; and there were occasionally shameful compliances by judges with the wishes of the king, and involving flagrant violation of the rights of the subject. In the time of Lord Coke, Barons of the Exchequer were appointed to hold office during good behaviour, *i.e.* practically for life, — other judges still holding during royal pleasure. Until the accession of William and Mary, it was in the power of the sovereign to select which tenure he might prefer, — *durante bene placito*, or *quamdiu bene se gesserint*. The Act of Settlement of that reign stipulated, "that . . . judges' commissions be made *quamdiu se bene gesserint*, and their salaries ascertained and established, but upon the address of both houses of Parliament, it may be lawful to remove them."[1] Commissions were still held to expire at the

prescribed by the constitution of Massachusetts." This was finally agreed to, as having been "ratified by the experience of a hundred and forty years." See Elliot, *Debates*, V. 328, 330; *Constitution of Massachusetts*, 1780, Pt. II. Ch. II. Sec. 1, Art. IX.

[1] 13 Will. III. c. 2, III. 7. Campbell says: "It was not until after the Revolution of 1688, which placed Dutch William on the

king's death.   But one of the earliest acts of George III. was to complete the independence of the judiciary by providing that judges should remain in office during good behaviour, notwithstanding any demise of the crown, and that their full salaries should be secured during the continuance of their commissions.

In the Constitutional Convention at Philadelphia it was proposed to make judges removable by the Presi-

throne, that any permanent check was placed upon the power of removal; and it was not until the reign of George III. that the present system was introduced, under which judges hold office during good behaviour. All this was settled in the Dutch republic two centuries before. . . . The supreme judges of the High Court of Appeals at The Hague, nominated by the Senate, and confirmed by the Stadtholder, executed their functions for life, or so long as they conducted themselves virtuously in their high office." — *Puritan in Holland, England, and America*, II. 450. However this be, the fact remains, that America received these matters from and through England, whether William III. is concerned or George III. As to the action of George III., see *King's Message*, March 3d, 1761; 1 Geo. III. c. 23; Walpole, *Memoirs*, I. 41; Cook, *History of Party*, II. 400. A precedent in favour of the establishment of an independent judiciary long before the time of "Dutch William," is the statute of Alfonso V. of Aragon, in 1442, providing that judges should remain such for life, they being removable only on sufficient cause by the king and Cortes combined. See Prescott, *History of Ferdinand and Isabella*, I. 108, Intro. Sec. 2, p. 74, 5th ed., Lond. 1849. Was the Dutch usage influenced by Spain, through Spanish relation to the Netherlands?   We have sufficient light on the direct cause of action in the Philadelphia Convention, from the remark of Hamilton in the *Federalist*, No. 78, in which he says, speaking of tenure of judges during "good behaviour," that it was a thing "conformable to the most approved of the State constitutions."

dent upon the application of both houses of Congress. The circumstances, however, were not the same as those which gave rise to the similar provision in the Act of Settlement, and the proposition failed of adoption. The Constitution of the United States reads : " The judges both of the superior and inferior courts shall hold their offices during good behaviour, and shall at stated times receive for their services a compensation, which shall not be diminished during their continuance in office." [1]

[1] *Constitution of the United States*, Art. III. Sec. 1.   The *Federalist*, No. 79, notes that " in the general course of human nature, a power over a man's substance amounts to a power over his will." Chief Justice Taney in a letter of February 15, 1863, objected to a national tax applying to justices of the Supreme Court, because it was an unconstitutional diminution of their salaries.   This letter was recorded in the minutes of the Supreme Court by an order of the court of March 10, 1863.   See Tyler, *Life of Taney*, 432. Hamilton, in the *Federalist*, No. 78, points out that " the complete independence of the courts of justice is peculiarly essential in a limited constitution."   Story declares, with reference to compensation, " without this provision the other, as to tenure of office, would have been utterly nugatory, and, indeed, a mere mockery." — *Commentaries on Constitution of the United States*, II. 424, § 1628. Tucker, treating of this clause of the Constitution says : " Whatever has been said by Baron Montesquieu, De Lolme, or Judge Blackstone, or any other writer, on the security derived to the subject from the independence of the judiciary of Great Britain, will apply at least as forcibly to that of the United States.   We may go further.   In England, the judiciary may be overwhelmed by a combination between the executive and the legislature.   In America, . . . it is rendered absolutely independent of, and superior to, the attempts of both to control or to crush it.   First, by the tenure of office, which is during good behaviour; these words (by a long train of decisions in England, even as far back as the reign of

In Section 2, Article III., of the Constitution, are described the powers of the national judiciary. "The
judicial power shall extend to all cases, in law and equity,
arising under this Constitution, the laws of the United
States, and treaties made or which shall be made under
their authority ; to all cases affecting ambassadors, other
public ministers and consuls ; to all cases of admiralty
and maritime jurisdiction ; to controversies to which the
United States shall be a party ; to controversies between
two or more States ; between a State and the citizens
of another State ; between citizens of different States :
between citizens of the same State claiming lands under
grants of different States, and between a State, or the
citizens thereof, and foreign states, citizens, and subjects.

"In all cases affecting ambassadors, or other public
ministers and consuls, and those in which a State shall
be a party, the Supreme Court shall have original jurisdiction. In all other cases before mentioned the Supreme
Court shall have appellate jurisdiction, both as to law
and fact, with such exceptions, and under such regulation, as the Congress shall make." [1]

The very first words of this section, "the judicial power
shall extend to all cases," imposes upon the national

Edward III.) in all commissions and grants, public or private, im-
parting an office, or estate, for the life of the grantee, determinable
only by his death or breach of good behaviour. Secondly, by the
independence of the judges in respect of their salaries, which cannot be diminished," etc.—Tucker's Blackstone, *Commentaries*,
App. 353, 354.

[1] *Constitution of the United States*, Art. III. Sec. 2.

judges a mode of action which is of English origin. English courts decide the issue of actual disputes only, and never lay down a general proposition except as arising from a "case," brought before them for settlement.   The success of the Supreme Court of the United States is largely a result of following this method of determining questions of constitutionality and unconstitutionality.   The process is slower, but it is freer from chance of political pressure, and far less provocative of jealousy than would be the presentation of abstract and emergent political propositions to a judicial tribunal; and yet this latter process is what a European foreigner thinks of when he contemplates a court of justice deciding an alleged violation of a constitutional rule or principle.

Thus also the rest of the same sentence of this second section of Article III. refers to legal usages of the mother-land : "The judicial power shall extend to all cases in *law and equity*, arising under the Constitution, laws, and treaties of the United States, and treaties made or which shall be made under their authority." [1]

[1] *Constitution of the United States*, Art. III. Sec. 2.   "The equity jurisdiction of the courts of the United States is independent of the local law of any State, and is the same in nature and extent as the equity jurisdiction of England from which it is derived." — *Gordon* v. *Hobart*, Sumner, II. 401.

Mr. Justice Miller, of the United States Supreme Court, forcibly says : "Not only did the framers of the new Constitution follow as well as they might the general polity of the English system, but they . evinced an ardent desire to preserve the principles which had been accepted as part of the general administration of the law among our

Mr. Justice Story asks : " What is to be understood by
' cases in law and equity,' in this clause ?   Plainly, cases
at common law, as contradistinguished from cases in
equity, according to the known distinction in the jurisprudence of England, which our ancestors brought with
them upon their immigration, and with which all the
American States were familiarly acquainted.   Here, then,
at least, the Constitution of the United States appeals to,
and adopts the common law, to the extent of making it
a rule in the pursuit of remedial justice in the courts of
the Union.   If the remedy must be in law, or in equity,
according to the course of proceedings at the common
law in arising under the Constitution, laws, and treaties
of the United States, it would seem irresistibly to follow,

ancestors.   This is shown in many of the provisions of the Constitution.   Among others, the article concerning the judicial powers of
the new government, establishes its jurisdiction as extending to all
cases in admiralty, and in law, and in equity, thus recognizing the
English separation of these three classes of legal controversies as
being governed by a separate jurisdiction.   At least such has been
the construction placed upon the instrument by the courts of the
country without much question.   It has been repeatedly decided
that the jurisdiction in equity, which was a very peculiar one under
the English system of legal administration, remains in the courts of
the United States as it was at the time they separated from that
country, and that one of the distinctive features of the difference
between law and equity — namely, that at law there is a right to a
trial by jury, and in equity there is none — has continued to the present day." — *Lectures on Constitution*, 488.   Judge Cooley, referring
to modern English usages, points to the effect of the jurisdiction acts
of 1873 and 1875; and of change in usage in certain States of the
American Union.   Cooley's Blackstone, II. Bk. III. 454, n. 11.

that the principles of decision, by which these remedies must be administered, must be derived from the same source.   Hitherto such has been the uniform interpretation and mode of administrating justice in civil cases in the courts of the United States in this class of cases." [1]

The seemingly American characteristic of the jurisdiction of national courts over controversies between States, had its origin in the colonial custom, by which disputes between one colony and another — which frequently arose before the War of Independence — were adjudicated by the Privy Council.   Such a case between Massachusetts and New Hampshire was settled by the Privy Council in 1679, and one between New Hampshire and New York in 1764.   In the case of Pennsylvania *v.* Lord Baltimore, the jurisdiction involved was recognized by Lord Hardwicke in the most deliberate manner.   And Blackstone thus states the law of the time : " Whenever a question arises between two provinces in America or elsewhere, as concerning the extent of their charters and the like, the king in his council exercises original jurisdiction therein upon the principles of feudal sovereignty." [2]   It was to take the place of this former jurisdiction of the crown, that the Constitution provided, " In all cases . . . in which a State shall be party, the Supreme Court shall have original jurisdiction." [3]

---

[1] *Commentaries on the Constitution of the United States,* II. 436.

[2] *Commentaries,* I. 231.

[3] *Constitution of the United States,* Art. III. Sec. 2.   " In extending the Federal judicial power to cases between two or more States,

It may be said in general, that the subjects coming within the reach of the federal courts, and the method of dealing with them, are very largely of a character familiar to English law. Powers which inhere in the British, or were exercised in the colonial, courts, are put into operation by the present tribunals to the extent of their jurisdiction. Customary writs are issued. Forms and procedure bear abundant evidence of old moulding. In fact, notwithstanding elements of differentiation, the entire American judicial and legal system, both State and national, is so essentially and confessedly of English origin, that consideration in minute detail is superfluous.[1] Perhaps no proof could be more to the point, than that the *Commentaries* of Sir William Blackstone are still

the Convention followed the example of the Articles of Confederation, which, although establishing no courts, provided that the United States in Congress assembled should be the last resort on appeal in all disputes and differences between two or more States." — *Publications of the American Academy*, No. 9, p. 234.

[1] Douglas Campbell (*Puritan in Holland, England, and America*, I. 62) says of this: " As the colonies grew, their jurisprudence naturally developed with them, and after they became independent States, their development was much more rapid. New law was required to meet new conditions of society. Sometimes the want was supplied by enactments of the legislature, at others by what Bentham aptly called judge-made law, the creation of the courts. The result is, that the legal system of America has changed about as much in the last two centuries as the face of the country itself. In England, too, the same change has been going on, in much the same directions, and from the same causes." Yet even he admits (p. 63): "England and America have, to-day, much the same legal principles."

"the best book in which to take a comprehensive view of the rudiments of English and American law."[1] And this legal influence is not merely a thing of the past, but continuous. "It is one of the links which best serves to bind the United States to England. The interest of the higher class of American lawyers in the English law, bar, and judges is wonderfully fresh and keen. An English barrister, if properly authenticated, is welcomed as a brother of the art, and finds the law reports of his own country as sedulously read and as acutely criticised as he would in the Temple."[2]

Referring to the next chapter, the provision in Article III. for trial by jury in criminal cases, we may consider the law of treason, which concludes the Article. Of the action of the Convention regarding this law, Story remarks : "They have adopted the very words of the statute of treason of Edward III., and thus by implication, in order to cut off at once all chances of arbitrary constructions, they have recognized the well-settled interpretation of these phrases in the administration of criminal law which has prevailed for ages."[3] The English judges originally were left to determine for themselves, by rules of the common law, somewhat vague in character, what was treason and what was not. Injustice often

---

[1] Cooley's Blackstone, *Commentaries*, I., preface, p. v. This statement comes from the pen of the leading legal writer of the present day in the United States.

[2] Bryce, *American Commonwealth*, II. 491.

[3] *Commentaries on the Constitution of the United States*, II. 555, § 1799.

resulted. And complaints and petitions were put forth
from time to time by the House of Commons calling
attention to the abuse. Finally, in 1352, a petition was
presented, the royal reply to which, entitled " A Declaration which offences shall be adjudged treason," consti-
tutes the statute.[1] This law of Edward III. was altered
and enlarged in later reigns. And an amendment to it,
referring to witnesses, which has been incorporated in
the American Constitution, dates from 1552 in the time
of Edward VI., when, in consequence of complaint from
persons under trial, that they were unable to defend
themselves, because not allowed to meet their accusers,
it was enacted that no one should be indicted for treason
in future, save on the testimony of two witnesses who
should be brought into the presence of the accused at
the time of his trial, unless he should willingly confess
the charges.[2] The Constitution reads : "Treason against
the United States shall consist only in levying war against
them, or in adhering to their enemies, giving them aid
and comfort. No person shall be convicted of treason

---

[1] 25 Edw., St. 5, c. 2. The petition prayed that "whereas the
king's justices in different counties adjudge persons indicted before
them to be traitors for sundry matters not known by the commons
to be treason, it would please the king by his council, and by the
great and wise men of the land, to declare what are treasons, in this
present Parliament." In later reigns the law of treason was often
extended to offences not mentioned in this statute of Edward III.,
but to reduce the crime to the limits of the ancient statute was
always a popular measure. With some modifications, this is the
law at the present time.

[2] 5 and 6 Edw. VI. c. 11.

unless on the testimony of two witnesses to the same overt act, or on confession in open court." [1]

Article IV., which takes up the general subject of States and territories, in their relation to each other and to the Federal government, touches a variety of matters confessedly of English derivation ; and even the State system itself, which usually has been considered an American peculiarity, must be conceded to be only a natural and necessary outgrowth of the old political separation of colony from colony, and of union under the crown. Colony and State have remained the same in substance, whether the higher administration has been centred in London or in Washington. And the identical principle is still in operation in the clusters of colonies of Canada, South Africa, and Australia, and has its analogies in the general structure of the British empire.

The concluding articles — the fifth, treating of amendments ; the sixth, detailing sundry matters of routine relating to the establishment of the Constitution itself ; and the seventh, providing for the ratification of that instrument — need not be dwelt upon, save as to points

[1] *Constitution of the United States*, Art. III. Sec. 3. "The interpretation of the phrases, 'levying war' and 'adhering to their enemies,' is a matter wholly for the court. The court is, then, empowered to defend the individual against prosecutions for any extraordinary treasons which Congress might attempt to construct." Burgess, *Political Science and Constitutional Law*, II. 148. See also *Hanauer* v. *Doane*, United States Reports, 12 Wallace, 342; *Ex parte Bollman* v. *Swartwout*, United States Reports, 4 Cranch, 75; *Carlisle* v. *United States*, United States Reports, 16 Wallace, 147.

which will come up in connection with kindred topics in
the next chapter.[1]

[1] Reference has already been made in this book to Douglas
Campbell's *Puritan in Holland, England, and America.* The
fact admitted by Mr. Campbell, that historians take a position
entirely at variance with his, seems not to have deterred him from
setting up a claim for Dutch influence in America; which claim, in
most of its particulars, must continue to lack the support of historians. A conspicuous feature, giving the key to the whole of his
work, is an argument in the introduction, intended to demonstrate
that American governmental institutions are not of English derivation. He says: " Instead of those of the United States being
derived from England, it is a curious fact, that while we have in the
main English social customs and traits of character, we have scarcely
a legal or political institution of importance which is of English
origin, and but few which have come to us by the way of England."
— I. 11. In proof of this astonishing assertion he proceeds, after
referring to certain religious and social matters, to illustrate by speci-
fying characteristics of the American Constitution. Let us briefly
look at these characteristics.

(1) Mr. Campbell intimates, that as the English Constitution is
unwritten, Americans could not have got a written constitution
from England; and seems to imply that they therefore got it from
the Dutch, who had a written compact in the Union of Utrecht, of
which he says much. Of course, nowhere in his work does he show
American continuity from this imagined Dutch original. And he
wholly ignores the real origin of written constitutions in America;
viz. the English charters granted by English sovereigns to English
subjects. These latter, with the English political usage growing up
under them, formed, as we have seen, the constitutions of colonial
days. All the States save Connecticut and Rhode Island, framed
the first State constitutions accordingly, — those two States retaining
the old charters, even into the nineteenth century. The national
Constitution, as a written document, is based on the written constitutions of the States, as these in turn were based on the written
English charters. And the latter had their source in English trade
charters, and not in any Dutch original whatsoever.

(2) He intimates that the American executive office is not of English derivation, because the President is a personal executive, and the English sovereign of to-day is controlled by a cabinet. In this he strangely confuses historical facts, and leaves altogether out of view the real evolution, through the colonial governorship and otherwise, from the older English kingship before the establishment of the Cabinet system.

(3) He intimates that the American Congress is not of English derivation, because the House of Lords of to-day has powers differing in some degree from those of the Senate, and the latter body is, in part, an executive or privy council; and because further a member of the House of Representatives is paid, and has a term of membership differing as to duration from that of a member of the House of Commons. Surely no serious answer need be accorded to arguments so trivial, in view of the fact of legislative evolution in organization, privileges, and power, traced in the foregoing Chapters III. and IV.

(4) Mr. Campbell says that "above all in America . . . sits the Supreme Court to see that the Constitution . . . is preserved intact. Its judges are appointed by the President and confirmed by the Senate, but they hold office for life or good behaviour." The foregoing chapter shows how far this can be claimed as proof that the American judicial system is not of English and Anglo-colonial evolution. He adds: "These features make up the peculiarities of the American Federal system, and differentiate it from other forms of government. All nations have an executive of some kind, most of them have judges and legislative bodies, so that in these general outlines there is nothing on which to base a theory of English origin. The question is whether our peculiar institutions, those distinctive of America, are derived from the 'mother-country.'" That is, of course, the sole question. And the aim of the present book — written before Mr. Campbell's appeared — has been to definitely settle the question in the affirmative, by the appeal to history.

CHAPTER VIII.

THE BILL OF RIGHTS.

THE English common law, which lies at the basis of English and American liberties, is the growth of centuries, and its maxims breathe the very spirit of the race. It is that "law of the land," to which the Magna Charta of King John referred for the guarantee of personal rights; and its essential principles are interwoven with the Petition of Rights of Charles I., and the Bill of Rights and Act of Settlement of the Revolution of 1688. So far as applicable to American conditions, "it was brought over by our ancestors," says Chancellor Kent, "upon their first emigration to this country."[1] And the royal

---

[1] "The common law of England, so far as it was applicable to our circumstances, was brought over by our ancestors upon their emigration to this country. The Revolution did not involve in it any abolition of the common law. It was rather calculated to strengthen and invigorate all the first principles of that law, suitable to our state of society and jurisprudence. It has been adopted, or declared in force, by the constitutions of some of the States, and by statute in others. And where it has not been so explicitly adopted, it is nevertheless to be considered as the law of the land, subject to the modifications which have been suggested, and to express legislative repeal."—Kent, *Commentaries on American Law*, II. 2S.

charters included it in their provision, that Englishmen
in the colonies should be entitled to the same privileges
as Englishmen at home.[1]

Formal declarations of rights, drawn from the common
law, were incorporated in the earliest colonial legislation.
Plymouth Colony, in the first of these, enumerated, among
other privileges, that justice should be impartially and
promptly administered, with trial by jury, and that no
person should suffer in life, limb, liberty, good name, or
estate, but by due process of law.[2] Connecticut, in 1639,
adopted an act closely similar. New York enacted, in
1691, that no freeman should be deprived of any rights,
or liberties, or condemned, save by the judgment of his
peers, or the law of the land ; that no tax should be levied
except by act of the legislature in which the colonists

---

[1] Kent summarizes the facts thus: "It was a provision in the
charters of the Virginia settlers granted by James I. in 1606 and
1609, and in the charter to the colonists of Massachusetts in 1629;
of the Province of Maine in 1639; of Connecticut in 1662; of
Rhode Island in 1663; of Maryland in 1632; of Carolina in 1663;
and of Georgia in 1732; that they and their posterity should enjoy
the same rights and liberties which Englishmen were entitled to at
home.   Such privileges were implied by the law, without any
express reservation.   The like civil and religious privileges were
conceded to New Jersey by the proprietaries in February, 1665."
— *Commentaries on American Law*, 12th ed. II. 2, n.

[2] "They insisted that they brought with them into this country
the privileges of English freemen, and they defined and declared
those privileges with a caution, sagacity, and precision that have not
been surpassed by their descendants.   Those rights were afterwards, in the year 1692, on the receipt of their new charter, reasserted and declared." — *Ibid.* II. 2.

were represented ; that trial by jury should be maintained, and that in all criminal cases there should be previous indictment by a grand inquest. Though the king repealed this act, another, of like import, was adopted in 1708.[1] Massachusetts, in 1641, promulgated a Body of Liberties, the first paragraph of which reads : " No man's life shall be taken, no man's honour or good name shall be stained, no man's person shall be arrested, restrained. banished, dismembered, nor anyways punished, no man shall be deprived of his wife or children, no man's goods or estate shall be taken away or anyway endangered under colour of law or countenance of authority, unless it be by virtue or equity of some express law of the country warranting the same, established by the General Court and sufficiently published, or in case of the defect of the law in any particular case, by the Word of God. and in capital cases, or in cases concerning dismembering or banishment, according to that word to be judged by the General Court." In like manner, declaration of rights was made by the legislature of Virginia in 1624 and 1676 ; by the legislature of Pennsylvania in 1682 ; of Maryland in 1639 and 1650 ; and of Rhode Island in 1663 ; and also by the proprietaries of Carolina in 1667, and of New Jersey in 1664, 1683, and at other dates. In 1638 the first assembly of Maryland declared Magna Charta to be the measure of their liberties.

The whole subject of privileges was forced into special prominence by the outbreak of the constitutional struggle

---

[1] *Laws of New York*, 1708.

between the colonies and England. And so it was that the congress of delegates from nine colonies, which met in New York in 1765, issued a general declaration of rights; and that a further and more formal pronouncement of the same character was put forth by the first Continental Congress in 1774. The latter became the basis of the bills of rights which eventually were incorporated into the constitutions of the new States. It declared "that the inhabitants of the English colonies in North America, by the immutable laws of nature, the principles of the English Constitution, and their several charters or compacts, were entitled to life, liberty, and property; and that they had never ceded to any sovereign power whatever a right to dispose of either, without their consent; that their ancestors, who first settled the colonies, were, at the time of their emigration from the mother-country, entitled to all the rights, liberties, and immunities of free and natural born subjects; and by such emigration they by no means forfeited, surrendered, or lost any of those rights; that the foundation of English liberty, and of all free government, was the right of the people to participate in the legislative power, and they were entitled to a free and exclusive power of legislation in all matters of taxation and internal policy, in their several provincial legislatures, where their right of representation could alone be preserved; that the respective colonies were entitled to the common law of England, and more especially to the great and inestimable privilege of being tried by their peers of the vicinity, according to the course of that law ; that they were entitled to the benefit of such English statutes as existed at the time of their colonization, and which they had by experience found to be applicable to their several local and other circumstances ; that they were likewise entitled to all the immunities and privileges granted and confirmed to them by royal charters, or secured by their several codes of provincial laws." [1]

It was widely anticipated by the public that the national Constitution drafted at Philadelphia would contain a full enumeration of such ancient rights. The members of the Convention seem not to have appreciated the force of this popular feeling ; considering that as the people themselves now possessed the power of making their own laws and of selecting those who should execute them, specific announcement of privileges which had grown out of old controversies with the crown was unnecessary. Sufficient provision was made in the body of the Constitution for taxation by the legislature only, for judgment in cases of impeachment, for the privilege of the writ of *habeas corpus*, for trial by jury in criminal cases, for the definition, trial, and punishment of treason with limitation of historical abuses in such connection, for the prohibiting of bills of attainder, *ex-post facto* laws, and laws impairing the obligation of contracts or imposing religious tests.[2] All these were so many declarations of rights

---

[1] *Journals of Congress*, I. ed., Phila. 1800.

[2] Regarding attainder and *ex-post facto* laws, Mr. Justice Miller remarks : " The prohibition against passing bills of attainder is one

for the protection of the citizens, not exceeded in value
by any which could possibly find a place in any bill of

which was intended to guard against a danger which has passed
out of the memory of the present generation.   Up to the time of
the formation of this Constitution, the Parliament of England had
been in the habit, by legislative enactments, of declaring individuals
attainted for treason, for murder, for conspiracies, and further
crimes, especially crimes against the government.   This declaration
of attainder by the legislative body was accompanied, either im-
pliedly, or by the express terms of the bill, with a deprivation of all
rights of property and of all capacity to transmit property by descent, or acquire it in that manner, in addition to punishments
such as death and other cruelties.   This kind of proceeding was
had, not in a court of justice, . . . but the legislature, the Parliament, either with or without inquiry, or with such insufficient inquiry as they chose to make, generally in the absence of the victim,
proceeded at once to make charges, decide upon the guilt of the
party, and announce the punishment, thus acting in all instances
as the sovereign, the legislative, and judicial power at the same time.

It was at one time suggested that *ex-post facto* laws, "equally
forbidden to the general government and to the States, might be
held to be any law which affected the rights of a person civilly or
criminally after those rights had been acquired or established in
accordance with existing laws.   This, however, is a mistake, and
the phrase '*ex-post facto* laws' has application alone to laws which
relate to crimes and criminal proceedings, because it was used in
that limited sense by our English ancestors long previous to the
formation of the Constitution.   The contemporary accounts of its
adoption show that such was the sense in which the Convention
understood it." — *Lectures on the Constitution of the United States,*
584–586.   The Supreme Court of the United States has decided for
this interpretation, in cases which have come before it, affirming
the English origin, as it constantly does in its decisions on constitutional and legal questions.   See *Calder* v. *Bull*, 3 Dall. 386;
Watson v. *Mercer*, 8 Pet. 88, 110; *Satterlee* v. *Matthewson*, 2 Pet.
380; *Kring* v. *Missouri*, 107 U. S. 221.

rights.[1] But as soon as the draft of the Constitution left the Convention, the lack of a formal bill was severely and persistently criticised by the people. And the promise that one should be added, as soon as the new government actually got under way, was found necessary in order to induce some of the principal States to ratify the instrument. The first ten amendments, therefore, were adopted as speedily as possible by the first Congress and the nation ; and to all intents they are to be regarded as a part of the Constitution in its original unity, as a product of the formative period.[2] Their position in this respect is essentially different from that of the amendments which are the outcome of subsequent national experience.

Thus there is not only a bill of rights in the Constitution of the United States, but that bill of rights was consciously demanded by the American people themselves against the judgment of their own Constitutional

---

[1] See *Federalist*, No. 84.

[2] " With a view of carrying into effect popular will, and also of disarming the opponents of the Constitution of all reasonable grounds of complaint, Congress, at its very first session, took into consideration the amendments so proposed; and by a succession of supplementary articles provided, in substance, a bill of rights, and secured by constitutional declarations most of the other important objects thus discussed " in the conventions of the States that adopted the Constitution. "These articles (in all twelve) were submitted by Congress to the States for their ratification, and ten of them were finally ratified by the requisite number of States, and thus became incorporated into the Constitution." — Story, *Commentaries on the Constitution of the United States*, I. 211, § 303.

Convention, and for the express reason that they regarded the liberties included therein as their liberties, because based upon old English law.

Let us take up consecutively these ten amendments. The first reads : " Congress shall make no law respecting an establishment of religion, or prohibiting the free exercise thereof; or abridging the right of the people peaceably to assemble, and to petition the government for a redress of grievances."[1]

The first clause of the amendment treats of the right of religious liberty, — a right the daughter-land was before the mother-country in establishing. The English Toleration Act of 1688[2] granted privileges to dissenters, which their active share in seating William of Orange on the throne was thought to have earned ; and though far from according religious freedom, it laid foundation for the future. Reactionary statutes passed in the latter part of the reign of Queen Anne were repealed in the early years of the House of Hanover ;[3] and from the accession of George II. dissenters were admitted to civil offices.[4] The laws against Roman

---

[1] In Charles Pinckney's " Plan " of a federal constitution, submitted to the Philadelphia Convention, was the following: " The legislature of the United States shall pass no law on the subject of religion, nor touching or abridging the liberty of the press." The amendment embraces recommendations of the conventions of New Hampshire, Virginia, and North Carolina.

[2] 1 Will. and Mary, c. 18.

[3] 5 Geo. 1. c. 4.

[4] This was done by means of the Annual Indemnity Acts passed in favour of those who had not qualified themselves under the Cor-

Catholics, also, were gradually softened in operation.[1]
Early in the reign of George III. modern principles
of toleration were enunciated in a judicial decision
of the Lords,[2] on which occasion Lord Mansfield declared, in moving the judgment of the House : "There
is nothing certainly more unreasonable, more inconsistent
with the rights of human nature, more contrary to the
spirit and precepts of the Christian religion, more iniqui-
tous and unjust, more impolitic, than persecution.   It
is against natural religion, revealed religion, and sound
policy."[3]   Regulations relating to dissent became more
and more relaxed.   And on the verge of the adoption
of the American Constitution, measures for the relief
of both Roman Catholics and Protestants were passed ;
and these were followed by a series of acts which
eventually removed all civil disabilities.

Of the condition of things in the colonies, Green
thus speaks : " Europe saw, for the first time, a state
growing up amid the forests of the west, where religious freedom had become complete.   Religious tol-

----

poration and Test Acts.   The first Indemnity Act was passed in
1727.   With few exceptions, similar acts were passed every year
thereafter, until the Test and Corporation Acts were repealed
in 1828.

[1] 1 Geo. I. c. 55, and 26 Geo. II. c. 33.

[2] *Chamberlain of London* v. *Allen Evans, Esq.*

[3] Cobbett, *Parliamentary History*, XVI. 313–327.   Among the
strong sayings of Lord Mansfield in this connection was the remark :
" Persecution for a sincere, though erroneous, conscience, is not to
be deduced from reason or the fitness of things."

eration had, in fact, been brought about by a medley
of religious faiths such as the world had never seen
before. New England was still a Puritan stronghold.
In the southern colonies the Episcopal Church was
established by law, and the bulk of the settlers clung
to it; but Roman Catholics formed a large part of the
population of Maryland. Pennsylvania was a State of
Quakers. Presbyterians and Baptists had fled from
tests and persecutions to colonize New Jersey. Luther-
ans and Moravians from Germany abounded among
the settlers of Carolina and Georgia. In such a chaos
of creeds, religious persecution became impossible."[1]

The boast was wont to be made, that the Puritans
of New England led the way in establishing by law
religious toleration. A similar claim is still put forth on
behalf of the Baptists of Rhode Island. Truth must
award the honour to Maryland, where action proceeded
from a combination of Roman Catholic and non-Roman
Catholic conditions.[2] This action of Maryland took

---

[1] *History of the English People*, V. 216.

[2] Douglas Campbell (*Puritan in Holland, England, and
America*) claims that religious liberty in America was of Dutch
origin; apparently on the ground that it existed in the Netherlands
at an early date. But he does not include Maryland in the sphere
of Dutch influence. And, in fact, the action in Maryland seems
to have had quite a different origin. Possibly Dutch example may
have had indirect influence elsewhere. Roger Williams, in establishing religious toleration in Rhode Island, was influenced not
improbably by the Dutch Anabaptists.

"Religious tolerance which prevailed in colonial Maryland, so
much vaunted, and so often contrasted with the narrow intolerance

place in 1649, and that of Rhode Island in 1663. In
the next year the proprietaries granted to the colonists
of New Jersey the widest toleration. Enactments
known as the Duke's Laws, issued in 1665 by an
assembly which met on Long Island at the call of
Governor Nichol, declared that no person professing
a belief in Christianity should be molested for his
judgment in matters of religion.[1] The same principles
were again promulgated in 1665, in the charter of
liberties established by the assembly, acting under the
Duke of York.[2] Charles II., in his charter of 1667,

common in New England, was evidently dictated by worldly prudence, rather than prompted by an advanced charity. It must be
remembered that at that time, the feeling in England was bitterly
hostile to the Papists, and that the grant of lands to Lord Baltimore
was from a Protestant monarch, and of a portion of the territory
claimed by Virginia, a Protestant colony. Considerations of prudence also forbade exciting the animosity of the Puritan colonies of
New England. Obviously, therefore, Lord Baltimore, whatever
might have been his disposition, could not, with safety, have founded
his new settlement upon a basis of intolerance." — Crane and
Moses, *Politics*, 119. However this may be, the claim of a Dutch
origin for religious toleration in America is unhistorical. The
honour belongs to Maryland.

[1] Thompson, *History of Long Island*, I. 132, ed. 1843.

[2] Douglas Campbell observes: "Of all the thirteen [original
States], two and two only — Virginia and New York — embodied
in their [new State constitutions] guarantees of religious liberty. . . .
The other States retained religious tests for their officials, or in some
form made religious discriminations. Virginia, in 1776, issued a
Declaration of Rights, which, it is claimed, formed part of her
constitution, laying down the principle " of religious liberty. " Still
the State retained its established Church until 1785, and in various

authorized the proprietaries of Carolina to accord religious liberty to non-conformists who did not by their non-conformity disturb the civil peace of the province. Massachusetts, in 1691, passed an act benefiting all but Roman Catholics; and the Quaker, William Penn, gave his colony, ten years later, a law guaranteeing freedom of conscience. Toleration similar to that of Massachusetts was provided in the charter granted by George II. to Georgia in 1732.

Thus when the Constitution of the United States was formulated, the principle of religious freedom had been for some time gathering strength. Partly from this cause, and probably yet more from the fact that no one Christian body was in sufficient numerical predominance to make an ecclesiastical establishment of it for the nation a political possibility, it was enacted; " Congress shall make no law respecting an establishment of religion,

other ways fell short of practising full religious liberty. New York, however, in its first constitutions adopted in 1777, proceeded at the outset to do away with the established Church. . . . Then followed a section much broader and more explicit than that of the Virginia Declaration of Rights." — *Puritan in Holland, England, and America*, I. 250. This author claims that the New York constitutional enactment is the basis of American religious liberty, and because it was an enactment of New York, gratuitously assumes it to be of Dutch origin, — though in truth it was but a logical outcome of the laws of the Duke of York, 1665, adopted under English influence. So far as the American Constitution is concerned, the first amendment seems to have originated in the draft of Mr. Charles Pinckney of South Carolina, proposed in the Philadelphia Convention. See Elliot, *Debates*, V. 131. See also action of New Hampshire convention.

or prohibiting the free exercise thereof."[1] In Article VI.
of the Constitution it had been laid down already : " No
religious test shall ever be required as a qualification
to any office or public trust under the United States,"
a reference to the English Test Act of 1673.[2]

The next provision in Article I. of the amendments
relates to freedom of public utterance and the press.
The invention of printing in the fifteenth century brought
with it a censorship, which was in the hands of the ecclesiastical power throughout Europe. After the Reformation,
this censorship devolved, in England, upon the crown ;
and a licenser was regularly appointed whose imprima-
tur was required for the lawful publication of any writing.
Printing was regulated further by royal proclamations
and grants of privilege.[3] The unlicensed issue of anything
deemed seditious or slanderous was punished by mutila-
tion and death.[4] And in the reigns of the first two

---

[1] *Constitution of the United States, Amendment I.*

[2] 25 Car. II. c. 2. The famous Test Act was passed " for preventing dangers which may happen from Popish recusants." It
worked much injustice.

[3] " All printing was interdicted elsewhere than in London, Oxford, and Cambridge; and nothing whatever was allowed to be
published until it had first been 'seen, perused, and allowed' by
the Archbishop of Canterbury, or the Bishop of London, except
only publications by the queen's printer, to be appointed for some
special service, or by the law printers, for whom the license of the
Chief Justices was sufficient." — Taswell-Langmead, *English Constitutional History,* 766.

[4] St. 23 Eliz. c. 2. See cases of Stubbe, 1579; Udal, 1591;
Barrow and Greenwood, 1593; Penry, 1593.

Stuarts, political and religious discussion was vigorously repressed by the Star Chamber. The Long Parliament used the weapon of censorship on the lines laid down by that obnoxious court, with such severity as to call forth from John Milton the *Areopagitica,* denouncing the suppression of truth by a licenser, and appealing for " the liberty to know, to utter, and to argue freely according to conscience, above all liberties." [1] After the Restoration, the Licensing Act, based upon the former parliamentary ordinances, was established for a period of three years, placing the regulation of printing in the control of the government of Charles II. [2] The act was continued by repeated renewals until 1679 ; [3] and was

---

[1] Milton, *Areopagitica,* 73, 74, *Arber's Reprints.*   In the British Museum are over 30,000 political newspapers and pamphlets that were printed in the twenty years between 1640 and the Restoration of Charles II.   Douglas Campbell notes that Milton in no way refers to Holland or to Dutch ideas in advocating liberty of the press.   *Puritan in Holland, England, and America,* II. 344, n. 2.

[2] 13 and 14 Car. II. c. 33.

[3] " After the Licensing Act had been temporarily suffered to expire in 1679, the twelve judges, with Chief-Justice Scroggs at their head, declared it to be criminal at common law to publish anything concerning the government, whether true or false, of praise or censure, without the royal license.   All newspapers were in consequence stopped; and the people were reduced, for political intelligence and instruction, to two government publications. . . . In the absence of newspapers, the coffee-houses became the chief organs through which the public opinion of the metropolis vented itself, while the inhabitants of provincial towns, and the great body of the gentry and country clergy, depended almost exclusively on news-letters from London for their knowledge of political events." — Taswell-Langmead, *English Constitutional History,* 768.

reaffirmed in 1685 by James II. for a term of seven years, and again, in 1692, by William and Mary. Efforts further to revive it proved unsuccessful, and it expired in 1694. From the latter date censorship has formed no part of English law.[1] This emancipation, having such vast results in later times, attracted slight attention at the moment. And in fact, though theoretically free, the press was still molested not a little. It steadily rose in influence, and in the first thirty years of George III. attained the beginnings of its present greatness.[2]

The last clause of Amendment I. deals with the right of petition. For many generations the exercise of the right was practically limited to redress of grievances, but

[1] Lord Macaulay declared that the emancipation of the press had "done more for liberty and for civilization than the Great Charter or the Bill of Rights." — *History of England*, IV. 542.

[2] It is not impossible that the example of Holland has aided the progress in America of the idea of freedom of the press. But although Douglas Campbell (*Puritan in Holland, England, and America*) strenuously asserts that Holland's example has so aided, he signally fails to establish the point, and no one else has really attempted to establish it. As a matter of fact, censorship of the press existed in the American colonies. In New England this lasted till about 1755. See Tyler, *History of American Literature*, I. 113. Thus, in 1723, Benjamin Franklin was forced to leave Massachusetts for Pennsylvania on account of a libel, and his brother was imprisoned. A declaration of the principle of entire freedom of publication was incorporated in the second constitution of Pennsylvania, in 1790, only just previous to the amendment to the national Constitution referred to in the text. This action of Pennsylvania distinctly referred to English laws and usage. In 1805 and in 1821 New York recognized this principle. Other States have made similar provisions.

just before the time of the Commonwealth, petitions on political subjects came into being, and many such were presented to Charles I. and to the Long Parliament. There was some intimidation by numerous bodies of petitioners, during that stormy period, and it was probably the memory of this that caused Charles II. to restrain, or rather to regulate, the right in such manner as to protect the government. In the Bill of Rights of William and Mary, the privilege received sanction in the declaration : " It is the right of the subject to petition the king ; and all commitments and prosecutions for such petitioning are illegal." [1] The present practice dates from 1779, just previous to the establishment of the American Constitution, when a widely organized attempt was made to procure the adoption of a certain measure in Parliament, by presenting numerously signed petitions from every part of England. This may properly be considered the beginning of the modern system of petitioning by which public measures and matters of public policy have been urged upon the attention of Parliament. The privilege came into special prominence in the colonies at the Revolutionary epoch, the Congress of 1774 distinctly claiming it in the Declaration of Rights : "They [the colonists] have a right peaceably to assemble, consider grievances, and petition the king, and that all prosecutions prohibiting proclamations and commitments for the same are illegal." [2]

The second amendment deals with the question of a

---

[1] 1 Will. and Mary, Sess. 2, c. 2.   [2] *Eighth Resolution.*

trained militia, and the right of the people to bear arms,
— a right involving the latent power of resistance to
tyrannical government.   From prehistoric days right to
bear arms seems to have been the badge of a Teutonic
freeman, and closely associated with his political privileges.   Such armed freemen made up the military host
of the tribe.   During Saxon times in England, there was
a fyrd, or national militia,[1] service in which was one of
the three duties — *trinoda necessitas* — to which every
alodial proprietor was subject.   This is met in full vigour
long after the Norman Conquest, working its way through
the superstratum of feudalism.   It continued side by
side with the feudal system, until, under Henry III. and
Edward I., the two were united in a general national
armament.   By the law known as the Assize of Arms,
in 1181, every freeman was required to provide himself
with a doublet of mail, iron skull-cap, and lance.   In the
reign of Queen Mary, this law was altered to provide for
arms of a more modern sort.[2]   James I. abrogated it.[3]
But although the militia languished for awhile, as the
standing army grew in efficiency, it was restored to vigour
in 1757.   The Bill of Rights provided : "The subjects
which are Protestants may have arms for their defence,
suitable to their conditions, and as allowed by law."[4]

[1] The *fyrd*, the armed folkmoot of each shire, was originally the
only military organization known to the English.

[2] 4 and 5 Phil. and Mary, c. 2 and c. 3.

[3] 1 Jac. c. 25, § 46.

[4] 1 Will. and Mary, Sess. 2, c. 2.   Blackstone remarks that this
declaration providing for the possession of arms "is a public al-

Upon this is based the second amendment to the Constitution, which reads: "A well-regulated militia being necessary for the security of a free state, the right of the people to keep and bear arms shall not be infringed."[1] And concerning it, Judge Cooley remarks: "It was adopted, with some modification and enlargement, from the English Bill of Rights of 1688, where it stood as a protest against arbitrary action of the late dynasty in disarming the people, and as a pledge of the new rulers, that this tyrannical action should cease. The right declared was meant to be a strong moral check against the usurpation of arbitrary power by rulers, and as a necessary and efficient means of regaining rights temporarily overturned by usurpation."[2]

The third amendment deals with the quartering of the troops on private citizens, a provision which speaks for itself, and the object of which is to secure the enjoyment

lowance, under due restrictions, of the natural right of resistance and self-preservation, when the sanction of society and the laws are found insufficient to restrain the violence of oppression." — *Commentaries*, I. 154.

[1] The convention of New Hampshire which acted on the adoption of the national Constitution, proposed as an amendment: "Congress shall never disarm any citizen, unless such as are, or have been, in actual rebellion." The conventions of Virginia and New York proposed: "That the people have a right to keep and bear arms; that a well-regulated militia, composed of the body of the people, trained to arms, is the proper, natural, and safe defence of a free state"; and "that any person religiously scrupulous of bearing arms, ought to be exempted, upon payment of an equivalent to employ another in his stead."

[2] *Principles of Constitutional Law*, 270.

of the great right of the common law, that a man's house
shall be his castle, privileged against civil and military
intrusion.   Among the tyrannies objected to in the Petition of Right of the time of Charles I. is, that "of late
great companies of soldiers and mariners have been dis-
persed into divers counties of the realm, and the inhabitants, against their wills, have been compelled to receive
them into their houses, and there to suffer them to
sojourn, against the laws and customs of this realm, and
to the great grievance and vexation of the people." [1]
By a law of Charles II. it was enacted "that no officer,
military or civil, or other persons shall quarter or billet
any soldier upon any inhabitant of this realm, without
his consent, and that every such inhabitant of this realm
may refuse to quarter any soldier, notwithstanding any
order whatsoever." [2]   Nevertheless, a complaint is to be
found in the Bill of Rights, that James II. had violated
fundamental liberties of the realm by, among other
things, "quartering soldiers contrary to law," [3] and a similar complaint against both king and Parliament is recorded
in the Declaration of Independence : " He [George III.]
has combined with others . . . giving his assent to their
pretended legislation, for quartering large bodies of

[1] 3 Car. I. c. 1, § 6.
[2] 31 Car. II. c. 1.
[3] 1 Will. and Mary, Sess. 2, c. 2.   The provisions of this statute and of the Petition of Right against the billeting of troops
are suspended every year by authority of Parliament, in the Mutiny
Act, which accords express permission to billet soldiers in inns and
victualling-houses.

armed troops among us." The language of the constitutional amendment is: "No soldier shall, in time of peace, be quartered in any house without the consent of the owner, nor in time of war, but in a manner to be prescribed by law."

The fourth amendment touches upon the question of protection against civil search without formal warrant, and the subject of general warrants.

The warrant — the paper which authorizes so grave an act as depriving a citizen of personal liberty — is necessarily surrounded with safeguards to protect the private individual against unjust and arbitrary police measures. The English race has been insistent with reference to these safeguards, and the warrant, as we now have it, is a characteristically English institution. A warrant must always name the person against whom it is directed. A general warrant, *i.e.* one that does not name the person, is contrary to English freedom.[1] But the latter point was not established until just before the American Revolution, — the illegal custom of the arresting of persons on general warrants lingering even into the reign of George III., when it received its death blow in the famous case of Wilkes. The question was raised by the printing of the libellous Number Forty-Five of the *North Briton*, the authorship of which was at first unknown. Lord Halifax, one of the secretaries of state, issued a general warrant describing no individual, but empowering the police to take whomever they might think guilty ; which resulted in

[1] See Lieber, *Civil Liberty and Self-Government*, 62.

the arrest of many innocent persons, and finally, among
them, of the culprit himself, — with seizure of his papers.[1]
He resisted on the ground that he had not been described
in the warrant. And after litigation which aroused the
excited sympathy of both England and the colonies, he
won legal decision in his favour, and obtained damages

---

[1] "There was a libel, but who was the libeller? Ministers knew
not, nor waited to inquire, after the accustomed forms of law; but
forthwith, Lord Halifax, one of the secretaries of state, issued a
warrant, directing four messengers, taking with them a constable,
to search for the authors, printers, and publishers, and to apprehend
and seize them, together with their papers, and bring them in safe
custody before him. No one having been charged or even suspected, no evidence of crime having been offered, no one was
named in this dread instrument. The offence only was pointed at;
not the offender. The magistrate, who should have sought proofs
of crime, deputed this office to his messengers. Armed with their
roving commission, they set forth in quest of unknown offenders;
and unable to take evidence, listened to rumours, idle tales, and
curious guesses. They held in their hands the liberty of every man
whom they were pleased to suspect. Nor were they triflers in their
work. In three days they arrested no less than forty-nine persons
on suspicion, — many as innocent as Lord Halifax himself. . . .
The messengers received verbal directions to apprehend Wilkes,
under the general warrant. Wilkes, far keener than the crown
lawyers, not seeing his own name there, declared it ' a ridiculous
warrant against the whole English nation,' and refused to obey it.
But after being in custody of the messengers for some hours, in his
own house, he was taken away in a chair, to appear before the
secretaries of state. No sooner had he been removed, than the messengers, returning to his house, proceeded to ransack his drawers,
and carried off all his private papers, including even his will and
pocket-book." — May, *Constitutional History of England*, II. 246,
247.

against those who, on a general warrant, had invaded his liberties.[1] The cause of freedom was vindicated. The courts decided against the validity of general warrants, and the decision was confirmed by the House of Commons and sustained by popular opinion.   The amendment to the Constitution reads: "The right of the people to be secure in their persons, houses, papers, and effects, against unreasonable searches and seizures, shall not be violated, and no warrants shall issue, but upon probable cause, supported by oath or affirmation, and particularly describing the place to be searched, and the person or things to be seized."

Amendments V. to X. inclusive read as follows : —

Article V. "No person shall be held to answer for a capital, or otherwise infamous crime, unless on a presentment or indictment of a grand jury, except in cases arising in the land and naval forces, or in the militia, when in actual service in time of war or public danger ; nor shall any person be subject for the same offence to be twice put in jeopardy of life or limb ; nor shall be

---

[1] Lord Chief Justice Pratt thus characterized the warrant: "The defendant claimed the right, under precedents, to force persons' houses, break open *escritoires*, and seize their papers, upon a general warrant, where no inventory is made of the things thus taken away, and where no offenders' names are specified in the warrant, and therefore a discretionary power given to messengers to search wherever their suspicions may chance to fall. If such a power is truly invested in a secretary of state, and he can delegate this power, it certainly may affect the person and property of every man in this kingdom, and is totally subversive of the liberty of the subject."

compelled in any criminal case to be a witness against himself, nor be deprived of life, liberty, or property, without due process of law; nor shall private property be taken for public use, without just compensation."

Article VI. "In all criminal prosecutions, the accused shall enjoy the right to a speedy and public trial, by an impartial jury of the State or district wherein the crime shall have been committed, which district shall have been previously ascertained by law, and to be informed of the nature and cause of the accusation; to be confronted with the witnesses against him; to have compulsory process for obtaining witnesses in his favour, and to have the assistance of counsel for his defence."

Article VII. "In suits at common law, where the value in controversy shall exceed twenty dollars, the right of trial by jury shall be preserved, and no fact tried by a jury shall be otherwise re-examined in any court of the United States than according to the rules of the common law."[1]

Article VIII. "Excessive bail shall not be required, nor excessive fines imposed, nor cruel and unusual punishments inflicted."

---

[1] Mr. Justice Miller, of the United States Supreme Court, says: "The first thing to be observed about this article is that it prescribes this mode of trial in '*suits at common law*.' It does not use the same words as the clause extending the judicial power 'to all cases *in law* and equity.' It is to be inferred, therefore, that trial by jury, as imposed by the Constitution, has relation to the common law as it was understood in England and to the right to such a trial in that class of cases." — *Lectures on Constitution of the United States*, 492.

Article IX. "The enumeration of the Constitution, of certain rights, shall not be construed to deny or disparage others retained by the people."

Article X. "The powers not delegated to the United States by the Constitution, nor prohibited by it to the States, are reserved to the States respectively, or to the people."

The provisions in these articles, intended to assure criminal justice, are mainly from the English common law. The expression, "twice put in jeopardy of life or limb," has descended from days when sanguinary punishments were frequent. The clause, "nor shall be compelled in any criminal case to be a witness against himself," was there placed to prevent repetition of the inquisitorial proceedings once practised in England. The requirement, that just compensation be made for private property taken for public uses, rests upon Magna Charta ; as does also the provision for speedy trial, and that no person be " deprived of life, liberty, or property without due process of law." [1]

---

[1] The expression "due process of law" is a technical one. "It has long been in use among law writers, and in judicial decisions, as implying correct and orderly proceedings, which are due because they observe all the securities of private right which are applicable in the particular case. In this sense it is synonymous with 'law of the land,' as used in the famous twenty-ninth chapter of Magna Charta. . . . The identity of the two in meaning and purpose is now well settled." — Cooley, *Principles of Constitutional Law*, 222. "As to the words from Magna Charta, after volumes spoken and written with a view to their exposition, the good sense of mankind has at length settled down to this: that they were intended to secure

The common-law origin and force of the claims in
the sixth amendment requiring that the accused be informed of the nature and cause of the accusation, and be
confronted with witnesses against him, is so understood
and admitted in practice, that surprise has been occa-
sioned that these specifications should have been thought
needful.   Of the succeeding provisions of this article for
"compulsory process of obtaining witnesses in his favour
and to have the assistance of counsel in his defence,"
the same cannot be said.   For it was a strange old
practice, derived from the Roman civil law, to allow a
party accused of capital offence no opportunity to clear
himself by the testimony of witnesses in his favour.   The
practice was denounced by Sir Edward Coke as unjust;
and soon after the accession of James I., the House of
Commons carried, amid some opposition from the crown
and upper house, a clause providing that in certain cases
witnesses might be sworn for, as well as against, the accused.   By a statute of William and Mary, the same
principle was established for cases of treason;[1] and in

the individual from the arbitrary exercise of the powers of govern-
ment, unrestrained by the established principles of private right and
distributive justice." — *Bank of California* v. *Okely*, 4 Wheat. 235.
See also *Murray's Lessee* v. *Hoboken Land Co.*, 18 How. 272, 276;
Taylor v. *Porter*, 4 Hill, (N.Y.) 140, 143; *Hoke* v. *Henderson*, 4
Dev. (N.C.) 1; *Kinney* v. *Beverley*, 1 Hen. & M. (Va.) 531;
James v. *Reynolds*, 2 Tex. 250; *Norman* v. *Heist*, 5 W. & S.
(Penn.) 171; *Davidson* v. *New Orleans*, 96 U. S. Rep. 97; Web-
ster in *Dartmouth College* v. *Woodward*, 4 Wheat. 518; Webster,
Works, V. 487.

[1] 7 Will. III. c. 3.   This statute provides that persons in-

the reign of Queen Anne, this was extended.[1] Yet, at
the period of the construction of the American Constitution, the law did not allow the privilege in ordinary
capital cases ; and the amendment, in extending it to all
classes of criminals without restriction, was, therefore,
an important improvement upon the usage of the mother-
country.   Another singular English deficiency — the failure in certain circumstances to give a prisoner under capital accusation the benefit of counsel for his defence —
was supplied in the American Constitution by the guarantee of counsel in all cases.[2]

The eighth amendment treats of excessive bail and
punishment, and is simply a transcript of a clause in the
Bill of Rights framed at the Revolution of 1688.   Its
object is to warn the national government against such

dicted for high treason shall have a copy of the indictment delivered to them five days at least before the trial, and a copy of the
panel of the jurors two days before the trial; that they shall be
allowed the assistance of counsel throughout the trial, and be
entitled to process of the court to compel the attendance of their
witnesses, who must be examined on oath.   It removes any doubts
as to the statute of Edward VI., by requiring the oaths of two
lawful witnesses, unless the prisoner shall willingly, without violence, in open court confess the charge, etc.

[1] 7 Anne, c. 21.

[2] In the first State constitutions of Maryland, New Jersey, Pennsylvania, Massachusetts, and Vermont, provision was made, guaranteeing counsel in all cases, and from these State provisions the
amendment to the national Constitution came.   This defect in the
English law, thus supplied by America, was remedied in the mother-
country by statute 6 and 7 Will. IV. c. 114.   See Cooley, *Constitutional Limitations*, 330–338.

proceedings as took place in England during the arbitrary Stuart period, — when a demand for enormous bail was often made against persons obnoxious to the court; who, failing to procure this, were thrown into prison. Excessive fines and amercements were also occasionally imposed, and vindictive and cruel punishments meted out. The clause in the Bill of Rights from which the amendment was drawn specifies: "That excessive bail ought not to be required, nor excessive fines imposed; nor cruel and unusual punishment inflicted."[1]

We come, in conclusion, to trial by jury — as provided in Article III. of the Constitution for criminal cases; and in the amendments, for criminal cases and civil actions alike — one of the most characteristic elements of the American constitutional inheritance from England.

The origin of this " bulwark of constitutional liberty " has been the topic of a great deal of learned discussion and of many antagonistic theories.[2] Probably the jury in

---

[1] 1 Will. and Mary, Sess. 2, c. 2.

[2] Philipps, *On Juries*, and Probert, *On the Ancient Laws of Cambria*, claim that the jury system originated among the Welsh, from whom the Anglo-Saxons borrowed it. Selden, Spelman, Coke, Turner, Philipps, and G. L. von Maurer regard it as an outcome of Anglo-Saxon invention. Bacon, Montesquieu, Blackstone, Savigny, and Nicholson — preface to Wilkins, *Anglo-Saxon Laws* — maintain that it is an importation from primitive Germany. Wormiers and Worsaae think it came from the Danes, who in turn derived it from the Norsemen. Hickes, Reeves, and others claim a Norse origin through the Normans; and Conrad Maurer points to a north German source. Of writers who admit its Norman origin, Daniels thinks the Normans found it in France. Möhl carries it

its earliest form, that of a body of sworn recognitors, was introduced into England by the Normans, they having borrowed it from the Franks. It is traceable to the capitularies of the Carolingian kings, and possibly through these, to the fiscal regulations of the Theodosian Code, — thus having some affinity to the Roman jurisprudence.[1] But although an importation, the system gained its real development in England alone, and gradually ceased to exist in Normandy and in the rest of France. From a simple beginning at the Conquest, it was consolidated in the reign of Henry III., and became one of the settled

---

back to the canon law of the Church, Meyer derives it from Asia by way of the Crusades, and Maciejowski derives it from the Slavic neighbours of the Teutonic invaders of England. *Entstehung der Schwurgerichte*, 11–19. Bourguignon says despairingly, " son origine se perd dans la nuit des temps." — *Memoire sur le Jury.* See Forsyth, *History of Trial by Jury;* Gneist, *Self-Government;* Glasson, *Hist. du Droit et des Inst. de l'Angleterre*, etc. Bishop Stubbs — *Constitutional History of England* — and other recent authorities accept the Carolingian and Theodosian origin, as stated in Palgrave, *English Commonwealth*, corrected and adjusted by Dr. Brunner, *Entstehung der Schwurgerichte.*

[1] See Smith, *Dictionary of Greek and Roman Antiquities:* " Codex Theodosianus." Brunner cites the Theodosian Code: " Super vacantibus ac caducis . . . certi etiam dirigantur qui cuncta solerter inquirant et cujus fuerint facultates et si nemo eas sibi jure nititur retentare. Ac si locum fisco factum esse claruerit occupatis prius bonis et rerum omnium descriptione perfecta . . . ; " *Codex Theodosianus*, X. 10, L. 11. " Ex privatorum . . . sollicitu dine contractum . . . illis . . . personis a quibus publici numeris injuncta curantur, nullum formitem calumniae patimur litis accendi. Cur enim continentiam venditionis alienae inquisitio palatina rimetur? " *Ibid.* L. 29.

institutions of the land, in close relationship with the old
Saxon procedure of the shiremoot. This king, who has
been called its father, applied it to every variety of fiscal
and legal transaction; and down to much later days it
was used largely in the assessment of taxation. The Constitutions of Clarendon give the earliest record in statute
law of its employment for criminal presentment and civil
inquest.[1]   Later, in the Assize of Clarendon, provision
was made that twelve men from each hundred, with four
from each township, should be sworn to present all
reputed criminals of their district in each county court, —
a jury of presentment, which may have been, in part, an
enlargement of a Saxon institution existing as far back as
the reign of Ethelred II., and which, as regulated by the
Articles of Visitation of Richard I., gave rise to the grand
jury of modern times. From a desire to still further
promote the security of justice, there arose a procedure
of having the testimony of this body examined by a
second body — the petit jury — and this procedure eventually became settled usage.[2]

But at first the process of trial by jury was different
in many respects from that with which we are now
familiar. Palgrave states this difference with admirable
clearness. "Jurymen in the present day are triers of
the issue; they are individuals who found their opinion
upon the evidence, whether oral or written, adduced
before them; and the verdict delivered by them is their
declaration of the judgment which they have found.

---

[1] A.D. 1164.   [2] A.D. 1194.

But the ancient jurymen were not impanelled to examine into the credibility of evidence ; the question was not discussed and argued before them ; they, the jurymen, were the witnesses themselves, who, of their own knowledge, and without the aid of other testimony, afforded their evidence respecting the fact in question to the best of their belief. In its primitive form a trial by jury was therefore only a trial by witnesses."[1] That is to say, the jurors decided from their own personal knowledge of the facts, or from tradition, without other witnesses than themselves. And, incidentally, this explains an important point, — namely, why the trial was properly held in the locality of the accused's residence, and the jury chosen from the vicinage in which the question arose.[2]

The development by which jurors ceased to be witnesses, and became judges of the fact, is common to both the criminal and the civil jury, and is traceable from the time of Edward III.[3] Out of the difficulty of securing twelve men acquainted with the matter in trial and able to give a unanimous verdict based on personal knowledge, grew the custom of permitting the jurors who were first summoned to add to their number persons having such knowledge.[4] And later on, jurors

[1] *English Commonwealth*, I. 243.

[2] "The testimony of the neighbourhood was appealed to for the purpose of deciding questions which related to matters of general concern." — Forsyth, *Trial by Jury*, 92.

[3] Year Books, 25 Edw. III.

[4] "The proceeding by assize was, in fact, merely the sworn testimony of a certain number of persons summoned to give evidence

without information were separated from those possessing it, the former becoming judges of evidence only,
and the latter witnesses ; a decision being given by the
former upon the testimony of the latter, and the law
in the case being decided by the presiding official in
the king's name.[1] By 1450 we have distinct evidence
that the mode of procedure was the same as that in
modern use,[2] though in occasional instances the ancient
functions of jurors lingered as late as to the accession
of the House of Hanover.

The Declaration of Independence complains of the
British government " for depriving us in many cases of
the benefits of trial by jury," and for " transporting us
beyond seas to be tried for pretended offences."

" Trial by jury," it has been said, " is justly dear to the
American people.   It has always been an object of deep
interest and solicitude, and every encroachment upon it

upon matters within their own knowledge.   They were themselves
only witnesses.   If all were ignorant of the facts, a fresh jury had
to be summoned; if some of them only were ignorant, or if they
could not agree, others were to be added — a process subsequently
called *afforcing* the jury — until a verdict could be obtained from
twelve unanimous witnesses." — Taswell-Langmead, *English Constitutional History*, 166.

[1] As a result of this " witnesses were examined and cross-
examined in open court; the flood gates of forensic eloquence were
opened, and full scope given to the advocate to exercise his inge-
nuity and powers of persuasion on the jurors, to whose discretion
the power of judging on matters of fact was now entrusted." —
Starkie, " Trial by Jury," *Law Review*, No. IV., August, 1845.

[2] Fortesque, *De Laudibus Legumæ Angæ*, c. 26.

has been watched with great jealousy." [1]   "The privilege in criminal cases has been looked upon as a necessary part of the liberties of the people, and a sentiment attaches to it which will scarcely suffer its value to be questioned.   Every State constitution preserves its suits in the State courts, and every new and revised constitution repeats the guaranty of it.   Even the common-law requirement of unanimity in the verdict, which is of more than doubtful value, is retained without inquiry or question, because it has existed from time immemorial." [2]

The proud words of retort to Montesquieu, with which Blackstone ends his panegyric on the jury system, are as applicable to America as to England; "A celebrated French writer, who concludes that Rome, Sparta, and Carthage have lost their liberties, therefore those of England in time must perish, should have recollected that Rome, Sparta, and Carthage, at the time when their liberties were lost, were strangers to the trial by jury." [3]

———————

Whatever may be in store for America, her *past* is closely inwrought with that of England.   Her laws, as her language, have descended to her.   For, though our ancient Teutonic race, in these new days, may encircle the globe, and find itself scattered on all continents and beside all seas, it will have ever one common home.

[1] *Parsons* v. *Bedford*, 3 Pet. 433, 446.
[2] Cooley, *Principles of Constitutional Law*, 237, 238.
[3] *Commentaries*, Book III. 379.

The Constitution of the United States possesses much
that is peculiar to itself. It is not the English Constitution of any age. Yet it is "heir of all the ages" of
English history. For the most part, as we have seen, it
applies to new conditions, time-tried principles of free
government.

It is well thus to call to mind that what is best and
noblest in American governmental institutions is safely
founded upon an historic past. The oak of English
freedom that the fathers of America transplanted, has
grown old and gnarled and stanch and great of girth, and
its firm roots have struck down deep into the soil.
Though clouds of social and political problem may
lower above it, it recks not of momentary sunshine or
passing tempest, — that sturdy oak, bounded by the succeeding circles of the centuries, and growing only more
strong with the ongoing of the years.

APPENDIX

APPENDIX.

CONSTITUTION OF THE UNITED STATES.

WE, the people of the United States, in order to form a more perfect union, establish justice, insure domestic tranquillity, provide for the common defence, promote the general welfare, and secure the blessings of liberty to ourselves and our posterity, do ordain and establish this Constitution for the United States of America.

ARTICLE I.

SECTION 1. All legislative powers herein granted shall be vested in a Congress of the United States, which shall consist of a Senate and House of Representatives.

SEC. 2. The House of Representatives shall be composed of members chosen every second year by the people of the several States, and the electors in each State shall have the qualifications requisite for electors of the most numerous branch of the State legislature.

No person shall be a Representative who shall not have attained the age of twenty-five years, and been seven years a citizen of the United States, and who shall not, when elected, be an inhabitant of that State in which he shall be chosen.

[Representatives and direct taxes shall be apportioned among the several States which may be included within this Union, according to their respective numbers, which shall be determined by adding to the whole number of free persons, including those bound to service for a term of years, and excluding Indians not taxed,

243

three-fifths of all other persons.] [1]   The actual enumeration shall be made within three years after the first meeting of the Congress of the United States, and within every subsequent term of ten years, in such manner as they shall by law direct.   The number of Representatives shall not exceed one for every thirty thousand, but each State shall have at least one Representative; and until such enumeration shall be made, the State of New Hampshire shall be entitled to choose three, Massachusetts eight, Rhode Island and Providence Plantations one, Connecticut five, New York six, New Jersey four, Pennsylvania eight, Delaware one, Maryland six, Virginia ten, North Carolina five, South Carolina five, and Georgia three.

When vacancies happen in the representation from any State, the executive authority thereof shall issue writs of election to fill such vacancies.

The House of Representatives shall choose their speaker and other officers; and shall have the sole power of impeachment.

SEC. 3.   The Senate of the United States shall be composed of two Senators from each State, chosen by the legislature thereof, for six years; and each Senator shall have one vote.

Immediately after they shall be assembled in consequence of the first election, they shall be divided as equally as may be into three classes.   The seats of the Senators of the first class shall be vacated at the expiration of the second year, of the second class at the expiration of the fourth year, and of the third class at the expiration of the sixth year, so that one-third may be chosen every second year; and if vacancies happen by resignation, or otherwise, during the recess of the legislature of any State, the executive thereof may make temporary appointments until the next meeting of the legislature, which shall then fill such vacancies.

No person shall be a Senator who shall not have attained to the age of thirty years, and been nine years a citizen of the United States, and who shall not, when elected, be an inhabitant of that State for which he shall be chosen.

---

[1] The clause included in brackets is amended by the XIVth Amendment, 2d section.

The Vice-President of the United States shall be President of the Senate, but shall have no vote, unless they be equally divided.

The Senate shall choose their other officers, and also a President *pro tempore*, in the absence of the Vice-President, or when he shall exercise the office of President of the United States.

The Senate shall have sole power to try all impeachments. When sitting for that purpose, they shall be on oath or affirmation. When the President of the United States is tried, the Chief Justice shall preside; and no person shall be convicted without the concurrence of two-thirds of the members present.

Judgment in cases of impeachment shall not extend further than to removal from office, and disqualification to hold and enjoy any office of honour, trust, or profit under the United States; but the party convicted shall nevertheless be liable and subject to indictment, trial, judgment, and punishment, according to law.

SEC. 4. The times, places, and manner of holding elections for Senators and Representatives shall be prescribed in each State by the legislature thereof; but the Congress may at any time by law make or alter such regulations, except as to the places of choosing Senators.

The Congress shall assemble at least once in every year, and such meeting shall be on the first Monday in December, unless they shall by law appoint a different day.

SEC. 5. Each house shall be the judge of the elections, returns, and qualifications of its own members, and a majority of each shall constitute a quorum to do business; but a smaller number may adjourn from day to day, and may be authorized to compel the attendance of absent members, in such manner, and under such penalties, as each house may provide.

Each house may determine the rules of its proceedings, punish its members for disorderly behaviour, and, with the concurrence of two-thirds, expel a member.

Each house shall keep a journal of its proceedings, and from time to time publish the same, excepting such parts as may in their judgment require secrecy; and the yeas and nays of the members of either house on any question shall, at the desire of one-fifth of those present, be entered on the journal.

Neither house, during the session of Congress, shall, without the consent of the other, adjourn for more than three days, nor to any other place than that in which the two houses shall be sitting.

SEC. 6. The Senators and Representatives shall receive a compensation for their services, to be ascertained by law, and paid out of the Treasury of the United States. They shall in all cases, except treason, felony, and breach of the peace, be privileged from arrest during their attendance at the session of their respective houses, and in going to and returning from the same; and for any speech or debate in either house they shall not be questioned in any other place.

No Senator or Representative shall, during the time for which he was elected, be appointed to any civil office under the authority of the United States, which shall have been created, or the emoluments whereof shall have been increased during such time; and no person holding any office under the United States shall be a member of either house during his continuance in office.

SEC. 7. All bills for raising revenue shall originate in the House of Representatives; but the Senate may propose or concur with amendments as on other bills.

Every bill which shall have passed the House of Representatives and the Senate shall, before it become a law, be presented to the President of the United States; if he approve he shall sign it, but if not he shall return it, with his objections, to that house in which it shall have originated, who shall enter the objections at large on their journal, and proceed to reconsider it. If after such reconsideration two-thirds of that house shall agree to pass the bill, it shall be sent, together with the objections, to the other house, by which it shall likewise be reconsidered, and if approved by two-thirds of that house, it shall become a law. But in all such cases the votes of both houses shall be determined by yeas and nays, and the names of the persons voting for and against the bill shall be entered on the journal of each house respectively. If any bill shall not be returned by the President within ten days (Sundays excepted) after it shall have been presented to him, the same shall be a law, in like manner as if he had signed it, unless the Congress by their adjournment prevents its return, in which case it shall not be a law.

Every order, resolution, or vote to which the concurrence of the Senate and House of Representatives may be necessary (except on a question of adjournment) shall be presented to the President of the United States; and, before the same shall take effect, shall be approved by him, or, being disapproved by him, shall be repassed by two-thirds of the Senate and House of Representatives, according to the rules and limitations prescribed in the case of a bill.

SEC. 8. The Congress shall have power, — to lay and collect taxes, duties, imposts, and excises, to pay the debts and provide for the common defence and general welfare of the United States: but all duties, imposts, and excises shall be uniform throughout the United States;

To borrow money on the credit of the United States;

To regulate commerce with foreign nations, and among the several States, and with the Indian tribes;

To establish an uniform rule of naturalization, and uniform laws on the subject of bankruptcies throughout the United States;

To coin money, regulate the value thereof, and of foreign coin, and fix the standard of weights and measures;

To provide for the punishment of counterfeiting the securities and current coin of the United States;

To establish post-offices and post-roads.

To promote the progress of science and useful arts, by securing for limited times to authors and inventors the exclusive right to their respective writings and discoveries;

To constitute tribunals inferior to the Supreme Court;

To define and punish piracies and felonies committed on the high seas, and offences against the law of nations;

To declare war, grant letters of marque and reprisal, and make rules concerning captures on land and water;

To raise and support armies, but no appropriation of money to that use shall be for a longer term than two years;

To provide and maintain a navy;

To make rules for the government and regulation of the land and naval forces;

To provide for calling forth the militia to execute the laws of the Union, suppress insurrections, and repel invasions;

To provide for organizing, arming, and disciplining the militia, and for governing such part of them as may be employed in the service of the United States, reserving to the States respectively the appointment of the officers, and the authority of training the militia according to the discipline prescribed by Congress;

To exercise exclusive legislation in all cases whatsoever, over such district (not exceeding ten miles square) as may, by cession of particular States, and the acceptance of Congress, become the seat of the Government of the United States, and to exercise like authority over all places purchased by the consent of the legislature of the State in which the same shall be, for the erection of forts, magazines, arsenals, dockyards, and other needful buildings; — and

To make all laws which shall be necessary and proper for carrying into execution the foregoing powers, and all other powers vested by this Constitution in the Government of the United States, or in any department or officer thereof.

Sec. 9. The migration or importation of such persons as any of the States now existing shall think proper to admit, shall not be prohibited by the Congress prior to the year one thousand eight hundred and eight, but a tax or duty may be imposed on such importation, not exceeding ten dollars for each person.

The privilege of the writ of habeas corpus shall not be suspended, unless when in cases of rebellion or invasion the public safety may require it.

No bill of attainder or *ex post facto* law shall be passed.

No capitation, or other direct tax shall be laid, unless in proportion to the census or enumeration hereinbefore directed to be taken.

No tax or duty shall be laid on articles exported from any State.

No preference shall be given by any regulation of commerce or revenue to the ports of one State over those of another; nor shall vessels bound to, or from, one State be obliged to enter, clear, or pay duties in another.

No money shall be drawn from the Treasury, but in consequence of appropriations made by law; and a regular statement and account of the receipts and the expenditures of all public money shall be published from time to time.

No title of nobility shall be granted by the United States; and no person holding any office of profit or trust under them shall, without the consent of the Congress, accept of any present, emolument, office, or title, of any kind whatever, from any king, prince, or foreign state.

SEC. 10. No State shall enter into any treaty, alliance, or confederation; grant letters of marque or reprisal; coin money; emit bills of credit; make anything but gold and silver coin a tender in payment of debts; pass any bill of attainder, *ex post facto* law, or law impairing the obligation of contracts, or grant any title of nobility.

No State shall, without the consent of the Congress, lay any imposts or duties on imports or exports, except what may be absolutely necessary for executing its inspection laws; and the net produce of all duties and imposts, laid by any State on imports or exports, shall be for the use of the Treasury of the United States; and all such laws shall be subject to the revision and control of the Congress.

No State shall, without the consent of the Congress, lay any duty of tonnage, keep troops or ships of war in time of peace, enter into any agreement or compact with another State, or with a foreign power, or engage in war, unless actually invaded, or in such imminent danger as will not admit of delay.

ARTICLE II.

SECTION 1. The executive power shall be vested in a President of the United States of America. He shall hold his office during the term of four years, and, together with the Vice-President, chosen for the same term, be elected as follows : —

Each State shall appoint, in such manner as the legislature thereof may direct, a number of electors equal to the whole number of Senators and Representatives to which the State may be entitled in the Congress; but no Senator or Representative, or person holding an office of trust or profit under the United States, shall be appointed an elector.

[The electors shall meet in their respective States, and vote by ballot for two persons, of whom one at least shall not be an inhabitant of the same State with themselves. And they shall make a list of all the persons voted for, and of the number of votes for each; which list they shall sign and certify, and transmit sealed to the seat of the Government of the United States, directed to the President of the Senate. The President of the Senate shall, in the presence of the Senate and the House of Representatives, open all the certificates, and the votes shall then be counted. The person having the greatest number of votes shall be the President, if such number be a majority of the whole number of electors appointed; and if there be more than one who have such majority, and have an equal number of votes, then the House of Representatives shall immediately choose by ballot one of them for President; and if no person have a majority, then from the five highest on the list the said House shall in like manner choose the President. But in choosing the President, the votes shall be taken by States, the representation from each State having one vote; a quorum for this purpose shall consist of a member or members from two-thirds of the States, and a majority of all the States shall be necessary to a choice. In every case, after the choice of the President, the person having the greatest number of votes of the electors shall be the Vice-President. But if there should remain two or more who have equal votes, the Senate shall choose from them by ballot the Vice-President.] [1]

The Congress may determine the time of choosing the electors, and the day on which they shall give their votes; which day shall be the same throughout the United States.

No person except a natural-born citizen, or a citizen of the United States at the time of the adoption of this Constitution, shall be eligible to the office of President; neither shall any person be eligible to that office who shall not have attained to the age of thirty-five years, and been fourteen years a resident within the United States.

In case of the removal of the President from office, or of his death, resignation, or inability to discharge the powers and duties of the said office, the same shall devolve on the Vice-President, and

---

[1] This clause in brackets has been superseded by the XIIth Amendment.

the Congress may by law provide for the case of removal, death, resignation, or inability, both of the President and Vice-President, declaring what officer shall then act as President, and such officer shall act accordingly, until the disability be removed, or a President shall be elected.

The President shall, at stated times, receive for his services a compensation, which shall neither be increased nor diminished during the period for which he shall have been elected, and he shall not receive within that period any other emolument from the United States, or any of them.

Before he enter on the execution of his office, he shall take the following oath or affirmation :

" I do solemnly swear (or affirm) that I will faithfully execute the office of President of the United States, and will, to the best of my ability, preserve, protect, and defend the Constitution of the United States."

SEC. 2. The President shall be commander-in-chief of the army and navy of the United States, and of the militia of the several States, when called into the actual service of the United States; he may require the opinion, in writing, of the principal officer in each of the executive departments, upon any subject relating to the duties of their respective offices, and he shall have power to grant reprieves and pardons for offences against the United States, except in cases of impeachment.

He shall have power, by and with the advice and consent of the Senate, to make treaties, provided two-thirds of the Senators present concur ; and he shall nominate, and by and with the advice and consent of the Senate, shall appoint ambassadors, other public ministers and consuls, judges of the Supreme Court, and all other officers of the United States, whose appointments are not herein otherwise provided for, and which shall be established by law; but the Congress may by law vest the appointment of such inferior officers, as they think proper, in the President alone, in the courts of laws, or in the heads of departments.

The President shall have power to fill up all vacancies that may happen during the recess of the Senate, by granting commissions which shall expire at the end of their next session.

Sec. 3. He shall from time to time give to the Congress information of the state of the Union, and recommend to their consideration such measures as he shall judge necessary and expedient; he may, on extraordinary occasions, convene both houses, or either of them, and in case of disagreement between them, with respect to the time of adjournment, he may adjourn them to such time as he shall think proper; he shall receive ambassadors and other public ministers; he shall take care that the laws be faithfully executed, and shall commission all the officers of the United States.

Sec. 4. The President, Vice-President, and all civil officers of the United States, shall be removed from office on impeachment for, and conviction of, treason, bribery, or other high crimes and misdemeanours. .

ARTICLE III.

Section 1. The judicial power of the United States shall be vested in one Supreme Court, and in such inferior courts as the Congress may from time to time ordain and establish. The judges, both of the Supreme and inferior courts, shall hold their offices during good behaviour, and shall, at stated times, receive for their services a compensation, which shall not be diminished during their continuance in office.

Sec. 2. The judicial power shall extend to all cases, in law and equity, arising under this Constitution, the laws of the United States, and treaties made, or which shall be made, under their authority; to all cases affecting ambassadors, other public ministers, and consuls; to all cases of admiralty and maritime jurisdiction; to controversies to which the United States shall be a party; to controversies between two or more States, between a State and citizens of another State, between citizens of different States, between citizens of the same State claiming lands under grants of different States, and between a State, or the citizens thereof, and foreign states, citizens, or subjects.

In all cases affecting ambassadors, other public ministers and consuls, and those in which a State shall be a party, the Supreme Court shall have original jurisdiction. In all the other cases before mentioned, the Supreme Court shall have appellate jurisdiction, both as to law and fact, with such exceptions, and under such regulations as the Congress shall make.

The trial of all crimes, except in cases of impeachment, shall be by jury; and such trial shall be held in the State where the said crimes shall have been committed; but when not committed within any State, the trial shall be at such place or places as the Congress may by law have directed.

SEC. 3. Treason against the United States shall consist only in levying war against them, or in adhering to their enemies, giving them aid and comfort. No person shall be convicted of treason unless on the testimony of two witnesses to the same overt act, or on confession in open court.

The Congress shall have power to declare the punishment of treason, but no attainder of treason shall work corruption of blood, or forfeiture, except during the life of the person attainted.

ARTICLE IV.

SECTION 1. Full faith and credit shall be given in each State to the public acts, records, and judicial proceedings of every other State. And the Congress may by general laws prescribe the manner in which such acts, records, and proceedings shall be proved, and the effect thereof.

SEC. 2. The citizens of each State shall be entitled to all privileges and immunities of citizens in the several States.

A person charged in any State with treason, felony, or other crime, who shall flee from justice, and be found in another State, shall, on demand of the executive authority of the State from which he fled, be delivered up, to be removed to the State having jurisdiction of the crime.

No person held to service or labour in one State, under the laws thereof, escaping into another, shall, in consequence of any law or regulation therein, be discharged from such service or labour, but shall be delivered up on claim of the party to whom such service or labour may be due.

SEC. 3. New States may be admitted by the Congress into this Union; but no new State shall be formed or erected within the jurisdiction of any other State; nor any State be formed by the junction of two or more States, or parts of States, without the consent of the legislatures of the States concerned, as well as of the Congress.

The Congress shall have power to dispose of and make all needful rules and regulations respecting the territory or other property belonging to the United States; and nothing in this Constitution shall be so construed as to prejudice any claims of the United States, or of any particular State.

SEC. 4. The United States shall guarantee to every State in this Union a republican form of government, and shall protect each of them against invasion; and on application of the legislature, or of the executive (when the legislature cannot be convened), against domestic violence.

ARTICLE V.

The Congress, whenever two-thirds of both houses shall deem it necessary, shall propose amendments to this Constitution, or, on the application of the legislatures of two-thirds of the several States, shall call a convention for proposing amendments, which, in either case, shall be valid to all intents and purposes, as part of this Constitution, when ratified by the legislatures of three-fourths of the several States, or by conventions in three-fourths thereof, as the one or the other mode of ratification may be proposed by the Congress; provided that no amendment which may be made prior to the year one thousand eight hundred and eight shall in any manner affect the first and fourth clauses in the ninth section of the first article; and that no State, without its consent, shall be deprived of its equal suffrage in the Senate.

ARTICLE VI.

All debts contracted and engagements entered into, before the adoption of this Constitution, shall be as valid against the United States under this Constitution as under the Confederation.

This Constitution, and the laws of the United States which shall be made in pursuance thereof, and all treaties made, or which shall be made, under the authority of the United States, shall be the supreme law of the land; and the judges in every State shall be bound thereby, anything in the constitution or laws of any State to the contrary notwithstanding.

The Senators and Representatives before mentioned, and the members of the several State legislatures, and all executive and judicial officers, both of the United States and of the several States, shall be bound by oath or affirmation to support this Constitution; but no religious test shall ever be required as a qualification to any office or public trust under the United States.

ARTICLE VII.

The ratification of the conventions of nine States shall be sufficient for the establishment of this Constitution between the States so ratifying the same.

Done in Convention by the unanimous consent of the States present,[1] the Seventeenth day of September, in the year of our Lord one thousand seven hundred and eighty-seven, and of the Independence of the United States of America the Twelfth.

IN WITNESS whereof we have hereunto subscribed our names.

G⁰ WASHINGTON,
Presidt. and Deputy from Virginia.

New Hampshire — John Langdon, Nicholas Gilman. *Massachusetts* — Nathaniel Gorham, Rufus King. *Connecticut* — Wm. Saml. Johnson, Roger Sherman. *New York* — Alexander Hamilton. *New Jersey* — Wil. Livingston, Wm. Patterson, David Brearley, Jona. Dayton. *Pennsylvania* — B. Franklin, Thos. Fitzsimons, Thomas Mifflin, Jared Ingersoll, Robt. Morris, James

---

[1] Rhode Island was not represented. Several of the delegates had left the Convention before it concluded its labours, and some others who remained refused to sign. In all, 65 delegates had been appointed, 55 attended, 39 signed.

The first ratification was that of Delaware, Dec. 7, 1787; the ninth (bringing the Constitution into force) that of New Hampshire, June 21, 1788; the last, that of Rhode Island, May 29, 1790.

Wilson, Geo. Clymer, Gouv. Morris. *Delaware* — Geo. Read, Richard Bassett, Gunning Bedford, Jun., Jaco. Broom, John Dickinson. *Maryland* — James M'Henry, Danl. Carroll, Dan. Jenifer, of St. Thomas. *Virginia* — John Blair, James Madison, Jun. *North Carolina* — Wm. Blount, Hugh Williamson, Rich'd Dobbs Speight. *South Carolina* — J. Rutledge, Charles Pinckney, Charles Cotesworth Pinckney, Pierce Butler. *Georgia* — William Few, Abr. Baldwin.

Attest : WILLIAM JACKSON, *Secretary.*

Articles in addition to, and amendment of, the Constitution of the United States of America, proposed by Congress, and ratified by the Legislatures of the several States, pursuant to the fifth Article of the original Constitution.

ARTICLE I.[1]

Congress shall make no law respecting an establishment of religion, or prohibiting the free exercise thereof; or abridging the freedom of speech, or of the press; or the right of the people peaceably to assemble, and to petition the Government for a redress of grievances.

ARTICLE II.

A well-regulated militia being necessary to the security of a free State, the right of the people to keep and bear arms shall not be infringed.

ARTICLE III.

No soldier shall, in time of peace, be quartered in any house, without the consent of the owner, nor in time of war, but in a manner to be prescribed by law.

ARTICLE IV.

The right of the people to be secure in their persons, houses, papers, and effects, against unreasonable searches and seizures, shall

[1] Amendments I.–X. inclusive were proposed by Congress to the Legislatures of the States, Sept. 25, 1789, and ratified 1789–91.

not be violated, and no warrants shall issue, but upon probable cause, supported by oath or affirmation, and particularly describing the place to be searched, and the person or things to be seized.

ARTICLE V.

No person shall be held to answer for a capital, or otherwise infamous crime, unless on a presentment or indictment of a grand jury, except in cases arising in the land or naval forces, or in the militia, when in actual service in time of war or public danger; nor shall any person be subject for the same offence to be twice put in jeopardy of life or limb; nor shall be compelled in any criminal case to be a witness against himself, nor be deprived of life, liberty, or property, without due process of law; nor shall private property be taken for public use, without just compensation.

ARTICLE VI.

In all criminal prosecutions, the accused shall enjoy the right to a speedy and public trial, by an impartial jury of the State and district wherein the crime shall have been committed, which district shall have been previously ascertained by law, and to be informed of the nature and cause of the accusation; to be confronted with the witnesses against him; to have compulsory process for obtaining witnesses in his favour, and to have the assistance of counsel for his defence.

ARTICLE VII.

In suits at common law, where the value in controversy shall exceed twenty dollars, the right of trial by jury shall be preserved, and no fact tried by a jury shall be otherwise re-examined in any court of the United States, than according to the rules of the common law.

ARTICLE VIII.

Excessive bail shall not be required, nor excessive fines imposed, nor cruel and unusual punishments inflicted.

ARTICLE IX.

The enumeration in the Constitution, of certain rights, shall not be construed to deny or disparage others retained by the people.

ARTICLE X.

The powers not delegated to the United States by the Constitution, nor prohibited by it to the States, are reserved to the States respectively, or to the people.

ARTICLE XI.[1]

The judicial power of the United States shall not be construed to extend to any suit in law or equity, commenced or prosecuted against one of the United States by citizens of another State, or by citizens or subjects of any foreign State.

ARTICLE XII.[2]

The electors shall meet in their respective States, and vote by ballot for President and Vice-President, one of whom, at least, shall not be an inhabitant of the same State with themselves; they shall name in their ballots the person voted for as President, and in distinct ballots the person voted for as Vice-President, and they shall make distinct lists of all persons voted for as President, and of all persons voted for as Vice-President, and of the number of votes for each, which lists they shall sign and certify, and transmit sealed to the seat of the Government of the United States, directed to the President of the Senate; — the President of the Senate shall, in the presence of the Senate and House of Representatives, open all the certificates, and the votes shall then be counted; — the person

[1] Amendt. XI. was proposed by Congress Sept. 5, 1794, and declared to have been ratified by the legislatures of the three-fourths of the States, Jan. 8, 1798.

[2] Amendt. XII. was proposed by Congress Dec. 12, 1803, and declared to have been ratified Sept. 25, 1804.

having the greatest number of votes for President shall be the President, if such number be a majority of the whole number of electors appointed; and if no person have such majority, then from the persons having the highest numbers not exceeding three on the list of those voted for as President, the House of Representatives shall choose immediately, by ballot, the President. But in choosing the President, the votes shall be taken by States, the representation from each State having one vote; a quorum for this purpose shall consist of a member or members from two-thirds of the States, and a majority of all the States shall be necessary to a choice. And if the House of Representatives shall not choose a President whenever the right of choice shall devolve upon them, before the fourth day of March next following, then the Vice-President shall act as President, as in the case of the death or other constitutional disability of the President.

The person having the greatest number of votes as Vice-President shall be the Vice-President, if such number be a majority of the whole number of electors appointed, and if no person have a majority, then from the two highest numbers on the list the Senate shall choose the Vice-President; a quorum for the purpose shall consist of two-thirds of the whole number of Senators, and a majority of the whole number shall be necessary to a choice. But no person constitutionally ineligible to the office of President shall be eligible to that of Vice-President of the United States.

ARTICLE XIII.[1]

SECTION 1. Neither slavery nor involuntary servitude, except as a punishment for crime whereof the party shall have been duly convicted, shall exist within the United States, or any place subject to their-jurisdiction.

SEC. 2. Congress shall have power to enforce this article by appropriate legislation.

[1] Amendt. XIII. was proposed by Congress Feb. 1. 1865, and declared to have been ratified by 27 of the 36 States, Dec. 18, 1865.

ARTICLE XIV.[1]

Section 1. All persons born or naturalized in the United States, and subject to the jurisdiction thereof, are citizens of the United States and of the State wherein they reside. No State shall make or enforce any law which shall abridge the privileges or immunities of citizens of the United States; nor shall any State deprive any person of life, liberty, or property, without due process of law; nor deny to any person within its jurisdiction the equal protection of the laws.

Sec. 2. Representatives shall be apportioned among the several States according to their respective numbers, counting the whole number of persons in each State, excluding Indians not taxed. But when the right to vote at any election for the choice of electors for President and Vice-President of the United States, Representatives in Congress, the executive and judicial officers of the State, or the members of the legislature thereof, is denied to any of the male inhabitants of such State, being twenty-one years of age, and citizens of the United States, or in any way abridged, except for participation in rebellion or other crime, the basis of representation therein shall be reduced in the proportion which the number of such male citizens shall bear to the whole number of male citizens twenty-one years of age in such State.

Sec. 3. No person shall be a Senator or Representative in Congress, or elector of President and Vice-President, or hold any office, civil or military, under the United States, or under any State, who, having previously taken an oath, as a member of the Congress, or as an officer of the United States, or as a member of any State legislature, or as an executive or judicial officer of any State, to support the Constitution of the United States, shall have engaged in insurrection or rebellion against the same, or given aid or comfort to the enemies thereof. But Congress may, by a vote of two-thirds of each House, remove such disability.

---

[1] Amendt. XIV. was proposed by Congress June 16, 1866, and declared to have been ratified by 30 of the 36 States, July 28, 1868.

SEC. 4. The validity of the public debt of the United States, authorized by law, including debts incurred for payment of pensions and bounties for services in suppressing insurrection or rebellion, shall not be questioned. But neither the United States nor any State shall assume or pay any debt or obligation incurred in aid of insurrection or rebellion against the United States, or any claim for the loss or emancipation of any slave; but all such debts, obligations, and claims shall be held illegal and void.

SEC. 5. The Congress shall have power to enforce, by appropriate legislation, the provisions of this article.

ARTICLE XV.[1]

SECTION I. The right of citizens of the United States to vote shall not be denied or abridged by the United States or by any State on account of race, colour, or previous condition of servitude.

SEC. 2. The Congress shall have power to enforce this article by appropriate legislation.

[1] Amendt. XV. was proposed by Congress Feb. 26, 1869, and declared to have been ratified by 29 of the 37 States, March 30, 1870.

INDEX

INDEX.